# The Legal Exhibitionist

## THE FAIRLEIGH DICKINSON UNIVERSITY PRESS SERIES IN LAW, CULTURE, AND THE HUMANITIES

Series Editor: Caroline Joan "Kay" S. Picart, M.Phil. (Cantab), Ph.D., J.D., Esquire Attorney at Law; Adjunct Professor, FAMU College of Law; former English & HUM professor, FSU

The Fairleigh Dickinson University Press Series in Law, Culture, and the Humanities publishes scholarly works in which the field of Law intersects with, among others, Film, Criminology, Sociology, Communication, Critical/Cultural Studies, Literature, History, Philosophy, and the Humanities.

*On the Web at http://www.fdu.edu/fdupress*

**Publications**

Joel Silverman, *The Legal Exhibitionist: Morris Ernst, Jewish Identity, and the Modern Celebrity Lawyer* (2022)
Matthew Sorrento and David Ryan, *David Fincher's* Zodiac*: Cinema of Investigation and (Mis)Interpretation* (2021)
T. Patrick Hill, *No Place for Ethics: Judicial Review, Legal Positivism, and the Supreme Court of the United States* (2021)
Caroline Joan "Kay" S. Picart, *Monsters, Law, Crime: Explorations in Gothic Criminology* (2020)
Elaine Wood, *Gender Justice and the Law: Theoretical Practices of Intersectional Identity* (2020)
Orit Kamir, *Betraying Dignity: The Toxic Seduction of Social Media, Shaming, and Radicalization* (2019)
Marouf A. Hasian, Jr., *Lawfare and the Ovaherero and Nama Pursuit of Restorative Justice, 1918–2018* (2019)
George Pate, *Enter the Undead Author: Intellectual Property, the Ideology of Authorship, and Performance Practices since the 1960s* (2019)
Victor Li, *Nixon in New York: How Wall Street Helped Richard Nixon Win the White House* (2017)
Marouf A. Hasian, Jr., *Kafkaesque Laws, Nisour Square, and the Trials of the Former Blackwater Guards* (2017)
Michaela Stockey-Bridge, *The Lure of Hope: On the Transnational Surrogacy Trail from Australia to India* (2017)

Ted Laros, *Literature and the Law in South Africa, 1910–2010: The Long Walk to Artistic Freedom* (2017)
Peter Robson and Johnny Rodger, *The Spaces of Justice: The Architecture of the Scottish Court* (2017)
Doran Larson, *Witness in the Era of Mass Incarceration: Discovering the Ethical Prison* (2017)
Raymond J. McKoski, *Judges in Street Clothes: Acting Ethically Off-the-Bench* (2017)
H. Lowell Brown, *The American Constitutional Tradition: Colonial Charters, Covenants, and Revolutionary State Constitutions 1578 – 1786* (2017)
Arua Oko Omaka, *The Biafran Humanitarian Crisis, 1967–1970: International Human Rights and Joint Church Aid* (2016)
Marouf A. Hasian, Jr., *Representing Ebola: Culture, Law, and Public Discourse about the 2013–2015 West Africa Ebola Outbreak* (2016)
Jacqueline O'Connor, *Law and Sexuality in Tennessee Williams's America* (2016)
Caroline Joan "Kay" S. Picart, Michael Hviid Jacobsen, and Cecil E. Greek, *Framing Law and Crime: An Interdisciplinary Anthology* (2016)
Caroline Joan "Kay" S. Picart, *Law In and As Culture: Intellectual Property, Minority Rights, and the Rights of Indigenous Peoples* (2016)

# The Legal Exhibitionist

## Morris Ernst, Jewish Identity, and the Modern Celebrity Lawyer

Joel Silverman

FAIRLEIGH DICKINSON UNIVERSITY PRESS
*Vancouver • Madison • Teaneck • Wroxton*

Published by Fairleigh Dickinson University Press
Copublished by The Rowman & Littlefield Publishing Group, Inc.
4501 Forbes Boulevard, Suite 200, Lanham, Maryland 20706
www.rowman.com

86-90 Paul Street, London EC2A 4NE, United Kingdom



*Fairleigh Dickinson University Press gratefully acknowledges the support received for scholarly publishing from the Friends of FDU Press.*

British Library Cataloguing in Publication Information Available

**Library of Congress Cataloging-in-Publication Data**

Names: Silverman, Joel (Joel Matthew), author.
Title: The legal exhibitionist : Morris Ernst, Jewish identity, and the modern celebrity lawyer / Joel Silverman.
Description: Lanham, Maryland : Fairleigh Dickinson University Press, [2022] | Series: The Fairleigh Dickinson University Press series in law, culture, and the humanities | Includes bibliographical references and index. | Summary: "The Legal Exhibitionist explores Morris Ernst's use of 'exhibitionism' to transform himself from insecure youth into America's most popular lawyer. Though Ernst later abandoned his progressive values to defend the FBI and a Dominican dictator and is today largely unknown, his story presaged the phenomenon of the modern celebrity attorney"—Provided by publisher.
Identifiers: LCCN 2021060152 (print) | LCCN 2021060153 (ebook) | ISBN 9781683933359 (cloth) | ISBN 9781683933366 (epub)
Subjects: LCSH: Ernst, Morris L. (Morris Leopold), 1888-1976. | Lawyers—New York (State)—New York—Biography.
Classification: LCC KF373.E7 S55 2022 (print) | LCC KF373.E7 (ebook) | DDC 340.092 [B]—dc23/eng/20220202
LC record available at https://lccn.loc.gov/2021060152
LC ebook record available at https://lccn.loc.gov/2021060153

# Contents

# Acknowledgments

When I completed an earlier version of this book in 2006, as my doctoral dissertation, I'd assumed that I'd be destined to join the numerous biographers (many of whom Morris Ernst himself encouraged to tackle his biography) who never managed that feat. Ernst's life and career not only spanned eight decades, but he was also constantly writing, dictating, speaking, and working. Moreover, at the time, his papers at the University of Texas at Austin's Harry Ransom Center hadn't been cataloged. And so I told myself that I would be content to have my dissertation "published" as a PDF online. I took on a fantastically rewarding administrative position at Yale in 2007, and though I returned to Ernst's life and career now and then, occasionally received kind emails from colleagues who had happened upon my work, and published an article based on one of my chapters, I thought that Ernst's story might remain a footnote: namely, he'd always be the guy who defended *Ulysses* in 1933.

But with the rise of Trumpism, the increased attacks on civil liberties, and the clear movement of the Supreme Court away from reproductive rights, it became clear to me that Ernst's story was more relevant than ever. This was, in one sense, unfortunate. Perhaps prior to 2001, and even up through the Obama years, Ernst's work in support of birth control, freedom of the press, and civil liberties seemed quaint, since so many Americans mistakenly assumed that those rights and freedoms were secure and permanent. (I count myself among that delusional mass, despite all of the evidence I now see to the contrary.) And yet those same rights have been seriously challenged in the United States over the past five years, and those challenges were decades in the making. I wanted to publish Ernst's story, not only because he worked tirelessly to *defend* those rights and freedoms, but also because he contributed to the culture that, to an important degree, ultimately *undermined* them. His endorsement of the FBI, his defense of conspiracy theories behind the disappearance of a Spanish, anti-totalitarian activist, and even his efforts to convert his fame into influence and to present himself as an authority on all matters of issues having no connection whatsoever to his legal work—creating, in essence, the primordial ooze from which the modern celebrity lawyer arose—damaged our democracy. And so, as the global pandemic cut me off from my world, I reentered Ernst's, and I hope I have done his story justice, both in terms of his contributions and his failings.

I'd never written a book before, and there were so many people who helped me along the way. I'm so grateful that Caroline Picart, the series editor of the Fairleigh Dickinson University Press Series on Law, Culture and the Humanities, took a chance on this unpublished author. Kay's publication list is daunting (20 books at the time of this writing) but she put me at ease and supported the project all the way through. Thanks, too, to James Gifford, my FDUP editor; Zach Nycum, associate editor at Rowman & Littlefield; and Megan DeLancey, production editor at Rowman & Littlefield, for their patience with this newbie and for shepherding my manuscript through to print.

My brother, Jonathan Silverman, always believed in this project and encouraged me early on to continue with the work I'd completed for the dissertation. Jonathan has offered not only ongoing moral support, but read and critiqued multiple drafts and helped me to greatly improve the manuscript. My mother, Beverly Silverman, my brother Jason Silverman, my aunt Cheryl and my nephew, Theo, have also been loving and caring boosters (and, additionally, excellent dinner company). I'm fortunate to have such a large and supportive extended family, including some published authors (Meryl Gordon, Walter Shapiro) and many aunts, uncles, and cousins (Marci, Debbie, Marty, Mindy, Mark, Suzanne, Andy) who always offered encouragement. While I wish my father, Melvin Silverman, were still with us, his spirit and love live on in these pages and in our hearts.

I am indebted to Stephanie Goldstein Begen, for her friendship and generosity. It's been fun to share "Morris stories" and new finds over the last 15 years, and I'm glad, Stephanie, that you still get chance to "be an Ernst" at least once each year. I'm also thankful to John Balz, Mary Batten, Paul Boyer, Roger Ernst, Arthur Joel Katz, Bernard "Buddy" Timberg, and Samuel Walker. We've sadly lost some of these souls over the last 15 years. I remain grateful for their time and their stories.

During my graduate years, I was fortunate to have the feedback and support of Janet Davis, Julia Mickenberg, Elizabeth Engelhardt, and Sarah Weddington. Mark Smith had my back; he was as supportive and thoughtful an adviser as one could hope for, and he reviewed countless drafts, challenging me not only to think critically about American history, but also to craft a narrative that might connect with an audience beyond the academy. My other UT Austin teachers, including Bill Stott, the late Bob Crunden, Robert Abzug, Richard Pells, and Shelly Fisher Fishkin, shared their scholarly strategies, which I drew upon as I researched and wrote about Morris Ernst's life. Bill Fagelson, my comrade-in-arms, and the indefatigable and brilliant

Jennie Burger helped keep me sane during those great years in Austin, even after I accidentally locked myself in their bathroom. My grad school colleagues, including Matt Hedstrom, Mark Metzler Sawin, Paul Erickson, Ole Bech-Petersen, Greg Barnhisel, Randy Lewis, and Siva Vaidhyanathan continue to inspire me. Pat Fox and the wonderful staff at the Harry Ransom Humanities Research Center (HRHRC) at the University of Texas at Austin were so nice and so generous with their assistance. UT also connected me with John Ruszkiewicz, who helped make me a better teacher and to see my own writing through a valuable new lens.

Over the years, the friendship of Robert Neal and Alisa Andrew, Meredith Gold and Jay Lindsay, Troy Resch and Zoe Cummings, Diane Fine and Carl Baum, Enola Iversen, and many other wonderful folks have helped to sustain me back when my family and I were new to New Haven and when I was new to this project. And then there are all the great friends and colleagues I met in New Haven: Jasmina Besirevic and Matt Regan, John Loge, Kyle Farley and Veronica Iacono, Alfred Guy, the late Debbie Tenney, Paula Resch, Jan Hortas, Kelly and Julia McLaughlin, George Levesque, Risa Sodi, Jeanne Follansbee and so many others. Thanks also go to so many other Yale colleagues, including Kate Lofton, Paul McKinley, Ryan Brasseaux, Michael Denning, Matthew Jacobson, Steve Pitti, and Alicia Schmidt Camacho. I've been especially blessed to count Mark Schenker among my friends and mentors. Mark has taught me a great deal about equity and stringency, and he shares my love (and Joyce's!) for wordplay, even if my groan-to-grin punning ratio is painfully unbalanced.

It's hard to believe that our son, Noah, was not yet a part of our lives when I began poking into the Morris Ernst papers. Noah is now a young adult; I'm proud to be his "Dr. Daddy." And most of all, I am incredibly fortunate to have been a part of Alba Estenoz's life for the past 30 years. Alba's determination to open her own dessert and tapas bar in 2020, after decades of serving as a pastry chef for restaurants in Austin, Madrid, and New Haven, was inspiring, and her grit and resilience during the pandemic was nothing short of heroic. Alba, I love you. . . . and remember: you promised you'd read this once I published it!

## *Chapter 1*

# Pre-Trial Jitters

In 1944, Morris Ernst was America's most famous living American lawyer. He had made a name for himself in the late 1920s and 1930s as a champion of civil liberties who successfully defended free speech, sexual education, birth control, and reproductive health, working first as a hungry practitioner in Greenberg, Wolff, and Ernst, the legal firm he co-founded; and later as co-general counsel for the ACLU. His landmark defense of James Joyce's *Ulysses* in 1933 cemented Ernst's reputation as *the* progressive attorney of the era, making it practically impossible, as Ernst himself declared, "for the censors legally to sustain an attack against any book of artistic integrity, no matter how frank and forthright it may be."[1] But it was his active self-promotion and exaggerations—what he called "exhibitionism"—that boosted his fame. In a 1940 interview, referencing his law education at NYLS's night school, he explained that upon entering the profession in 1912, "Very quickly I realized the inadequacy of my part-time preparation . . . . I started to make up for it by exhibitionism and have never recovered."[2] As part of his efforts to promote himself, Ernst befriended newspaper writers, authors, actors, politicians, and practically anyone whose work carried some weight in popular culture. He counseled Groucho Marx, Edna Ferber, E. B. White, and James Thurber; his clients often became his friends, and his friends became clients. Most lawyers in small firms promote themselves for business purposes, but Ernst converted self-promotion into an art. He became a regular fixture at the Stork Club, the Algonquin, 21, and other New York City nightclubs, where he might relax with Heywood Broun, coax Walter Winchell to drop Ernst's name into his weekly column, or sell Harold Ross on a brief *New Yorker* piece. He held cocktail parties in his Manhattan home, with a wide array of guests from many fields and political backgrounds, and invited luminaries out to his Nantucket summer compound. And very quickly, Ernst's exhibitionism, together with his brilliant legal talents, helped him attain a level respect he found wanting in his youth. Every opportunity to talk about censorship and sex was, for Ernst, a chance to demonstrate his own sexual expertise and spread his own name. In a 1932 article he published in *The Nation*, Ernst could declare that sex had won in America; it followed that Ernst, who had so frequently defended sex, was its champion.[3]

One of the prime reasons for Ernst's success was his undeniable charisma and charm. He literally entertained the public. Ernst made the law and the art of lawyering seem exciting. The world-renowned psychoanalyst Marie Jahoda fondly wrote that Ernst "has an amazing gift for making even national income figures sound more exciting and meaningful than the latest murder story."[4] Ernst's friends often recognized his exaggerations or flair for drama, but they didn't fault these traits—at least, not initially. Vice President Henry Wallace, whom Ernst often advised, once gently corrected some mistakes Ernst had published in his latest book, but then immediately forgave them. "Your sense of the dramatic is so perfect that the truth modifies itself to suit your purpose," Wallace wrote. "For that reason you can write a more interesting book than I. As long as the truth is not seriously hurt, why should anyone complain?"[5] And while defending his clients, Ernst turned courtrooms into classrooms and laymen into colleagues. His was the persona of the energetic teacher, who genuinely wanted laymen to learn the law. On one national radio broadcast he declared:

> It is about time the laymen were not mystified by us lawyers. . . . What I am concerned with is getting the public informed. I am fearful that the lawyers will never have any real motive for reforming the law. Why should we change our pleasant little racket? The pressure will have to come from you lay people. How else can we educate the public? The newspapers are very ineffective and to a great extent the public has lost faith in the integrity of the press.[6]

Ernst here suggested that he was wise to the "racket" of the law and, as opposed to the other tricksters in the legal world, that he was willing to shed light on its inner workings. In his delineation, Ernst was the educator who, unlike journalists or other lawyers, would demystify the law and thus liberalize his profession by opening it up to the common man.

Yet Ernst was not a pedantic teacher, and therein lies the secret to his success as a performer. He was eager, amusing, interesting, and *likeable*. "We had fun educating judges and juries," Ernst once wrote, and the hint of whimsy here provides some additional insight into Ernst's popularity. In the 1930s and 1940s, at a moment of great economic, political, and social upheaval, Ernst's was a fresh voice—a teacher, a social critic, a brilliant showman, and a talented speaker who suggested ways to fix the errors behind economic depression and political strife. He was ever willing to provide advice, ideas, and suggestions, and asked little in return. He became a man whom people liked and wanted to know, and through radio broadcasts, newspaper and magazine articles (as both author and subject), public speaking engagements, and books, he promoted his causes, and himself, thereby creating a model for the modern American celebrity lawyer.

By the late 1950s, however, Ernst's star had begun to fade. His brand of boyish enthusiasm, which his contemporaries had heretofore graciously viewed as a side product of restless intellect and an eagerness to please, was no longer interpreted in such positive terms. As early as 1944, *Life* recognized that "Ernst readily admits to being an exhibitionist," but that "he might not so readily admit that his exhibitionism betrays, in inverted form, a sense of inferiority."[7] More importantly, Ernst chose what seemed like a strikingly different direction in his choice of clients and causes, devoting more time and energy on burnishing the reputation of FBI Director J. Edgar Hoover and attacking Communists than on promoting feminist issues or defending free speech. He remained generous with his time and advice, but his favors, his motives, and his integrity now came under scrutiny. Meanwhile, his focus on the common man and his defense of progressive causes, two features that had helped bring the recognition he so sorely desired, diminished. And yet, though Ernst was no longer out in front of the media to publicize or defendthose same progressive causes, he continued his exhibitionism. Roger Baldwin, who worked closely with Ernst at the ACLU, once joked of Ernst: "He must know some unimportant people, but if so he never mentions them."[8] Ernst's intense need to drop names, together with his decision to steer away from the kind of causes that he could use to connect him with everyday Americans, led him to make choices that undermined his efforts to remain a respected and popular American personality.

Though Ernst may have unwittingly complicated the writing of his story by exaggerating his own power, the very existence of those widely reported exaggerations are all the more interesting because, objectively, there was no need whatsoever for Ernst to exaggerate his accomplishments. By almost any measure, by the end of World War II he was eminently successful in his profession. He had not only won almost every obscenity case he argued (many of which were landmarks), but he had also demonstrated his ability to master numerous different legal topics and had written articles and books on everything from banking to unions. He regularly appeared at the White House in the 1940s and had argued before the Supreme Court. He had advised mayors, governors, and presidents. Artist Peggy Bacon sketched him, and novelist Phillip Wylie included him as a character in his murder mystery spoof.[9] He was in great demand for debates on radio broadcasts and for public speaking engagements. While his 1944 *Life* profile hinted at some of the coming blows to his credibility and popularity, responses to the article were warm and positive, and this wartime article, circulated among millions of readers, secured his popularity. Why, then, would a man like Ernst, who was universally (and rightfully) recognized as a successful attorney and a powerful opponent of censorship, find it necessary to suggest that he had more influence than he really had? Why would a man who really did have the ear of a president need to inflate his own importance? Why would he risk his hard-earned reputation as a civil liberties pioneer by feeding confidential documents to the FBI and by representing a Caribbean dictator?

Though we may never know all of the answers to these questions, there is sufficient evidence to suggest that at the root of his choices was, indeed, a sense of inferiority. Ernst's insecurity was perhaps complicated by his own Jewish background and by changing popular assumptions about masculinity, and his need for exhibitionism grew out of a desire for respect that would never fully be realized, at least in his own perception. By drawing from primary sources, including an unpublished transcript of Ernst's taped 1961 interview with a historian, along with letters, interviews with relatives and former associates, and a memoir written by his nephew, this first chapter begins to flesh out Ernst's path toward becoming a celebrity social justice lawyer, with a view to squaring his background with the persona he would later present in his writings. Chapter 2 describes Ernst's successful defense of birth control activist Mary Ware Dennett in the "Sex Side of Life" trial, as well as the societal contexts that led to it. This case challenged what Ernst would describe as Victorian values—and, along with those values, the assumptions that certain boys and men might be inherently savage. Chapter 3 tells the story of *People v. Sideri,* in which Ernst defended doctors and nurses who were arrested after police raided their birth control clinic. *Sideri* illustrates why the idea of contraception could remain threatening to some men and women; it also demonstrates that Ernst could craft talking points that advanced his clients' causes while promoting himself as a modern man. The case against Radclyffe Hall's novel *The Well of Loneliness*, described in chapter 4, raised the specter of defending a lesbian text in 1929. Ernst's success with *Well* was due in part to his research into homosexuality and on his apparent acceptance of the fluidity of gender identity as well as a perception that society was changing more quickly than the law. Chapter 5 presents the famed 1933 case of *Ulysses,* which rightly codified Ernst's reputation as a superb legal advocate—making the case not just for his client, but for the rights of artists and, indeed, citizens everywhere. Ernst was the ideal attorney to argue this case, both because he could relate on a personal level with fictional outsiders and because, professionally, he had learned to translate otherness for a general audience. Chapter 6 presents the famous "Birth of a Baby" trial, which indubitably shows Ernst at the height of his fame and respect in obscenity law. Ernst was glad to take on this case for the boost to his celebrity and to his firm's profits. Yet in contrast to Ernst's prior cases, the *Life* case feels artificial and staged. While the case did legitimize public depictions of pregnancy and birth, *Life*'s motives in publishing this pictorial, and Ernst's motives in defending the magazine, struck some contemporaries as mercenary and self-serving. Chapter 7 reveals how Ernst's anti-communism, combined with his insatiable thirst for access and influence, led him to make questionable choices in clientele as he tried to navigate changing cultural conditions, guessing wrong and ultimately staining his reputation and credibility. He embraced J. Edgar Hoover and the FBI and possibly informed on his colleagues, eventually exchanging over 300 letters with the agency. Finally, chapter 8 describes Ernst's reputational decline. In 1958, Ernst accepted a huge challenge: to defend Rafael Trujillo, the murderous dictator of the Dominican Republic, against charges that he disappeared one of his political enemies in New York City. This was a public charge, not a legal one, and Ernst's subsequent extralegal report, for which he was paid an enormous sum, was largely dismissed as a whitewash. Though that period marked the end of his days of legal relevance, he retained enough cultural currency that he could still receive invitations to appear on the *Merv Griffin Show* and public radio shows to promote his latest book or opine on the events of the day. But despite his considerable achievements, his landmark work in obscenity law, and his impact on civil liberties, his legacy has been largely forgotten. To America's first modern celebrity lawyer, this lack of recognition would have been the ultimate tragedy.

This chapter will provide some background on Ernst's childhood and early career, framing it with a discussion about the way gender and ethnicity shaped the life of a small, ambitious Jewish boy into the civil liberties lawyer who, during the thirties and forties, became perhaps America's most famous attorney. Using the contextual lenses of American studies, this book combines the historical recounting of Ernst's greatest free speech trials with an emphasis on historical and theoretical contexts. It serves as a window into a changing United States that was confronting long-held assumptions about the nature of public mores. Those assumptions ranged from the role of women, to what constituted "obscenity," to the nature of gender and sexuality, and their roles in shaping human perceptions, behavior, and, especially in Ernst's case, American law. That a boy who considered himself an outsider became an insider through his tireless efforts shows the strange and important role Ernst had in shaping the world from the Great Depression through World War II. That much of his work benefited a feminist agenda might be partially an accident of his background, but is also a logical extension of these complicating forces all Americans, and particularly those historically marginalized, confronted.

## EARLY INSECURITIES: JEWISHNESS AND MASCULINITY

Morris Leopold Ernst was born on August 23, 1888, in Uniontown, Alabama. Ernst's father, Carl Ernst, came from what Morris Ernst called a "peasant village" in Pilsen, Bohemia, and joined his brother in Alabama to operate Ernst Brothers & Mayer, a general merchandise store.[10] In Uniontown, Carl Ernst married Sarah Bernheim, the daughter of a well-to-do German immigrant. According to Morris Ernst, family "legend" held that when his family moved to New York City in 1890, they had $200,000 socked away.[11] It seems improbable that Carl Ernst, who arrived in Alabama poor and uneducated, was able to earn and save so much money from running a general store. More likely, a good amount of whatever money the Ernsts had saved came from the maternal side of the family. Ernst's description of his father's success as "legend" is important because Ernst's boyhood belief in his father's ability apparently came crashing down in 1907, along with the family fortunes, after the younger Ernst entered college.[12] This failure may have had implications for Morris's development, perhaps contributing to an almost obsessive search for recognition and validation.

After the family moved to New York, Carl Ernst applied his retail business experience to real estate and for many years amply supported the family. The Ernsts had enough money, for example, to send Morris away to Camp Marienfeld in New Hampshire. Morris recalled the camp as "shockingly modern," since the boys went around nude (and barefoot to boot).[13] While a nudist camp for boys was indeed modern, the Ernsts' decision to send their boy out to the country fit the contemporary middle-class concern about providing boys with what Jeffery P. Hantover calls "proper masculine socialization."[14] Hantover suggests that turn-of-the-century middle-class adults worried about the effect that an urban environment, smaller families, and the long absences of working fathers would have on boys, since all of these factors could increase boys' contact with, and (according to this early twentieth century line of thinking) subsequent feminization from, their mothers. The rural back-to-nature camp environment, where "boys could be boys" and could literally immerse themselves in dirt and aggressive play was, as historian E. Anthony Rotundo writes, anathema to the clean, quiet and domesticated household kept by many nineteenth-century middle-class women.[15] The addition of nudity would presumably also highlight the difference between Ernst and his non-Jewish, and non-circumcised, fellow campers. Ernst grew up during the 1890s, a decade that was "widely perceived as encompassing an acute 'crisis of masculinity.'"[16] As Harry Brod and others have suggested, during the late nineteenth century, industrialization, urbanization and the influx of

**Figure 1.1. Morris Ernst and his sister, Magdalen, visiting family in Pilsen, early 1890s.**

immigrants were beginning to have a serious impact on the way in which men and women perceived themselves. Fewer men were their own bosses, and this decrease in autonomy had an impact on the way that Americans would perceive gender in the coming era. As Michael Kimmel explains,

> Rapid industrialization, technological transformation, capital concentration, urbanization, and immigration—all of these created a new sense of an oppressively crowded, depersonalized, and often emasculated life. Manhood had meant autonomy and self-control, but now fewer and fewer American men owned their own shops, controlled their own labor, owned their own farms.[17]

Within the male-dominated power structure, women had more say over their own lives and, as Joseph Pleck argues, with men more likely to be absent from the home for business or travel, mothers had more influence on their children.[18] "In my youth," Ernst later recalled in an interview with Edward R. Murrow, "no boy saw much of his father, when he worked 70 hours a week."[19] Even as married women's influence thus expanded at home, the increasing spectacle of single women in the public sphere raised the specter of emasculation for some men. As women entered the workforce, though the jobs they took were hardly threatening to white male hegemony, some men thought it an omen of grave portent for male power. The slippery slope of feminine earning power could, in some men's minds, lead to women calling the shots.

One solution for such men was a kind of masculine quarantine. By 1900, when Ernst was entering adolescence, "a severe sociosexual wrench was evident" and the role of mothers and wives "was beginning to transcend its accustomed domain and threaten not just the masculine establishment but the whole of masculine identity."[20] During this era, in response to these anxieties over masculinities, "men's only" clubs increased. Concerns over masculinity may have also led to the founding of the Boy Scouts. Originally founded in England by Lord Robert Baden-Powell in 1907, the Boy Scouts began organizing its male troops in America in 1910 and quickly built up a large membership. According to Hantover, its rapid acceptance through the nation was due to the fact that Scouting was "perceived . . . as an agent for the perpetuation of manliness among adolescents; the Boy Scouts provided an environment in which boys could become 'red blooded' virile men."[21] Such was the conflict between the traditional, Victorian embrace of female domesticity, and the emerging interest in male self-segregation.

Morris did not enter the Boy Scouts, but Camp Marienfeld served the same purpose. After Ernst's mother contracted tuberculosis in 1901 and was sent away in the hopes that she would be cured, Carl Ernst likely didn't know quite what to do with his children.[22] Perhaps summer camp was a necessary solution for a one-parent household with a working father, or perhaps Carl Ernst was unequipped to deal with his two children on his own. Either way,

Morris was shipped off, and this experience was momentous enough that he vividly recalled it 60 years later. The summer away from home surrounded by naked boys seems to have reinforced the young Ernst's insecurities. As a boy, at least, this emphasis on the physical was uncomfortable to Ernst and was intertwined with his sense of himself as timid. "As I look back at it," he told one interviewer, "I was a shy and bashful boy."[23] That inevitably led to loneliness. "I was usually desolate for a friend," he later wrote. "I recall no confidants in my youth . . . I was frightened and lonely for sure."[24] Even when he was in his seventies, Ernst easily recalled how he was mocked during his formative years for his appearance. "I had been brought up to believe that I was ugly," he revealed. "I had uncles who always kidded me about my big Jewish nose which did my ego no good." Like many Jews at the turn of the century, Ernst's uncles and relatives were likely seen, in Kimmel's words, as "too bookishly effete and too physically puny to truly measure up" to contemporary manly ideas, and they apparently directed their own insecurities at the young Morris.[25] He also recalled being taunted by outsiders as well: "I was told that I was Jewish, and for that reason, inferior."[26]

It is thus understandable that Ernst, who found no palatable models of masculinity in his immediate environment, looked toward popular culture for a hero. Like many boys in the late nineteenth-century, Ernst idolized the manly Theodore Roosevelt.

> The earliest hero that I remember is Teddy Roosevelt . . . I wasn't a fighting type. I never shot a gun in my life, even to this time . . . so I doubt that Teddy was my hero because of his San Juan Hill episode, although just because I am a physical coward and don't like guns and shooting, and physical pain and blood, maybe he was my hero. I rather guess that he was my hero because of his great energy, and because he was very outspoken and very indiscrete.[27]

A number of scholars have argued that Roosevelt had an important influence on popular notions of masculinity in the late nineteenth and early twentieth centuries.[28] Gail Bederman argues that there is a direct link between Roosevelt's numerous pronunciations on manhood and his bellicose forays into military conflict as president. Roosevelt's much-touted military and personal adventures—the San Juan Hill episode that Ernst cites, or Roosevelt's hunting trips in Africa, for example—became the stuff of many young men's imaginations.[29] Boys pretended that they were Teddy Roosevelt, achieving manliness through strenuous and dangerous exploits. Part of the appeal for a boy like Ernst would have been Roosevelt's legendary transformation from frail youth to powerful adult. Although the disconnect between an unathletic and scrawny boy like Ernst and the barrel-chested Roosevelt was enormous, Ernst could still see Teddy as a hero to be emulated.

Ernst apparently gained some confidence in himself while attending the Horace Mann school in New York, which introduced him to an eclectic crowd of individuals. It was here that Ernst met Heywood Broun, who later became a powerful and popular newspaper columnist and Ernst's lifelong friend and client.[30] Ernst thrived at Horace Mann. He played cello and helped Burnet Corwin Tuthill, who later became a famous conductor, establish his first orchestra in high school.[31] During these years, he even gained enough confidence to undertake a challenging trip to Europe by boat, where he and a cousin hiked around the continent. Spurred on by his cousins, Ernst applied to Harvard when only 15 years old. He failed all of his entrance exams, however, and instead attended Williams College.

Ernst would reminisce about his inability to gain admittance to Harvard throughout his life. In fact, he proudly kept a copy of the rejection letter on his desk for all of his clients to see and publicized its existence in interviews and in his own memoirs. He thus used this rejection from Harvard to suggest, private school and powerful friends aside, that regardless of such connections, he was a man of the people rather than a member of the effete elite. Ernst later lamented that he lacked the kind of academic refinement that his wife gained at college, and he came to idolize men like Supreme Court Justice Felix Frankfurter who had a Harvard pedigree. In fact, Yale law professor Fred Rodell claimed Ernst's inability to attend a "first-class" law school actually "gnawed" at him.[32] But whatever Ernst's true feelings about his education, he decided to exploit such failures in an attempt to raise his stature as a relatable man.

One important person in Ernst's development was Ted Lewis, a professor at Williams. Lewis, a Welsh immigrant, had been a professional baseball player known as "the Pitching Professor" before entering academia, and Ernst adored him:

> To me he represented the Horatio Alger legend of rags to riches in the very best sense of the word "riches." My own sports were tennis and bowling, so I had a very real envy of the athlete who performed publicly in the arenas of our more highly competitive team contests. I was also rather lonely, envying the more sophisticated students at Williams, although I remember my college days as generally quite happy. So I listened to Ted's words with acute and magnified attention, both in the classroom and across the table in his modest kitchen, to which he sometimes invited me.[33]

Ernst attributes his progressive take on government—the idea that it was the duty of the state to help out its less fortunate members—to his discussions with Lewis. In his introduction to *The Teacher*, a collection of essays he edited, Ernst proclaimed, "I shall die in debt to Ted Lewis." But notice, as Ernst describes his teacher, the package this philosophy came in: "Tall and lean, preserving the appearance of an athlete in training, (Lewis) was a handsome man whose maturity impressed me at the time, although I suppose he was only about ten years my senior."[34] Lewis, in other words, represented to Ernst the important trappings of masculinity: athleticism, public performance, popularity, intellectual aptitude, and kindness. "I was in youthful awe of Ted's athletic prowess," he later mused.[35] Ernst couldn't hope to attain true athleticism, but he learned that he could certainly vie for the other rewards he associated with Lewis's manliness.

Such lessons were not immediately applicable at Williams. Despite his academic success, Ernst continued to crave the attention granted to the athletes and fraternity men and tried desperately to fit in. "If you look at my picture of my freshman class," he said, "I wore my hat in the oddest fashion because I wanted to look as if I was a collegiate type which I wasn't. All through college I envied the captains of the football teams and the athletes."[36] Joe L. Dubbert interprets the rise in organized sports and this new emphasis on athleticism during the progressive era as "an important line of defense against effeminization."[37] If Ernst's insecurities about athletics seem particularly acute, it may be due to such cultural pressures.

In addition to feeling physically out of place, in 1907 Ernst faced new economic pressures which must have added to his unease. When his father's real estate investments soured, Ernst began working full-time, first at a shirt factory, and then at a furniture store. While Ernst had hoped to enter law school like his friends at Williams, in 1909, when he graduated from Williams, that goal must have seemed unattainable. Though he would later write cheerfully about these years, even praising his father in print, privately Ernst winced at the very suggestion that he grew up privileged. After *Life* magazine published its 1944 spotlight about him and made such a suggestion, Ernst took pains to emphasize that, contrary to *Life's* assertion, Carl Ernst had "lost every nickel he ever had."[38] Ernst may have exaggerated his father's financial losses. DeWitt Stetten Jr., who was Morris Ernst's nephew, recalled that Carl Ernst and his brother "alternated between prosperity and bankruptcy."[39] At least some of that money helped send his son to camp in New Hampshire, to private school, and to Williams College. Given this degree of financial support, Morris Ernst's bitterness over the family's change in fortunes seems odd. The extent of Ernst's disappointment in his father is initially hard to gauge. On the one hand, he spoke sympathetically of his father's difficult experiences in Europe and the obvious sacrifices immigrants like Carl Ernst made:

> The people who left poverty, or being hit over the head by local police, as my father must have been in his peasant home in Pilsen, when they got to this land of freedom, they had ambitions not for themselves so much as for their children.

> To this end their whole life was dedicated—saving up enough so that his kids would get an education when he didn't have [*sic*].[40]

Ernst here talks approvingly of the sacrifices of immigrants; indeed, he acknowledges the limitations his father faced. In Ernst's last memoir, written in 1968, he called his father "a kind man, generous and sentimental."[41] On the other hand, the garrulous Ernst, who refused few invitations to talk in public, and was by all accounts a most vocal and vivacious character, was unable to speak with his own father. "We didn't talk much at all," he recalled in an unpublished interview. "I had no real communication system with my father."[42] Comparing his parents, he considered his mother "the strong person." This is a revealing assessment, given that Ernst said that he didn't know his mother very well because "she got sick when I was quite young."[43] According to the *New York Times* obituary, Sarah Ernst contracted tuberculosis in 1901, when Ernst was about 13 years old.[44] Perhaps Ernst was romanticizing his mother; after all, his memory of her was fuzzy. Though he was 19 years old when she died in 1908, she had spent a good portion of his childhood at "the leading health resorts in Europe" in the hopes of curing the illness she had contracted seven years earlier.[45] But his remark that she "was the strong one" seems to be a swipe at his father (if his mother was "the *strong* one," that is, his father must have been "the *weak* one"). Ernst's comment about the "legend" of the money his father earned also seems to detract from the romantic image of the sacrificing immigrant.

While working full-time, Ernst also worked toward his law degree at New York Law School by taking night classes. In 1912, despite the change in family finances, Ernst earned his degree and married his first wife, Susan Leerburger. He then joined two other friends from his college days at Williams College, and in 1915 they founded the law firm of Greenbaum, Wolff, and Ernst. As a Jewish lawyer in 1915, Ernst was fortunate to be able to start his own firm, as there were few other alternatives for Jews who wished to practice. Jews who wanted a legal career in the early twentieth century knew that discrimination virtually eliminated any possibility of being hired by a non-Jewish firm. In documenting the entry of Jews into the legal profession, Jerold Auerbach points out that during this period, the doors of most New York law firms were closed to Jews.[46] Similarly, in her biography of Supreme Court Justice Abe Fortas, Laura Kalman explains why Fortas looked to Jewish firms for work after graduating from Yale Law School in the early twentieth century: as a Jew he was all but barred from other firms.[47] As late as 1939, Ernst himself approached Supreme Court Justice Harlan Stone on behalf of other Jews in an attempt to counter such restrictions.[48] Certainly, Jewish firms did exist, but since Jews were unable to apply to non-Jewish firms, the competition for a position in the top Jewish firms was fierce. The only other real option for young Jewish attorneys—particularly those lawyers like Ernst who earned their law degrees at night school—was to create a firm of their own.[49]

Ernst provides little information about the first years of his firm and even less about his personal life. In later years, when he offered readers autobiographical tidbits, he wrote very little about his first wife, Susan. Perhaps the memories were too grim: like Ernst's mother, his wife contracted tuberculosis. Susan died in 1920, leaving Ernst alone with their two-year-old daughter, Constance. In 1923, he married Margaret Samuels, a newspaper writer from Mississippi; the couple would have two more children, Roger and Joan.

Greenbaum, Wolff, and Ernst soon established its credibility as an all-purpose corporate firm. Ernst spent his first ten years as a kind of general practitioner, working on cases relating to banking regulations, taxes, jewelry legislation, and so forth. By the mid-1920s, Ernst's firm was also representing several progressive causes, and Ernst quickly became the most prominent member of the team. He rose in stature both by tackling controversial issues involving sex education, birth control, lesbianism, marital sexuality, and reproductive health, and by using the media to promote his name. This entry into obscenity law better fit his growing need to perform before and excite an audience. Readers were interested in reading for themselves the titillating details in books that the government had deemed obscene, and Ernst noticed that book sales shot up after a text had been challenged. The public was also interested in what the flamboyant lawyer had to say. Ernst quickly found his opinion in demand and offered it liberally in interviews, as an author in magazines and books, as a speaker at public forums, and as a debater on the radio. Some of the most controversial, and thus exciting, cases of this ilk stemmed from issues that would become critical issues in the modern feminist movement, such as reproductive health, female sexuality, and birth control.

## FEMINIST WORK FOR MASCULINE RESPECT

Though Ernst employed his exhibitionism in the service of garnering personal and professional respect, in the process he also helped gained legitimacy for certain feminist causes. In representing numerous women's causes, Ernst was performing what Harry Brod calls "pro-feminist" work. Brod distinguishes between "pro-feminist" men, whom he identifies as those men who believe feminism to be "of, by, and for women" but that men should support it; and "profeminist" men, who see their own stake in feminism and participate in feminist politics "of, by, and for men."[50] A "profeminist" man, according to Brod's definition, is thus actively engaged in advancing feminist issues. Ernst did in fact actively support many women's issues, both inside and outside the courthouse. As a lawyer, he promoted texts that expanded the cultural boundaries of acceptable sexual practices and worked to get those new standards codified into law. As a cultural critic, he publicly recognized gender inequities and proposed that the government make it financially attractive for women to work by paying working mothers a stipend to cover the cost of childcare. He was an early proponent of having female jurors. And as a businessman, he literally gambled on the success of Harriet Pilpel, who in 1936 became the first female lawyer hired by his law firm. Ernst promised his skeptical partners that he would personally pay out the difference if Pilpel failed to bring in enough income, a bet he won.[51] Rather than attempt to quarantine himself from femininity, as some contemporaries had done with all-men and all-boys organizations, Ernst embraced it—at least, professionally—and soon discovered that the strategy of publicly supporting issues of importance to women helped him win the recognition and respect he so desired. Unable to emulate the physical qualities of his hero Theodore Roosevelt, and insecure and lonely as a boy, Ernst discovered a knack for the law and worked hard to dominate it. In the process, he merged his newfound talent for argumentation with his passion for social justice and his desire to become intimate with New York's power brokers and celebrities. As clients became friends, social connections led to more social connections, and media coverage begot media coverage, Ernst embodied the beloved image of the underdog who, through the dint of effort and perseverance, overcomes the odds and reaches the top of his profession. Though his affluent background and his Williams education might seem to suggest otherwise, his NYLS law degree, earned at night school while Ernst held down a full-time job, helped cement that image. Ernst could thus persuasively present himself as a common man, an image only bolstered by his support of popular progressive issues in the 1920s and 1930s.

Despite any protestations to the contrary, of course, Ernst knew that he was exceptional. Indeed, as historian Brett Gary writes, at that moment in American history when literary and sexual modernism were both gaining what Gary calls "legal legitimacy," he emphasizes Ernst's enormous achievement in gaining that legitimacy: "There's one guy who's orchestrating all of this: Ernst."[52] Likewise, Jay A. Gertzman has called Ernst "the most influential and politically powerful of the era's First Amendment advocates."[53] The civil liberties scholar Samuel Walker, in assessing Morris Ernst's contributions to reproductive rights, calls Ernst "a real pioneer."[54] Though Ernst's success thus makes it more appropriate to label him as "exceptional," rather than "representative," his fame and popularity was contingent on his image as a kind of common man who had access to the powerful and influential. Like modern-day congressmen who are thoroughly political animals and yet publicly disassociate themselves with "politics as usual" in Washington, Ernst could avow "a love affair with the law" and still tell a roomful of doctors that "lawyers are the basic parasites of the day . . . a standing army of 170,000 human beings organized primarily to prevent change and progress."[55] While the public found such pronouncements endearing, Ernst was anything but common.

In terms of race, class, ethnicity, and even geography, Ernst's experiences as a man in the early twentieth century were similarly exceptional. That is, Ernst's ability to forge a new kind of manly conception as a Jewish lawyer in New York is not necessarily applicable to, say, the Pullman Porters in Washington (whom Ernst would represent in the 1920s). He was, however, constantly meeting with and learning from men who differed from him, and these experiences informed Ernst's exhibitionist tendencies. In other words, it did not matter that Ernst could not possibly have remembered his infancy in Alabama; he was born in the South (and married a Jewish woman from Natchez, Mississippi) and knew to promote this fact when discussing matters of interest to Southerners. Ernst's progressive credentials as a defender of civil liberties earned him an honorary Pullman Porter's membership, an honor which, as he recounted his adventures for the public, also became a proud part of that identity. Ernst's identity was forged by sheer will and by his interactions with people who came from a diverse and broad range of backgrounds. Like novelists who draw from their environment and experiences to make fictional characters live on the page, Morris Ernst had a knack for successfully bending both the truth and his own image to his benefit.

The fact that Ernst's life, career, and experiences were so extraordinary suggests how difficult it was for other men of his background to reach his level of recognition. He thus offers rare insight into the cultural demands that numerous twentieth-century Jewish men faced. In the first place, by examining Ernst, one can see how much pressure some men felt to attain recognition and acceptance *as* men. Though Ernst enjoyed a degree of success that men from similar backgrounds might never know, many of those other men certainly must have felt just as ostracized by and excluded from certain American masculine ideals they faced while coming of age in the late nineteenth century. These Jews, Stephen H. Norwood writes, faced "hoary stereotypes of Jewish males' physical incapacity, cowardice, and effeminacy that dated almost from the beginning of the Second Diaspora."[56] Secondly, one realizes how incredibly hard Ernst had to work to achieve such recognition. The man was, as his law partners said, a dynamo.[57] He had to be. His social and professional schedule was packed; he saved a fraction of time by making his clients into his friends, and vice versa, but this arrangement also meant that Ernst was constantly performing. If he worked hard to achieve recognition as a lawyer, he had to work even harder to attain respect as a Jewish man.

To better understand Ernst, then, it is necessary to explore how and why he sought, gained, and lost respect and recognition during the twentieth century.

And to do so, it is necessary to delve into the roots of his celebrity, his talent of self-promotion, and his profound interest in remedying social injustice. In studying his life, it becomes clear that his rise to fame was predicated on his lust for the limelight and an intense need to rub shoulders with the powerful. As Roger K. Newman has written of Ernst, "this access became part of his essence."[58] In part, that access and his celebrity grew out of Ernst's passion for civil liberties and his willingness to take on unpopular and risky cases. He argued in favor of issues such as sexual education and birth control, defended texts depicting lesbian relationships, and represented progressive, activist women such as Marie Stopes, Mary Ware Dennett, and Margaret Sanger. He studied sexuality in order to better argue his cases, became a fan of sexologist Alfred Kinsey, and eventually dedicated an entire book to Kinsey's groundbreaking study of male sexuality. At a time when the average man was ignorant about the reproductive health of his wife or girlfriends, Ernst was thus well versed in sex.

This intimate understanding of sexuality, together with Ernst's drive to be seen and heard, made Morris Ernst a new kind of Jewish American man in the twentieth century, even if his contemporaries did not always envision him in contemporary masculine terms. Again and again, in the media coverage Ernst so aggressively sought, journalists invariably mentioned his smallness (despite the fact that his 1921 passport application placed him at the above-average height of "5 feet, 8–1/2 inches") and alluded to his ethnicity.[59] *Time* magazine, for instance, constantly drew attention to Ernst's size, describing him as "swarthy, small and solidly built"—"swarthy" being a code word for "non-white"—or as "lively, liberal little Manhattan Lawyer Morris Ernst."[60] In 1934, when artist Peggy Bacon included Ernst in *Off With Their Heads!*, her aptly titled book of portraits, she included a tiny drawing of Ernst as a jack-in-the-box—not an image most people would immediately associate with strength or masculinity.[61] *Life* described Ernst as a "smallish, darkish man."[62] Even in a favorable 1938 *Scribner*'s portrait of Ernst, the prominent historian Marquis James, described Ernst as a small man.[63] But by taking on controversial cases that resonated with the progressive spirit of the age and by promoting himself in the media, Ernst carved out a masculine niche that also resonated with changing attitudes about gender. For a relatively brief and shining moment, Ernst transcended cultural expectations about masculinity and earned the recognition and acceptance that had been unavailable to him as a young man.

Given his purported status as an outsider and his itch for public recognition, law was the perfect career choice for Morris Ernst. The law afforded him the opportunity to perform in front of audiences and use his mind, rather than his body, to try to outmaneuver his opponents. Ernst couldn't slay wild animals like Teddy Roosevelt and, in fact, hated the sight of blood, but as a lawyer he could defeat opponents and demonstrate his superiority through argumentation. Moreover, in getting the public to acknowledge his success and his knowledge of sexuality, he was effectively gaining recognition as a man. He thus drew strength from winning and from using that knowledge and his promotional acumen to gain the attention of the powerful and the famous, on the one hand, and of the general public on the other. The fact that he chose such contentious issues to defend and that he could, in the course of a trial, reveal his intimate knowledge of sexuality, helped make him an interesting person to know.

Before turning specifically to the case of Morris Ernst, it will be instructive to examine the background on the intellectual foundation of masculinity studies and the meaning of terms such as "gender" and "masculinity" as they apply in this analysis. Robert A. Nye points out that through the first decades of the twentieth century, gender was a stable concept. That is, people understood one's gender to be the same thing as one's sex; this identity was natural, and it did not change. There was, in other words, an understanding that gender was binary—you were either a male heterosexual or a female heterosexual and there were no other constructions of gender. Homosexuality as a term and a concept did not even emerge until the late nineteenth century although, as Caroll Smith-Rosenberg has demonstrated, there is clear evidence that erotic relationships between women long predate the use of the term "lesbian."[64] Nye attributes the changing realization that gender was fluid in part to the technological and medical advances of the past fifty years:

> The art of the cosmetic surgeon now permits the external markers of the body's sex to be enlarged, suppressed, reshaped, or spectacularly invigorated by drugs. As a consequence, we now think of sex as infinitely malleable, as an unreliable indicator of sexual orientation, and as a signifier of gender rather than the other way around . . . . These developments have divided sex, gender, and sexuality into separate ontological and analytical categories and have produced the situation in which gender, as the more stable feature of personal and social identity, has begun to replace sex as the common descriptor in everyday discourse for women and men, male and female.[65]

Though Nye is right that sex and sexual orientation today seem more malleable, the roots for this uncertainty or anxiety about identity in gender reach further back in history. For instance, as Laura Doan has documented, during the 1920s, when many British women dressed in a decidedly masculine way, their contemporaries did not read this fashion as a sign of sexual orientation.[66] The very fact that women chose this "masculine" style, however, suggests that at least some men and women in this era were raising questions about what constituted masculinity and femininity. And though Karen Halttunen does not deal directly with such questions of gender identity, her study of nineteenth-century advice manuals serves as a reminder that in the Victorian era, when Ernst and his clients and adversaries were born and raised, identity was frequently interrogated. Halttunen points to the insecurity that Victorians had about the fact that "confidence men" and "painted ladies" could wheedle their way into proper society. This anxiety, she writes,

> arose out of a crisis of social identity faced by these men and women who were on the move both socially and geographically. In what was believed to be a fluid social world where no one occupied a fixed social position, the question "Who am I?" loomed large; and in an urban social world where many of the people who met face-to-face where strangers, the question "Who are you really?" assumed even greater significance.[67]

In other words, anxieties about identity—and the idea that one type of person could "pass" for another—existed long before plastic surgery and hormone treatment became widely available, and those were the types of anxieties with which Ernst would have had to contend, both personally and professionally.

Men in the 1920s and 1930s, regardless of sexuality, race, ethnicity, or social status, were members of a society that adhered to certain shared assumptions about what constituted a man and were ultimately evaluated in terms of these shared assumptions. In Ernst's era, men might dismiss this construction, but they could not escape it. Men might grumble about the influence of women in society, or join a men's only club, or enroll their sons in the Boy Scouts, but women's thoughts and attitudes and bodies were increasingly heard and seen in the public sphere, and they weren't going away. During this period, men and women were aware that the process of masculinity was in flux: hence the rise of men's clubs and the Boy Scouts and other "men-only" associations, as well as the redefinition of masculine women's fashions and a more liberal display of the female body. Accordingly, those who were unnerved and threatened by these changes attempted to cajole their fellow citizens into rejecting ideas and policies that promoted the newer features of manliness, while their opponents tried to codify laws that seemed to allow for a freer, if not terribly enlightened by our contemporary standards, interpretation of gender roles.

The modern idea that gender is flexible and fluid—an interpretation which may have contributed to Ernst's triumphant defense of the lesbian novel *Well of Loneliness*—explains how Ernst gained confidence and became successful in defending women's issues. By adopting this assumption about gender, Ernst unwittingly, if temporarily, fashioned himself as a kind of sexual renaissance man. Cases relating to obscenity in general, and sexuality in particular, boosted both Ernst's confidence and his credibility and raised his standing in the public's eye.

As an early-twentieth-century Jewish American man, Ernst's strategy of exhibitionism stemmed from insecurities relating to his sense of himself as a man. Like the late twentieth-century men that Susan Faludi presents in her analysis of modern masculinity, Ernst felt the need to overcompensate for his own perceived weaknesses by literally showing off. The men and boys who hunt for fame in Faludi's book do so as a strategy; they are, in effect, writing their own masculine script in which they become the actors; they want to be celebrities because they believe it will provide them with power and transform them into active, rather than passive, participants in their world. Faludi, in other words, suggests that men seek fame and notoriety to validate their own masculinity. Fame, in this construction, appears to be the only route to power for many modern men, who feel most manly—or imagine that they will feel more like men should—when they are in the spotlight. Ernst, too, used the media, and in doing so, raised his cultural capital by associating himself publicly with controversial cases relating to sex. Ernst's constant efforts to be linked to the powerful and famous and his search for controversy also hint at some type of overcompensation.

Though Faludi's reading of how masculinity informs the pursuit of fame is thus useful, I depart from what Bryce Traister identifies as the "two-pronged crisis theory" of masculinity.[68] As Traister explains, one prong of crisis theory "locates instability at the base of all masculine identities constructed within American cultural matrices" while the other prong posits that gender is "always performative and contingent."[69] In simpler terms, crisis theory suggests that masculinity is forever changing and is therefore unstable at its core. This theory has been especially popular with poststructuralists, who use the idea of instability or crisis to suggest that one can never really nail down gender. The crisis theory of masculinity helps explain why Faludi sees modern masculinity as betrayed or threatened; times and cultural demands have changed and, in Faludi's telling, men simply do not know where they stand in their society.[70] Or, as Faludi explains it, the shift from a utilitarian society to a society based in commercial culture and the resulting constraints on masculinity have made men feel worthless.[71] Given the fact that the very meaning of "utilitarian" necessarily changes with time, some will find Faludi's overarching claim to be questionable, but her detailed documentation of the way in which men search for recognition through celebrity does help to explain Ernst's almost obsessive self-promotion.

Whereas Faludi provides the motive for Ernst's remarkable transition from insecure youth to exhibitionist lawyer, Judith Butler provides the means. Butler's major contribution to the field of gender studies is the concept of performative masculinity. While Faludi and Butler may seem to be different in almost every other way, at heart they share the same philosophical belief: that masculinity is in crisis. Butler, however, explicitly presents gender as a strategy:

> That gender reality is created through sustained social performances means that the very notions of an essential sex and a true or abiding masculinity or femininity are also constituted as a part of the strategy that conceals gender's performative character and the performative possibilities for proliferating gender configurations outside the restricting frames of masculinist domination and compulsory heterosexuality.[72]

Put another way, gender is a strategy of performance which empowers those whose identities fall outside the frames, or popular expectations, of heterosexuality. Though here Butler is analyzing drag queens in particular, her analysis, as other scholars have noted, is applicable elsewhere. Ernst created his own gender reality, through "sustained social performances"; in his case, his performances in the courtroom, in the media, in his own books and articles, in the New York clubs, and so on. In doing so, he navigated around the "restricting frames of masculinist domination" and presented himself as an actor, rather than a spectator. Traister rightfully attributes the performative nature of masculinity to Butler's poststructuralist work; because Butler assumes that gender is unstable, her work also fits into his crisis theory.

If masculinity is forever unstable and in crisis, however, then instability and crisis become the norm, and every male action necessarily constitutes a response to a crisis. Traister rebuts the crisis theory of masculinity by citing recent examples of male-on-male violence, and asks whether the idea of gender in crisis could ever explain, for instance, hate crimes. "I just do not know," Traister argues, "whether the vicious masculinity behind these crimes is enduring a 'crisis' in any way comparable to that of their victims."[73] In Ernst's case, his performative masculinity—what he called exhibitionism—stemmed not from a crisis, but from his ability to pursue the narrow avenues of masculine opportunity during the first half of the twentieth century. Though he may have been insecure, and though he faced adversity and definite challenges in his drive toward success, Ernst's identity stemmed from innovation, rather than crisis.

Another clue about Ernst's motivations came from the esteemed historian, John F. Kasson, who has written about masculinity in the early twentieth century. In his analysis of the images of masculinity popularized by Harry Houdini, Eugen Sandow, and Edgar Rice Burroughs, Kasson illustrates how these three men "repeatedly dramatized the transformation from weakness to supreme strength, from vulnerability to triumph, from anonymity to heroism, from the confinement of modern life to the recovery of freedom."[74] In this sense, Ernst's transformation was most akin to Houdini's. Harry Houdini was born in Budapest in 1874 as Erik Weisz (later changed to "Ehrich Weiss").[75] In 1876, Ehrich's father, Rabbi Mayer Samuel Weiss, immigrated to the United States, and the rest of the family joined him two years later.[76] Ehrich's father was unable to keep his job as a rabbi in Appleton, Wisconsin, and in vain moved the family from place to place in search of a congregation. Like Ernst, Ehrich Weiss associated his father with financial struggle and disappointment, and Kasson argues that the younger Weiss's ambition "sprang from the painful sight of his father's failure."[77] Again, like Ernst, Weiss found that performance could help him navigate the churning waters of masculine expectation:

> In its play with appearance and reality, deception and illusion, imposture and grandiosity, magic offered a means by which (Houdini) could negotiate his anxieties and fantasies about manliness in a household in which he both desired and feared to take his father's place. The magician was a role by which he could sustain a fantasized self of miraculous powers. More specifically, it offered a grandiose *masculine* role by which Ehrich could proclaim his complete independence, even invulnerability. This was, in addition, an *assimilated* role. The downward spiral of his father's career would not be his. Tricking others could fortify his sense of mastery and of mental and bodily integrity. The line between an actor playing the role of a magician and a boy imagining an imposture as a masculine hero might for Ehrich Weiss have been a fine one [emphasis in the original text].[78]

Ernst himself had a connection with Houdini, as his cousin, Bernard M. L. Ernst was Houdini's lawyer. Houdini encouraged Morris Ernst to take magic lessons at a cocktail party both men attended in the early 1920s.[79] Ernst enrolled in magic classes, joined the Society of American Magicians, and saw the applicability of magic in the courtroom. "The advocate can learn much from the conjurer, whose art depends on—and exposes—man's lack of ability to tell what is real, and what illusion," Ernst wrote in 1968.[80] "The magician knows that the more intent the mind—upon the wrong thing—the easier it is to fool. I tell someone to go to the corner of the room and not think of the number 2; it's really difficult if not impossible."[81] Lawyers could use illusion, Ernst wrote, to change the way testimony was perceived. Though Ernst stopped paying his dues to the Society of American Magicians because, he said, of "my inability to really become a worth while magician" [*sic*], his short-lived career as a student of magic had taught him, to paraphrase Vice President Wallace, how to shape reality.[82] But much like a magician, Ernst formulated a pattern that would focus the attention of the audience on one corner of his life (in Ernst's case, his knowledge of sexuality, his famous, powerful friends, etc.) and away from another (his physical attributes, his insecurities, his background, and so forth).

The final clues to Ernst's success come from Ernst himself. As Ernst would suggest in his 1960 introduction to the "biography" of his law firm, when he was in his early seventies, the public persona one reveals in their memoirs is not always reliable. "Of course no one ever writes an honest autobiography or retains anyone so to do," Ernst wrote. "Only a masochist would enjoy a record of his defeats."[83] Ernst wrote and co-authored over twenty-five books and countless articles, including memoirs and published diaries. While he wrote some of these texts in the third person, Ernst would frequently cite his own casework and would refer to himself anonymously as "the defense attorney."[84] Many of his books were co-authored by other lawyers and writers, but regardless of whether there was another hand in the crafting of the texts, the tone throughout these works paints the picture of a breezy and confident man of the people. Whether or not he uses the first person, Ernst's public persona is consistently that of a modern man who is intimate with the power brokers and yet can relate to the little guy. Perhaps this image of the scrappy intermediary who can speak *to* the powerful but *with* the common man is the true essence of Ernst—or, at least, perhaps this is the man whom Ernst ultimately became. In exploring what Ernst called his "inadequacy," one begins to realize how Morris Ernst became successful—and, perhaps, why his influence waned during the last decades of his life. To Ernst, exhibitionism meant not only exploiting his connections to the media, speaking to the public, and writing memoirs; it also meant taking on controversial clients and flaunting his relationship with the powerful and famous. One contemporary wrote that, with the possible exception of the British intellectual Harold Laski, "no living man can compete with Ernst when it comes to first-naming the famous."[85] Exhibitionism not only provided a shield for Ernst's supposed inadequate legal training; it was also his means of compensating for his insecurities as a Jewish man in early-twentieth-century America, and thus became an integral part of his masculine script.

To overcome his insecurities, rooted as they were in Ernst's status as a second-generation Jewish immigrant, in his relationship with his father, in the illness and absence of his mother during his childhood, in his sudden loss of financial support, and even in his physical attributes, Ernst sought out fame and controversy. The resulting confidence he seemed to gain was thus a product of both his enormous legal talent and the connections he forged with the powerful and famous. The next chapters demonstrate Ernst's success in presenting his clients as victims of outdated mores and the misguided authorities who followed them. Though he would increasingly publicize his relationships with powerful cultural and political figures, from the late 1920s through the 1940s, he made it clear that he was on the side of the common man, and the resulting, heady mix—the guy who calls out the overreach of authorities and describes his own profession as a "racket," yet who influenced leaders at the highest levels of government—gained Ernst national fame, along with the respect and recognition he'd always coveted.

## NOTES

1. Morris L. Ernst, foreword to James Joyce, *Ulysses* (New York: Vintage Press, 1961), v–vi.
2. Paul Boyer, *Purity in Print: Book Censorship in America From the Gilded Age to the Computer Age*, second ed. (Madison: The University of Wisconsin Press, 2002), 147.
3. Morris L. Ernst, "Sex Wins in America," *The Nation,* August 10, 1932, 122–124.
4. Marie Jahoda to Dr. Seymour Siegel, January 26, 1955, Box 454, Morris Leopold Ernst Papers, MS-1331, Harry Ransom Center, University of Texas, Austin (hereafter cited as "MLE"). The letter identifies Siegel as the director of WNYC.
5. Henry Wallace to Morris Ernst, May 1, 1945, Box 477, MLE.
6. Unpublished script of an April 4, 1935, radio debate with Tom Stix, held at the Algonquin Hotel and broadcast live on WOR radio, Box 11, MLE.
7. Fred Rodell, "Morris Ernst: New York's Unlawyerlike Liberal Lawyer is the Censor's Enemy, the President's Friend," *Life*, February 21, 1944, 107.
8. Cited in Roger K. Newman, "Morris Leopold Ernst," *Dictionary of American Biography*, New York: Charles Scribner's Sons. 1995, *Gale in Context: U.S. History*, https://link.gale.com/apps/doc/BT2310013962/UHIC?u=29002&sid=bookmark-UHIC&xid=29bdbed3.
9. Anonymous, *The Smiling Corpse. Wherein G.K. Chesterton, S.S. Van Dine, Sax Rohmer and Dashiell Hammett Are Surprised to Find Themselves at a Murder* (New York: Farrar & Rinehart Incorporated, 1935). Book critic John Chamberlain, who himself appears in the novel, identified the author as Phillip Wylie; Chamberlain wrote that his source was Walter Winchell (who is also a character in the book). See John Chamberlain, "Books of the Times," *New York Times*, March 11, 1935. Wylie later wrote *Generation of Vipers*, a nonfiction book in which he promoted the idea of "Momism," a theory that too much mothering weakened America.
10. Morris L. Ernst, unpublished family history, 2, Box 877, MLE. Jon Balz first alerted me back in 2004 to this treasure trove hidden within the then-uncatalogued collection of Ernst's papers. Along with random papers and articles, this box contains an untitled bound transcript of Ernst's long taped interviews in June 1961, recorded when Ernst was 72, in which he reveals more details about his childhood than in any of his published writings.
11. Ernst, unpublished family history, 4, Box 877, MLE. Morris Ernst's sister, Magdelan Ernst Stetten, put the family savings at $150,000—still an enormous sum in 1890. Bernard M. (Buddy) Timberg, "The Ernsts and The Bloomingdales: A Special Report"; unpublished family history, 1973; shared with the author by Buddy Timberg.

12. Ernst, Unpublished family history, 4, Box 877, MLE.
13. Ernst, Unpublished family history, 26, Box 877, MLE.
14. Jeffrey P. Hantover, "The Boy Scouts and the Validation of Masculinity," in *The American Man*, ed. Elizabeth H. Pleck and Joseph H. Pleck (New York: Prentice-Hall, Inc., 1978), 290.
15. E. Anthony Rotundo, "Patriarchs and Participants: A Historical Perspective on Fatherhood in the United States," in *Beyond Patriarchy: Essays By Men on Pleasure, Power, and Change*, ed. Michael Kaufman (New York: Oxford University Press, 1987).
16. Harry Brod, "The Case for Men's Studies," in *The Making of Masculinities: The New Men's Studies*, ed. Harry Brod (Boston: Allen & Unwin, 1987), 47.
17. Michael Kimmel, *Manhood in America: A Cultural History* (New York: The Free Press, 1996), 83.
18. Joseph H. Pleck, "American Fathering in Historical Perspective," 86, in Michael S. Kimmel, ed., *Changing Men: New Directions in Research on Men and Masculinity* (Newbury Park: Sage Publications, Inc., 1987), 83–97.
19. Morris L. Ernst and Margaret S. Ernst, interview by Edward R. Murrow, *Person to Person*, CBS, January 6, 1956.
20. Joe L. Dubbert," Progressivism and the Masculinity Crisis," Rept. in Elizabeth H. Pleck and Joseph H. Pleck, eds., *The American Man* (Englewood Cliffs: Prentice-Hall, Inc., 1980), 309–310.
21. Hantover, 287.
22. "Mrs. Carl Ernst Dead," *New York Times*, February 15 1908, 14. According to the *Times*, Sarah Bernheim Ernst died of tuberculosis she contracted in 1901 while doing charity work.
23. Ernst, Unpublished family history, 39, Box 877, MLE.
24. Morris L. Ernst, *Untitled: The Diary of My 72nd Year* (New York: Robert B. Luce, Inc., 1962), 206.
25. Michael S. Kimmel, "Masculinity as Homophobia: Fear, Shame, and Silence in the Construction of Gender Identity," 280–281, in Stephen M. Whitehead and Frank J. Barrett, eds. *The Masculinities Reader* (Malden: Polity Press/Blackwell Publishers, 2001), 266–287.
26. Morris L. Ernst, *A Love Affair With the Law: A Legal Sampler* (New York: The Macmillan Company, 1968), 127.
27. Ernst, Unpublished family history, 23, Box 877, MLE.
28. See, for example, Rachel Adams and David Savran, "Introduction to Part 3: Representations," in *The Masculinity Studies Reader*, ed. Rachel Adams and David Savran (Malden: Blackwell Publishers, Inc., 2002); E. Anthony Rotundo, *American Manhood: Transformations in Masculinity from the Revolution to the Modern Era* (New York: Basic Books, 1993); Michael S. Kimmel, "The Contemporary 'Crisis' of Masculinity in Historical Perspective," in *The Making of Masculinities: The New Men's Studies*, ed. Harry Brod (Boston: Allen & Unwin, 1987); and John F. Kasson, *Houdini, Tarzan, and the Perfect Man: The White Male Body and the Challenge of Modernity in America* (New York: Hill and Wang, 2001).

29. Gail Bederman, *Manliness and Civilization: A Cultural History of Gender and Race in the United States, 1880–1917* (Chicago: The University of Chicago Press, 1995), 170–205.

30. Freda Kirchwey, Ernst's friend and the future editor of *The Nation*, which Ernst's firm represented (and for which Ernst wrote numerous articles), also attended Horace Mann, but it is unclear when the two met each other.

31. Ruth Houston, "A Dream Come True: Papa Tuthill and Memphis Music," 9. Unpublished fellowship thesis, Rhodes College, 2004. Burnett Corwin Tuthill founded what eventually became the Memphis Symphony Orchestra. He was the son of William Burnet Tuthill, the chief architect of Carnegie Hall. Oddly enough, though Ernst loved to drop names, and though he occasionally mentioned the fact that he had played cello as a boy, he never discussed Tuthill or his father.

32. Rodell, "Morris Ernst," 107.

33. Morris L. Ernst, "Foreword," in *The Teacher*, ed. Morris L. Ernst (New York: Prentice-Hall, 1967), 11.

34. Ibid.,12.

35. Ernst, *Love Affair With the Law*, 28.

36. Ernst, Unpublished family history, 39, Box 877, MLE.

37. Dubbert, "Progressivism," 309.

38. Morris L. Ernst to Roy Larsen, February 18, 1944, Box 128, MLE. Larsen was *Life*'s publisher.

39. Dewitt Stetten Jr., *How My Light is Spent: The Memoirs of DeWitt Stetten, Jr.*, Office of NIH History, 1983. history.nih.gov/articles/DeWittStettenMemoirs.pdf. NIH.

40. Ernst, Unpublished family history, 5, Box 877, MLE.

41. Ernst, *Love Affair With the Law*, 5.

42. Ibid., 8.

43. Ibid., 9, 15.

44. "Mrs. Carl Ernst Dead," *New York Times*, February, 15 1908, 14.

45. Ibid.

46. Jerold S. Auerbach, "From Rags to Robes: The Legal Profession, Social Mobility and the American Jewish Experience," *American Jewish Historical Quarterly* 66, no. 2 (1976): 266–268.

47. Laura Kalman, *Abe Fortas: A Biography* (New Haven: Yale University Press, 1990).

48. According to Auerbach, with this goal in mind, Ernst asked Stone "to meet with the partners of Wall Street firms in an attempt to ease restrictive hiring practices." See Auerbach, "Rags," 267–8n.38.

49. Edward S. Shapiro notes that as late as 1942, about one-third of the corporations that advertised in the *New York Times* and the *New York Herald* stipulated that they wanted only Christian employees. See Edward S. Shapiro, *A Time for Healing: American Jewry Since World War II*, ed. Henry L. Feingold, 5 vols., vol. V, *The Jewish People in America* (Baltimore: The Johns Hopkins University Press, 1992), 6.

50. Harry Brod, "To Be a Man, or Not to Be a Man—That is the Feminist Question," 207–208, in Tom Digby, ed., *Men Doing Feminism* (New York: Routledge, 1998) 197–212.

51. Roger Ernst, telephone interview by author, July 5, 2005. Roger Ernst was the son of Morris and Margaret Ernst. See also Joan Cook, "Harriet Pilpel, 79, Lawyer, Dies; An Advocate of Women's Rights," *New York Times*, April 24, 1991: D23. Pilpel became a senior partner at Ernst's law firm. She was later appointed general counsel of Planned Parenthood and earned a reputation as one of the country's major proponents of women's rights. Pilpel argued over 20 cases before the U.S. Supreme Court and was well-known to regular viewers of William F. Buckley Jr.'s television show, *Firing Line*.

52 New York University, "Faculty Profiles: Brett Gary," March 7, 2006: http://education.nyu.edu/education/steinhardt/db/profiles/1278.

53. Jay A. Gertzman, "The Moral Absolutist & the 'Average Person'," *JURIST* 4. No. 4 (April 2001): http://jurist.law.pitt.edu/lawbooks/revapr01.htm#Gertzman.

54. Samuel Walker, telephone interview with author, May 22, 2006.

55. Morris L. Ernst, "The Law Catches Up With Science," Speech to the Society of Medical Jurisprudence, October 14, 1937, Box 267, MLE. Cited in John Balz, "Legally Yours: The 'Unlawyerlike' Lawyer Morris Ernst Goes Public with Birth Control," Remarks Prepared for the American Society of Legal History Conference, October 28–30, 2004. Ernst often mentioned his "love affair with the law," and in 1968 even used that phrase as a title for his last memoir.

56. Stephen H. Norwood, "'American Jewish Muscle': Forging a New Masculinity in the Streets and in the Ring, 1890–1940," *Modern Judaism* 29, Number 2, May 2009, 167.

57. "GREENBAUM, WOLFF & ERNST-A brief history of the firm," Box 846, MLE.

58 Newman, "Morris Leopold Ernst."

59. Samantha Barbas, citing an undated Williams College grade report (perhaps reflecting a not yet 17-year-old Ernst?) puts his height at "only five feet, six inches." Either way, it is inconceivable that Ernst, who voraciously consumed any news report about him, would not have noticed and internalized the consistent media focus on his size. Samantha Barbas, *The Rise and Fall of Morris Ernst, Free Speech Renegade* (Chicago: University of Chicago Press, 2021) 15. A copy of Ernst's 1921 passport application is available here: "United States Passport Applications, 1795–1925," *FamilySearch* (https://familysearch.org/ark:/61903/1:1:QKDF-CZCP).

60. "Compact Disgust," *Time*, September 7, 1931; "Guild vs. AP," *Time*, December 16, 1935.

61. Peggy Bacon, *Off With Their Heads!* (New York: Robert M. McBride & Company, 1934).

62. Rodell, "Morris Ernst," 97.

63. Marquis James, "Morris L. Ernst," *Scribner's*, July 1938.

64. Caroll Smith-Rosenberg, "The Female World of Love and Ritual: Relations between Women in Nineteenth-Century America," in *History of Women in the United States*, v.10: *Sexuality and Sexual Behavior*, ed. Nancy F. Cott, *History of Women in the United States* (New Providence: K.G. Saur, 1993).

65. Robert A. Nye. "Locating Masculinity: Some Recent Work on Men," *Signs* 3 (Spring 2005): 1937(26).

66. Laura Doan, "Passing Fashions: Reading Female Masculinities in the 1920s," *Feminist Studies* 24, no. 3 (1998).

67. Karen Haltunen, *Confidence Men and Painted Women: A Study of Middle-Class Culture in America 1830–1870* (New Haven: Yale University Press, 1982).

68. Bryce Traister, "American Viagra: The Rise of American Masculinity Studies," *American Quarterly* 52, no. 2 (2000).

69. Ibid.

70. Susan Faludi, *Stiffed: The Betrayal of the American Man* (New York: William Morrow and Company, Inc., 1999), 34–35.

71. Jes Burns, Interview with Susan Faludi, *Etude* (The University of Oregon), Autumn 2004. http://etude.uoregon.edu/autumn2004/faludi/index.html.

72. Judith Butler, *Gender Trouble: Feminism and the Subversion of Identity* (New York: Routledge, 1990), 141.

73. Traister, "American Viagra," 292.

74. Kasson, *Houdini*, 8.

75. Ibid., 80.

76. Ibid.

77. Ibid., 84.

78. Ibid., 86–87.

79. Ernst joined the Society of American Magicians and that he cancelled his membership in 1928. Morris L. Ernst to Richard Van Dien, April 5, 1928. Box 414, MLE.

80. Ernst, *Love Affair With the Law*, 85.

81. Ibid.

82. Morris L. Ernst to Richard Van Dien, April 5, 1928, Box 414, MLE. Bernard M. L. Ernst had told Morris Ernst that his dues to the Society were overdue, and Morris wrote Van Dien to inform him that he had resigned years earlier. Van Dien, Houdini, and Bernard M.L. Ernst all served as presidents of the Society.

83. Morris L. Ernst, 1955 Foreword to GREENBAUM, WOLFF & ERNST-A brief history of the firm prepared for the occasion of its 40th Anniversary and a postscript thereto following its 45th Anniversary on May 15, 1960, Box 846, MLE.

84. In his 1940 book on censorship, for example, Ernst wrote in the third person about many cases that he had personally argued, including those treated in this book. See Morris L. Ernst and Alexander Lindey, *The Censor Marches On: Recent Milestones in the Administration of the Obscenity Law in the United States* (New York: Doubleday, Doran & Company, Inc., 1940).

85. Rodell, "Morris Ernst," 97.

## *Chapter 2*

# The Sex Side of Life

### COURTING THE MEDIA AND ATTACKING THE CENSORS

In the early 1920s, Ernst's energy and excitement for legal and public affairs soon garnered attention in New York City. Roger Baldwin, a founder of the ACLU, began consulting with Ernst on legal affairs, and in 1923, Baldwin had recruited Ernst to serve as treasurer for the American Fund for Public Service.[1] By 1926, Ernst had joined the ACLU Executive Committee, and was increasingly involved in free speech cases, pro bono.[2] One of Ernst's earliest opportunities to apply his strategy of exhibitionism more broadly came in 1929, after the Justice Department indicted a New York grandmother for mailing obscenity. The accused was Mary Ware Dennett, a well-known birth control activist, and the text in question was a sexual education pamphlet titled "The Sex Side of Life." The stated fear was that Dennett's tract would provoke sexual assault. Assistant District Attorney James E. Wilkinson would declare as much when the case later went to trial: "Why," he stated, "there's nothing a boy could see, on reading this book, except a darkened room and a woman! And suppose it falls into the hands of an abnormally minded boy. Why, the first thing he will do will be perhaps to waylay a beautiful girl . . . and . . . *attack her!*"[3] The state thus based its decision to indict Dennett on the assumption that certain men were savage and that texts like "The Sex Side of Life" endangered women and girls by inciting men and boys to rape and violence. In an era when Americans like Wilkinson still envisioned masculinity as a wild, threatening force, and the meaning of masculinity was being contested, it is not surprising that the State wanted to ban "The Sex Side of Life." Vice societies and obscenity hunters believed that indecency was symptomatic of the desecration of the traditional Victorian moral code and sought to protect children, whom they felt were most at risk.

By employing the relationships he'd cultivated with influential journalists, Ernst effectively helped convert the indictment of Dennett into a *cause célèbre.* As a published writer, an ACLU attorney, and an outspoken supporter of freedom of the press and freedom of speech, he enjoyed the company of writers such as Heywood Broun, Dorothy Thompson, and Freda Kirchwey, and he effectively tapped his media connections to help massage public opinion to his client's benefit. Ernst was able to curry favor with his friends in the media, whom he knew would pounce on the controversy. He, in turn, would influence their reporting and reap the benefits of favorable coverage. In the process, he moved the court to accept the more liberal interpretation of free speech, and he indirectly influenced the public's assumptions about what kind of speech was acceptable. At the same time, Ernst showcased his extensive knowledge of sexuality and represented a kind of foil to the type of male brute the prosecution feared.

In 1918, when Dennett first published "The Sex Side of Life: An Explanation for Young People," the censors ignored it. A text like Dennett's, which was first published in a medical journal, could still be understood as "private," since it was presumably in the hands of medical experts and not the general public. It was not until eleven years later, after the pamphlet had already been distributed to thousands of readers and adopted for use by churches and youth organizations such as the Young Men's Christian Association (YMCA), that the state indicted Dennett for violating the federal obscenity statute.[4] One of the prosecution's main arguments was that Dennett's pamphlet could improperly stimulate boys because it suggested that sex was intermingled with love.

In spite of Assistant District Attorney Wilkinson's alarming predictions about the potentially violent response of an "abnormally minded boy" to sex education, Americans were starting to envision more modern approaches to gender and sexuality that were at odds with this threatening image. Dark rooms inhabited by savage, animalistic men might exist, but perhaps modern thought and education could shed light on such rooms. The justice system, playing catch-up with societal norms, was slowly ratifying more modern ideas about gender and sexuality that had replaced those standards. The court broke with conventions, and in doing so it established a new measure for evaluating sex education texts, effectively deflating, if not demolishing, the argument that sex education invariably led men and boys to rape and disease. This case, then, begins to hint at how and why conceptions of gender identity slowly began to change in the courts, and how once-private notions were presented publicly. In addition, the case shows how, by exploiting the controversy generated by a profeminist text, Morris Ernst would bolster his own career to emerge as the preeminent censorship lawyer of the era.

## CHILDHOOD AND CIVILIZATION

During the 1910s, when Dennett first published her sex education pamphlet, the dominant theory on adolescence was that sexual control was crucial to children's maturation. Psychologist G. Stanley Hall, who founded the American Psychological Association in 1892 and published the hugely influential two-volume textbook, *Adolescence*, was pivotal in popularizing this perspective.[5] He argued that boys were essentially savage and needed to be civilized. City life, especially, was full of temptation, and so self-control was crucial in forging solid morals.[6] Fears of what Barbara Dafoe Whitehead calls "unruly sexual energies" were predicated on the assumption that masculinity was wild.[7] As Allan Brandt has shown, this assumption carried into adulthood, and even informed the way in which early twentieth-century doctors treated their adult patients. "Just as education for men followed the Victorian assumption that men were sexually aggressive," Brandt writes, "instruction for women focused on the notion of the passionless, dutiful woman."[8] For parents who were steeped in such assumptions, the question left unanswered by Hall's depiction of adolescence was how to impose such sexual control. That question grew in urgency as the increasing influence of Sigmund Freud and his disciples transformed notions of male childhood by suggesting that children, even from infancy, were inherently sexual beings.

Members of vice societies and their supporters found this reworking of sexuality threatening. Vice societies had first emerged in the late nineteenth century in response to the changing moral landscape of the city.[9] Paul Boyer describes how, during that era, some transplants to city life lamented what they saw as a moral vacuum. "The familiar sources of guidance and support—family, church, close-knit community—had been left behind," Boyer explains, and he suggests that vice societies grew out of concerns about the potential for social unrest and the related anxiety about the potential danger of so-called street urchins.[10] The twentieth-century Freudian portrait of the child as a sexual being could only have intensified such fears. The idea that sexuality was organic and inborn for women and men alike was also troubling. If sexual desire was innate in both women and men, then, perhaps they were more similar than previously thought. If so, perhaps because of such similarities, women could participate more fully in politics, enter the labor force, and be active in other traditionally masculine spheres.

More importantly for vice societies, the Freudian take on sexuality meant that women, who had often been depicted as passionless models of purity, might be as receptive to sin as men, and thus would abdicate their role as the domestic moral force who could rein in their husbands' and boys' inappropriate passions. Accordingly, progressives envisioned sexual education as a means to restrain sexual behaviors and instill sexual control rather than a tool to enlighten.[11] In this context, it is understandable why "The Sex Side of Life," which offered parents and their children graphic details about the human reproductive system and advice on sexual relations, might be interpreted as obscene. With her very detailed drawings of the male and female reproductive systems, Dennett transgressed the comfort zone of vice hunters, who worried that such details would stimulate young readers. In addition, if taken to its logical conclusion, Dennett's pamphlet offered its young readers a picture of a world in which, at least in the realm of sexual love, men and women were equals.

In the 1920s, as Dennett's pamphlet was first being circulated, sexual education was a relatively new phenomenon. Although by 1929 "The Sex Side of Life" had been in circulation for over a decade, toward the end of the 1920s sex education was by no means ubiquitous. By 1922, 46.6 percent of American secondary schools provided some type of sex education.[12] It was only in the late nineteenth century that women's rights and social purity proponents began to discuss the need for sexual education. Reformers like Lucinda Chandler, responding to fears about prostitution and venereal disease, stressed that children needed to learn about sex from parents or other respected authorities—or else they would learn about it "from the gutters," an argument that Morris Ernst would later repeatedly echo both in his books and in the courtroom.[13] The initial battles of these social reformers, who included religious leaders, suffragists, and temperance advocates, targeted the more obvious and threatening signs of sexual immorality, such as prostitution. The Progressive era, which spawned a reform movement dedicated to getting government involved in social and economic problems, witnessed a new focus on venereal disease.[14] In 1904, Dr. Prince Morrow published *Social Diseases and Marriage,* calling for a social hygiene movement to combat sexually transmitted diseases. He revealed, to the shock of contemporaries, that the incidence of venereal disease was greater in wives than in prostitutes. Morrow estimated that a full three-quarters of adult men had contracted gonorrhea. Although he traced the original source of these diseases to prostitutes, his point was that the wives were innocent victims. Brandt suggests that Morrow and other social hygienists thus "came to view venereal disease as a threat to the very foundations of the Victorian, child-centered family; the susceptibility of innocent women and children seemed not only criminal, but treasonous."[15]

This interpretation of the family owed much to the Victorian conception of gender, according to which women were passive and virtuous and responsible for taming the animalistic passions of men. Physicians like Morrow "accepted a common image of women as innocent, weak and helpless"—and given that such progressives believed that motherhood was a woman's primary domestic duty, and that physicians, as Brandt illustrates, "considered the male sexual drive with foreboding," venereal disease was therefore doubly threatening.[16] Morrow's solution was to educate the masses and to erase the stigma associated with venereal disease so that those who were inflicted would seek treatment.[17] Morrow was at the forefront of medical professionals to warn that when it came to sexually transmitted diseases, "secrecy and privacy have been placed above the interests of the public health." [18] The efforts of physicians like Morrow resulted in the creation of the American Social Hygiene Association, which envisioned the public school system as the ideal environment to educate the young on the horrors of venereal disease.[19]

Before World War I, however, the public was not yet ready to discuss educating children about sex. While the social hygienists gained important allies including, most notably, the National Education Association's endorsement in 1912, those in league with the vice societies strongly opposed open discussion of sexuality in any form. This is not surprising, given that vice societies were the fruit of nineteenth-century anxieties about city life among the rich and middle class.[20] In fear of social uprisings, and assuming that moral decay could lead to such unrest, wealthy patrons like John D. Rockefeller, J. P. Morgan, and William E. Dodge were among the successful businessmen who incorporated vice societies and pushed for anti-obscenity legislation. These types of laws often stemmed from the long-standing assumption that it was the responsibility of the wealthy to establish the moral boundaries of society. As legal scholar Kermit Hall argues, "(t)he upper classes in colonial society considered it part of their moral responsibility to impose appropriate forms of morality on the lower orders." As in colonial times, such laws "served as a handy instrument of social control."[21]

Anthony Comstock, the son of a wealthy farmer and mill owner in New Canaan, Connecticut, came to personify the vice societies. After his brother died at the Civil War battle of Gettysburg, Comstock joined up and served for a year and a half. Once the war ended, he moved from job to job, seeking employment in New Canaan; New Haven; and finally, New York City. At the age of 21 he took a job as a grocery clerk in New York, and here he found his calling. It was in New York that he saw his fellow employees trading shocking books and pictures back and forth. As he recalled, a friend of his was "led astray and corrupted and diseased" after he bought an obscene book and went to a brothel.[22] Comstock visited the bookseller, bought a book, and then brought the police to seize the bookseller's stock. He continued doing so on a small scale and published his findings. In 1872, the YMCA rewarded Comstock for his efforts. The YMCA's wealthy patrons, who had themselves battled against saloons and obscene literature, encouraged Comstock to establish a new YMCA committee known as the New York Society for the Suppression of Vice. Comstock did so and the YMCA appointed him as its secretary.[23] The following year, in 1873, he successfully lobbied Congress to push through the law that became known as the Comstock Act, which forbid the mailing of obscene materials.[24] During the early years of the twentieth century, despite the policy recommendations made by Prince Morrow and other medical professionals, there was still widespread belief that venereal diseases were the wages of sin, and that it was immoral even to suggest that sexually transmitted diseases were curable. Discussions of venereal disease in themselves, therefore, could theoretically fall under the very broad definition of obscenity under the Comstock Act, a fact of intimidation which hampered the social hygiene movement by making the topic of sexually transmitted disease continue to appear unseemly, if not criminal.

World War I provided social hygienists with the evidence they needed to push the idea of teaching sexual education in public schools. The experience of soldiers during the war ultimately lent weight to the argument that children should be educated about sex. Military officials were shocked by the number of incidents of venereal disease, which they initially attributed to wartime prostitution or "comfort girls." After further study, however, the military determined that the overwhelming majority of cases of sexually transmitted diseases were contracted on the homefront, before soldiers even entered the service. The revelation during World War I that five out of six infected soldiers contracted venereal disease *before* the war began sent the government scurrying for a solution. Congress responded in 1918 by creating the Division of Venereal Diseases, a federally funded organization which focused on the prevention of sexually transmitted diseases. The idea behind the organization was to reach future soldiers while they were children and before they became sexually active.[25] Backed by the U.S. Public Health Service, social hygienists now anticipated further government support for their cause.[26]

But after World War I ended, Congress did not renew funding for the control of venereal disease, a decision Brandt attributes to a movement away from the idea that the federal government should take responsibility for Americans' health.[27] Congress slashed funding for the Venereal Disease Division: in 1920, the agency received about $4 million; by 1926, it received less than $60,000.[28] Though social hygienists now focused on introducing sexual education in public schools, the quality and depth of the information they provided was weak and insufficient. While much more permissive than their opponents in the vice societies, these reformers saw sexual instruction as little more than the means to eradicate, or at least help curb, sexually transmitted diseases. As James H. Jones argues in his biography of sexologist Alfred C. Kinsey, in the early twentieth century, social hygienists who fought for sexual education "had no intention of teaching young people human reproduction, human anatomy, birth control techniques or the like." Instead, their aim was to give students just enough information for them to avoid premarital sex. In the words of contemporary reformer Maurice Bigelow, social hygienists believed that information about sex and venereal disease could be taught to children "without the slightest consciousness on their part that what they are receiving is sex instruction."[29] When tied to disease prevention, complete with frightening pictures of the ravaging effects of venereal disease, sexual education was often welcomed by community leaders and politicians. Even so, the movement to incorporate sexual education in the classroom was still met with resistance. If American parents were generally receptive to the idea of educating children about the dangers of venereal disease, they were nervous about the unintended consequences they believed might arise from providing children with too much information.

Social hygienists shared these concerns. After all, their overarching goal was not to increase sexual liberty but rather to eliminate venereal diseases by instilling a sense of sexual self-control in children, a task that took on increasing importance as parents and reformers alike witnessed their social and cultural environments changing. Waves of immigration in the late nineteenth century brought new attitudes toward sexual morality, which many white middle-class Americans found threatening. Victorian ideas about what it meant to be "civilized" were linked to concerns about sexuality and sexual control.[30] Historian Jeffrey Moran has demonstrated that these concerns "represented the quest for stability and certainty in the midst of an unsettled, industrializing, urbanizing America."[31] With the influx of immigrants, who often embraced and lived by different mores, entrenched and established Americans who upheld traditional Victorian mores felt increasingly threatened. As John D'Emilio and Estelle Freedman observe in their *History of Sexuality in America*, "foreigners became the scapegoat for the sexual anxieties of the native-born."[32] It was one thing to instill a code of sexual ethics in one's own children, but what about foreign-born kids? After all, in urban areas, immigrants were increasingly in contact with native-born children.

With these anxieties inflamed by the changing ethnic and racial makeup of the cities, some Americans believed that adolescents, whom they viewed as not yet fully formed moral beings, as well as those adults who suffered from some spiritual weakness, might be tempted by the impure foreign influences entering America. Certainly, professional anti-Semites and white nationalists declared as much publicly. In the 1920s, for example, the pro-Klan *American Standard* bemoaned the "dreadful narcotizing of moral modesty" and pinned responsibility on Jews for this hit on morality: "Jazz is a Jewish creation. The mush, the slush, the sly suggestion, the abandoned sensuousness of sliding notes, are of Jewish origin. Monkey talk, jungle squeals, grunts and squeaks and gasps suggestive of cave love are camouflaged by a few feverish notes and admitted to homes where the thing itself, unaided by the piano, would be stamped out in horror."[33] The message was that immigrants, Jews, and non-whites threatened to wear down American restraint and, subsequently, purity.

Figure 2.1. Morris Ernst, as sketched in 1921 by the German-Jewish artist Hermann Struck.

For censors and vice societies, the answer to protecting all children, then, was to obliterate any kind of image, idea or activity that might thwart their attempts to foster and nourish self-control in young people. In actuality, the social hygiene movement "was not a plea for sexual liberation but a demand for sexual control, a major counterattack by late Victorians who were intent on holding the line against the moral chaos of the city."[34] By taking a hard-line approach to sexuality, in some cases scaring children with descriptions of the ravages of venereal disease, social hygienists were hoping to reach children before they became corrupted by urban influences, including prostitution, dancing, and the threatening sexual mores of newcomers.

Inherent in this approach was a particular assumption about what it meant to be a man. As E. Anthony Rotundo illustrates, toward the end of the nineteenth century, the cultural understanding of manliness was changing, with "a growing tendency to look at men as creatures of impulse and passion, even as animals or savages."[35] Male passions, which many had considered to be threatening earlier in the century, were valued at the century's end. Cultural spokesmen like President Theodore Roosevelt, the psychologist James Cattell, and novelist Jack London would suggest, in Rotundo's words, that "civilization had so fully repressed their passions that their very manhood—their independence, their courage, their drive for mastery—was being suffocated" and, accordingly, with the dawn of the twentieth century, such men lauded and upheld the animalistic connection with such passions.[36] Rotundo classifies this response as "a male rebellion against the cultural standards that middle-class men of previous generations had helped to sustain."[37] The key to keeping these masculine ideals of civilization and savagery in balance was self-control. If there was anything that reformers hoped would emerge from bringing sex into the classroom, it was sexual self-control, which would, in their estimation, keep the boys from becoming too animalistic and the girls from enticing the boys.

By the time that Ernst defended Dennett, however, the savage nature of masculinity was no longer a foregone conclusion. Estelle B. Freedman's study of the sexual psychopath phenomenon from 1920 to 1960 confirms that public attitudes toward masculinity no longer assumed that all men possessed an animal or uncontrollable nature. According to Freedman, the popular understanding of the sexual deviant was that he was either "inadequately masculine (the effeminate homosexual) or hypermasculine (the sexual psychopath)."[38] Thus the animal nature of man had become an aberration, rather than the norm, and the mid-twentieth century sexual psychopath was now understood as "overly masculine" and was therefore a member of a small subgroup.

The changing attitudes about what constituted "normal" manhood were part of a larger sea change in sexual mores and practices. As immigrants brought new ideas and behaviors to American cities which were at odds with the accepted Victorian notions of decency, newspapers brought both nativist and romanticized images of these newcomers into the homes of Americans, instilling fear or pity in readers. As women slowly entered the labor market, there was more opportunity for social intercourse with men, particularly in the cities.[39] The resulting conversations could be quite shocking to contemporaries. Christine Stansell illustrates how, on the fringes of middle-class society, modern men and women would openly discuss sexual matters in public cafes and clubs. Many of these modernist ideas, if not always accepted, would percolate into the larger cultural landscape. For instance, Gertrude Stein would become world famous and a darling of the campus lecture circuit for creating texts which broke with traditional literary conventions. Stein was a lesbian, a fact she neither promoted nor hid, and her ability to gain acceptance in the mainstream was itself evidence that traditional sexual conventions were also slowly being challenged by twentieth century pressures. Finally, during the 1920s and 1930s, European sexologists such as Havelock Ellis and Magnus Hirschfield became respectable in the United States, and their professional analyses were joined by American studies of sexuality performed by R. L. Dickinson and Katharine Bement Davis.[40] In light of the increased visibility of women and immigrants into the workplace, a stronger feminist voice in society and an increasing consensus that sexuality could be understood through science, the social and economic bearings for the traditional male role seemed to be eroding.[41]

The courts, however, had not yet codified these changes. Morris Ernst pointed out how the failure of courts to acknowledge the new attitudes toward sexuality led to contradictions in the law. In *To the Pure,* a groundbreaking 1928 indictment of censorship he co-wrote with William Seagle, Ernst illustrated how such contradictions could actually favor one sexual behavior by punishing another. In his discussion of the federal Mann Act of 1910, which forbade "the transportation of women in interstate commerce for immoral purposes," he pointed out that no corresponding state law existed in New York. As a result, while *intrastate* sex was acceptable, *interstate* sex could be a criminal act: "(I)t is lawful for a man to take his mistress from Brooklyn to Manhattan, or from Albany to New York for illicit relations, nevertheless . . . it is crime for the very same New Yorker to take his mistress for the purpose from Manhattan to Jersey City."[42] Furthermore, an 1888 federal law that made "the sending of any obscene letter" a criminal offense created some very strange scenarios:

> Under the law of 1888 if a man in Brooklyn writes a love note to his mistress in Manhattan to come and spend Wednesday night with him there, he is guilty of a felony which subjects him to both five years imprisonment and five thousand

> dollars fine. But, now observe that if instead of sending the passionate love note, he actually visits his mistress in Manhattan and has sexual intercourse with her, he commits no crime at all since fornication is not criminal under the laws of the State of New York.[43]

One supposes that such an argument could have been used to call for a federal law against "fornication" and, accordingly, a censor could argue that the problem was actually that existing laws weren't stringent enough and should be extended to cover the crime of fornicating. By 1928, Ernst had not taken a clear stance on the legality of different sexual activities; he had initially set his sights on obscenity laws and focused mainly on the censorship of texts. Yet it was clear that Ernst did not condemn such behavior; two decades later, Ernst would more explicitly promote Kinsey's work to push the boundaries of what sexual behaviors were "normal."[44]

Although Ernst's ostensible intention of presenting the example of the Brooklynite's sexual dilemma was simply to illustrate the inconsistencies in the laws, the plausible extension of his argument was that the problem with contemporary attitudes toward sexuality stemmed not from this libidinous New Yorker but rather from the federal law that attempted to regulate his passion. The assumption, too, was that the "mistress" was an almost inert object. Ernst does not reverse the scenario and suggest what might befall the mistress should she write a letter or visit her male lover, because the danger of either event occurring according to the assumptions inherent in the federal law is minimal. Women, in this legal representation, are unwitting victims of uncontrollable male lust, but what does this depiction say about men? Clearly, the laws Ernst cited were written with the Victorian conceptions of masculinity and femininity in mind; the law viewed men as predators and women as prey.

All these issues manifested themselves in Dennett's trial. "The Sex Side of Life" was original, and menacing, because it injected pleasure into sexuality, and the admission that sex was pleasurable offended Victorian sensibilities on three counts. First, the idea of sex as enjoyable did not jibe with the notion of women as passionless vessels. This threw a wrench into the argument that women were to be confined to house and home, since it was presumably male passion that allowed men to do battle in the heretofore masculine spheres of business and politics. Second, by emphasizing that sex was pleasurable, Dennett was undermining the assumption that the primary function of sex was procreation, thus cheapening sex and lowering it to the status of a nickelodeon. Third, Dennett's pamphlet targeted children, and while social hygienists sought a muted level of sexual education, this approach, in the minds of some contemporaries, encouraged children to have sex. Like the social hygienists who argued for sexual instruction in the schools, Dennett wrote "The Sex Side of Life" to reach children while they were young. Unlike her predecessors, however, she intended to introduce, rather than erase, romance and passion into the lesson.

Prior to 1918, Dennett's professional life had been dedicated mainly to promoting birth control, but she became interested in sexual education when her eldest son became a teenager. She looked for an adequate guide to sex for her two boys in the New York Public Library and was disappointed with the texts she found. In her pamphlet's introduction, meant for adult parents and teachers, she wrote that what other sexual education texts lacked was

> the frank, unashamed declaration that the climax of sex emotion is an unsurpassed joy, something which rightly belongs to every normal human being, a joy to be proudly and serenely experienced. Instead there has been an inference that sex emotion is a thing to be ashamed of, that yielding to it is an indulgence which must be curbed as much as possible, that all thought and understanding of it must be rigorously postponed, at any rate till after marriage.[45]

Those who wished to maintain Victorian norms were using words of shame, such as "self-abuse" rather than "masturbation," to intimidate twentieth-century Americans into clinging to antiquated moral standards. Dennett's challenge of these standards, and her claim that sex was "an unsurpassed joy," brought her into direct opposition with Victorianism, and twentieth-century American Victorians attempted to silence her with the single word "obscene."

While her son's entrance into puberty directly spurred Dennett to write about sex for a young audience, it was Dennett's divorce, and the tragedy that led up to it, that motivated her to write about sex in this style. One can better understand both Dennett's focus on sexual education and why Ernst viewed her as an ideal client for a test case by examining her personal and professional life in more detail. Born in 1872 to a middle-class family in Worcester, Massachusetts, Dennett did not fit the mold of the ideal Victorian upbringing. Nineteenth-century girls were to grow up as pure vessels which would be transplanted from their parents' to their husband's home. Girls would learn the art of domesticity from their mothers, and then would themselves become a domesticizing force on their husbands and children.[46] In Dennett's case, economic realities intruded on this Victorian model. Dennett's father, a merchant, died of cancer when Dennett was only 10 years old. Her mother became an entrepreneur whose business, which entailed taking young ladies on tours of Europe, left Dennett and her sisters mostly in the care of aunts. Dennett attended a finishing school in Northampton, Massachusetts, and then studied at the school of the Boston Museum of Fine Arts. She did not immediately follow the trajectory of many contemporary middle-class women, who left their parents' home only to move into their husband's house. Instead, she accepted a teaching position in Philadelphia at Drexel Institute and moved into her own apartment, which she would later share with her sister.

While her biographer rightly suggests that Dennett was challenging nineteenth-century trends in search for a more independent lifestyle, as a young adult she was by no means a bohemian. Her fiancée was William Hartley Dennett, a well-connected architect who had studied with Charles Eliot Norton at Harvard. Although she opted for an education and career in the arts, her life later followed the traditional path described by Stansell: after marrying, she placed his career over her own and became more helpmate than partner. She and her husband apparently enjoyed a happy marriage, but three increasingly difficult births transformed her personally and professionally. Dennett's second son died when he was only three weeks old, and her health was seriously threatened after her third son was born. Her doctor told her that another birth could kill her, but he was either unwilling or unable to provide her with birth control information. At this time, in 1905, it was illegal to send information about birth control through the U.S. postal service. Under the Comstock Act, anyone mailing anything deemed by the postmaster to be an "obscene, lewd, lascivious, indecent, filthy or vile article, matter, thing, device, or substance" could face a fine of up to $5,000 and/or a prison sentence of up to five years. Although physicians who served the upper class were known to provide their wealthy clients not only with birth control information but birth control paraphernalia, and some even performed abortions, Dennett's doctor was silent. The only recourse, as the Dennetts saw it, was abstinence. Mary Ware Dennett's post-partum condition required surgery and as she lay in bed recuperating, her husband increasingly enjoyed the intimate company of the wife of a family friend.

After recovering, as Dennett found herself spending less and less time with her husband, she threw herself into a cause that must have been very attractive to a jilted wife: the suffrage movement. Those fighting for the vote believed that it would put men and women on an equal footing, and given that the balance of power had clearly shifted in her own marriage, this idea was appealing to her. Her success as a writer and speaker attracted the attention of the movement's leaders, who in 1910 encouraged her to move to New York City to take on the position of Secretary of the National American Woman Suffrage Association. Once in New York, she divorced her husband and obtained permanent custody of her children.[47] As a divorced working woman living apart from her children, her separation from the nineteenth-century model of woman and mother was complete. She befriended modernist women like Jessie Ashley, the wife of "Big Bill" Haywood, the leader of the Industrial Workers of the World (IWW). But Ashley was a passionate activist in her own right, and was one of the few female attorneys active in the first decades of the twentieth century. Ashley and fellow feminists Charlotte

Perkins Gilman, Rose Pastor Stokes, Elizabeth Gurley Flynn, and Crystal Eastman were among the members of the political supper club known as Heterodoxy, and Dennett soon began to attend the Heterodoxy meetings in Greenwich Village. The Heterodoxy Club was founded in 1912 to provide feminist women with a forum to discuss the political and personal issues of the day.[48] Dennett's close contact with the more extreme Heterodites, combined with the continuing influence of her ex-husband, modified her views somewhat.

Hartley Dennett's justification for his affair was casually rooted in Jacob Beilhart's free love philosophy.[49] Beilhart instituted a religion he called "Universal Life," which he based on his conviction that he was a faith healer, and which aimed to attain what he called "the Fruit of the Universal Spirit."[50] He created a utopian colony outside of Lisbon, Ohio, and attracted spiritualists and others to build a farming community with him. After rumors of "free love" and some legal challenges arose in Ohio, Beilhart transplanted the Spirit Fruit Colony to Ingleside, Illinois, around 1904. The publicity surrounding the colony, along with Beilhart's own writings, carried his philosophy cross-country, and men and women like Hartley and Mary who felt shackled by conventional gender stereotypes and expectations found something appealing in Beilhart's dictums. For instance, Beilhart referred to himself as the "masculine nature that lives in the feminine nature that she may become free," a suggestion of gender fluidity not widely communicated during that era.[51] Hartley and his girlfriend, who remained married to a Dennett family friend, were inspired by a Wellesley, Massachusetts, utopian colony opened by a Spirit Fruit Society member. Hartley eagerly shared with Mary his exciting new views about the need to eliminate boundaries of love and to adhere to the ideal of free choice.[52] Mary Ware Dennett's biographer suggests that, despite her anger at her ex-husband for his affair, she continued to love him throughout her life. The point is important because she came to agree with some of the same arguments that he and the Heterodites made about love, relationships and marriage that he invoked to justify his decision to desert her. These ideas, in turn, would inform "The Sex Side of Life."

After working in the suffrage movement, Dennett turned her attention to birth control, a cause which, given her own tragic experience with birth, was highly personal for her. In 1915, together with Ashley and Clara Gruening Stillman, she formed the National Birth Control League (NBCL), the first national birth control organization in the United States.[53] It was in this role that she first clashed with the provisions of the Comstock Act. The 1873 law prohibited the mailing of a wide range of "obscene, lewd, or lascivious" items, including "any article or thing designed or intended for the prevention of conception."[54] The law effectively stifled Dennett and her colleagues, who had to respond to constant requests for birth control information with a form letter stating that the law prohibited the clinic from distributing such information. In 1918 she became the executive secretary of the NBCL, and exploited World War I fears and prejudices about immigration to sell the idea of birth control. "Birth control," one NBCL advertisement claimed, "means race conservation. It means having children as they are wanted and can be cared for."[55] Dennett saw that the Comstock Act was the major obstacle to circulating birth control information, and she became obsessed with a quixotic, one-woman campaign to change the law. After NBCL attempts to change New York law failed, Dennett decided to try to change the federal obscenity statute instead. She resigned from the NBCL and founded the Voluntary Parenthood League in 1919. Her main goal was simple: to amend the law to repeal the phrase "prevention of contraception." She personally lobbied members of Congress and found that many Congressmen personally supported her cause but were unwilling to publicly take action. Frustrated, she began to attack members in letters, even resorting to name-calling. This was an era in which the active image of man was predicated on a more passive role for women, and those women who did not adhere to cultural expectations could quickly lose any political capital they possessed.

Perhaps mindful of her own relationship with her ex-husband—if she and Hartley had envisioned sex differently, or if they had known about birth control, might their marriage have remained intact?—and with a view to shielding her sons from misconceptions about sex, she wrote down the facts of life, including her own drawings of male and female sexual organs. Dennett had studied art and her depictions of genitalia were clear, accurate and quite detailed. After previewing the pamphlet with her eldest son, she was satisfied with her work and distributed copies to friends. Encouraged by their response, she submitted it to the *Medical Review of Reviews*, which published it in 1918.

Why did it take the post office over a decade to indict Dennett for mailing "The Sex Side of Life"? Some of that delay between initial publication and indictment can be attributed to audience. Within the pages of the *Medical Review of Reviews,* the pamphlet would be viewed as a scholarly publication and, accordingly, was deemed to be in professional hands and out of the public domain. But Dennett and others the distributed the pamphlet to parents, and when demand increased, she began to sell it. While there was little chance that an adolescent was reading the *Medical Review of Reviews*, once the pamphlet was being distributed by the YMCA and church groups, it was on the public radar.

Additionally, her association with "radical" causes, such as the suffragette movement and birth control, would not have endeared her to the government. As Richard Polenberg demonstrates in *Fighting Faiths*, radicals and activists who couldn't be arrested for their political activities were frequently brought to trial on obscenity charges.[56] Ernst himself pointed this out in *To the Pure.* Because sexuality seemed so threatening, Ernst argued, activists who publicly denounced government policies were more vulnerable to prosecution if they spoke openly or embraced radical sexual ideals. In other words, a sexual radical was assumed to also be a political, economic, and religious radical (or vice-versa). "The man who publicly upholds birth control, the single standard, free love, compassionate marriage, easy divorce, and legitimization is a man prone to play with subversive ideas on private property, to be attracted by criminal syndicalism," Ernst wrote. "When such an individual is attacked under the sex censorship, it is assumed that no very great tenderness for his rights need be shown."[57] Thus, while Ernst felt that Comstock and his disciples were contemptible, his larger complaint was with the legal system, which rewarded vice societies with prosecutions and fines, and the government itself, which sanctioned the censors' cause.

In addition, Dennett had pointedly irritated government officials on at least two occasions. First, prior to publishing the pamphlet, in her attempt to amend the Comstock Act she had stepped on some toes. Frustrated in her attempts to persuade congressmen to support her bill to exempt contraceptives from the obscenity clause, she resorted to ultimatums. Dennett circulated a letter in which she threatened that if her bill did not come up for action, congressmen would be "held responsible," and that she would expose their "cowardice." Her empty threat—"Would this sort of public attention be your preference?"—could not have endeared her to the men on Capitol Hill.[58] From today's perspective, her antagonistic response should strike many as brave and praiseworthy, but at a time that male authority dominated Washington politics, and when it was by no means clear that a modification of the obscenity clause held popular support, Dennett's aggressive approach seems self-defeating. Second, in her effort to have her pamphlet freed from the obscenity clause, she baited postal officials. After a 1920 obscenity ruling forbade her from mailing the pamphlet with second class postage, she demanded information on the ruling. When officials failed to respond with the details she requested, she insulted the post office. In a 1922 article she wrote for the *Birth Control Herald*, she insisted that the government could not enforce obscenity laws and that the postmaster general and the Department of Justice employees were thus "unfaithful and inefficient public servants."[59] Dennett's biographer sees a correlation between this taunt and the postmaster general's subsequent decision to ban "The Sex Side of Life." While there is no direct evidence that these activities resulted in her indictment, they certainly made some powerful men wary of her. Some congressmen must have associated Dennett with what many contemporaries considered the wacky, extreme free love proponents like Beilhart and Dennett's own ex-husband.

Since it later emerged that she was indicted by the complaint of a male government employee posing as a woman—that she was ensnared, if not technically entrapped, by the government—it is at least worth remembering that in earlier years she was a woman who made waves, and perhaps enemies, in her aggressive and combative interactions with male authorities.

## ERNST AS COUNSEL FOR SEX AND EDUCATION

Whatever its origin, Morris Ernst was personally delighted by the indictment. Ernst and Dennett had first met in his capacity as co-general counsel for the ACLU. During a birth control campaign, before "The Sex Side of Life" had been seized, Ernst had suggested that she use the pamphlet for a test case. Having already become convinced of the importance of publicity in winning controversial obscenity cases, he warned Dennett that the success of the case would require intense media scrutiny. She initially resisted; according to her biographer, Dennett had never recovered from the very public airing of her divorce. When she eventually decided to accept Ernst's offer to use the pamphlet for a test case on censorship, Ernst had withdrawn that offer, since he believed that Dennett was not fully committed to the legal defense of her text. But the indictment erased all doubts for both lawyer and defendant. For Ernst, in fact, this case was a dream come true. If he won, he would liberate sexual education and also make a name for himself. It was also an opportunity to argue against what he viewed as an outdated and ignorant moral code. Ernst denigrated Victorianism and lamented the fact that influential twentieth-century Americans seemed to be living in a nineteenth-century world.[60] To achieve his goal of disabling the Victorian grasp on society, Ernst acted as a bridge between activists, like Dennett, who exploded the Victorian conception of sexuality; and those judges and juries who felt threatened by this rejection of existing moral standards. As a man, Ernst was able to bring a female activist into the courtroom and, eventually, legitimize her feminist agenda.

In his 1940 recollection of the "Sex Side of Life" trial, Ernst recalled that the censors' objection was that Dennett

> had advocated the dissemination of basic biologic facts, and had dared to assert that physical love might be not only noble and beautiful but pleasurable. She had expressed the hope that birth control would some day be legally recognized. She had suggested that venereal diseases were curable, and that masturbation would not necessarily consign an adolescent to eternal damnation.[61]

The government painted such assertions as obscene. Although the prosecution initially had prepared to argue two points, namely, that Dennett had mailed a pamphlet and that this pamphlet was obscene, Dennett had already freely admitted to mailing out "The Sex Side of Life," and so the prosecution's only task was to persuade a jury that the ideas contained within the pamphlet fell under the federal definition of obscenity.

After insisting on representing Dennett without payment, Ernst immediately took the case to the media, working though the numerous friends he had cultivated in the literary and journalism community. These included his childhood friend Heywood Broun, who had co-written a scathing 1927 biography of Anthony Comstock. Broun, whom the *New York Times* called "one of the most widely read newspaper columnists in America," would later help found the American Newspaper Guild and already wielded considerable influence in media circles.[62] Ernst believed that the courts' decisions "have nothing to do with justice" but that, instead, "the point of view of the judge derive[d] from the pressure of public opinion."[63] And so Ernst endeavored to ensure the existence of that public pressure. While doing so was, in hindsight, in the best interest of his client, so too was it a means for Ernst to promote his own reputation and image as a modern man.

Fortunately for both attorney and client, Ernst's performance would resonate with the public. Early on, *United States v. Dennett* revealed the stark contrast between the government's pessimistic model of masculinity in crisis and Ernst's optimistic portrait of men and women released from the bonds of ignorance. In January 1929, as he attempted to have the obscenity charges dismissed, Ernst made a case not just for "The Sex Side of Life," but for the importance of sex education in general.[64] Children, he told Judge Grover Moscowitz, would eventually learn about sexuality, and "it is far preferable to have them get the material in a intelligent, clean way than to pick it up from somebody whispering a dirty four-letter Anglo-Saxon word."[65] He portrayed sexual education as a right for adolescents and adults, telling reporters the following day, "If this is suppressed, it means that our children will have to go to the gutter for their sex education."[66]

Ernst drew upon the words and actions of accepted institutions to argue his points. The federal government itself, he pointed out, had issued numerous educational pamphlets, "many of which are as frank in detail, and as specific as to terms" as Dennett's.[67] He cited one such government pamphlet titled "Healthy Manhood," which did, indeed, mention masturbation, and which reassured readers that "while the practice of masturbation is sexually weakening and morally debasing and while the boy who refrains from the habit makes the better man in maturity, the evil effects of masturbation should not be exaggerated."[68] Regardless, the government's pamphlet did recycle myths about masculinity in general and masturbation specifically:

> Every young man should understand that from a biological standpoint, from the age of 12 to 21 the body of the boy is being made into the man, and that nature has no large amount of vital energy that may be safely wasted in excesses of any kind during the adolescent period, for all the forces of the body are needed for rebuilding. Sexual excesses particularly during that period are certain to be followed by a dwarfing or stunting effect on the mental and physical development of the man. Self-control is necessary.[69]

As a Jewish man who had been made painfully aware of his inability to fulfill the idealized image of the tall, strong man that dominated his youth, this passage may have had special meaning for Ernst. He knew from his pre-trial research into sexual education that the government was perpetuating myths, and as media coverage of the trial brought him increased attention and recognition, his own success would prove the lie of this "dwarfing or stunting" effect.

Another title that Ernst submitted into evidence was the pamphlet "Manpower," which similarly associated masculinity with a beefy ruggedness with which Ernst did not personally relate. "Manpower," issued in the 1920s by the United States Public Health Service, allows a glimpse into the mentality of those who found Dennett's pamphlet objectionable. The cover of "Manpower" has a drawing of a burly, rugged white man who wears outdoorsy hiking clothes; he is pursuing just the kind of healthy physical outdoor activity that the pamphlet claims is necessary to maintain one's sexual self-control. The man seems to have just conquered a mountain, and as he rolls up the sleeve of his right arm, his left arm in a fist, he seems to be seeking his next conquest (which, readers were led to believe, was assuredly not of a sexual nature). This image of the burly, athletic man was precisely the type of image Ernst could not personally embody. But as the Victorian ideal of sexual self-control lost appeal, Ernst's knowledge of sexuality offered an alternative to the physically imposing, but sexually ignorant, "Manpower" model.

"Manpower" was ultimately useful to Ernst because it did state, like Dennett's own pamphlet, that "masturbation . . . does not produce the terrible effects some persons say it does."[70] But many of the ideas about sex that arose in the government's pamphlet conflicted with Dennett's and Ernst's positions. For example, while "Manpower" did tell its readers that "self abuse" would not produce terrible effects, the pamphlet also left little doubt that masturbation was wrong and shameful. According to "Manpower," "If a man uses his reason, stops and thinks, he knows that he must either indulge his sex appetite or control it. For an unmarried man indulgence means self-abuse or prostitution, both of which endanger his health and rob him of his self-respect."[71] Masturbation is thus likened to prostitution, and "prostitution," which the pamphlet implies is intercourse with any woman other than one's wife, inevitably leads to venereal disease.[72] Clearly, "Manpower" saw no alternative to married sexual relations. In addition, the government's pamphlet suggested that men who do not control their sexual urges before marriage threaten their own manpower. "The man needs the full power of his will to keep his sex desires from leading him into practices that weaken and destroy himself and others," the government warned.[73]

While Ernst clearly understood the causes of tensions between censors and educators, and could accurately gauge the pulse of the public, his greatest strength in the "Sex Side of Life" case lay in his ability to translate the feminist ideas of his client into a more palatable narrative for the public. In *To the Pure* he foreshadowed his strategy in *United States v. Dennett* when he declared that, in fact, the government is not truly concerned with indecency per se. "Our first clue out of the labyrinth," he and Seagle wrote, "is to realize that the State has no concern with the crime of obscenity as a literary problem. The State as a political agent is not primarily interested in literature, and literary purity is not in itself its first solicitude. . . . Politically, the safety of the State is the first rule of its existence."[74] Why did government concern itself with morals? For his explanation, Ernst pointed to Darwinism, materialism, and the secularization of society. "With the religious test of life undermined," he wrote, "the Victorian world set out upon a quest for a secular system of ethics, and discovered its basis naturally in sex. With the powers of the state also limited, the family was of peculiar importance as a medium through which to bind the conscience of the individual, and the deep loyalties of the family become paramount."[75] The argument followed that, since the legitimacy of government seemed to rest in large part on the legitimacy of the family, and since obscenity seemed to lead its victims astray from family morals, therefore obscene materials threatened the very bedrock of ethics upon which the government rested. The issue was safety. This was the assumption upon which rested Ernst's case. He would argue that, far from threatening the welfare of the society, Dennett's text actually contributed to the health and welfare of citizens.

At trial, however, he would initially be unable to present any concrete evidence that demonstrated how Dennett's pamphlet was actually being used. Rather than handle the case himself, Judge Moscowitz, in the words of the legal scholar Laura M. Weinrib, punted.[76] Moscowitz personally thought "Sex Side of Life" was not obscene, Weinrib writes, but perhaps influenced by his own, unrelated legal problems, thought it best to have the case heard before a jury—and then, before another judge.[77] After months of delays, the prosecution won the first round by convincing the trial judge, Warren B. Burrows, to stifle Ernst's witnesses, who would have indicated how and where the pamphlet was distributed.[78] In his argument at the trial, Ernst tried to chip away at the assumptions that lay beneath the word "obscene." Since the 1929 understanding of "obscene" was that it described a violation of community standards, Ernst attempted to demonstrate that "The Sex Side of Life" had been ordered by and sent to upstanding community institutions. Given that the YMCA, the YWCA, numerous churches and the Union Theological Seminary had helped distribute 30,000 of Dennett's pamphlets during the previous 11 years, to condemn her pamphlet was to condemn each of those institutions.[79]

When the case went to trial in April 1929, Ernst's attempt to include this institutional evidence was roundly rejected by the judge, who agreed with the prosecution's objection that the question of the distribution of the pamphlets was "incompetent, irrelevant, and immaterial."[80] This ruling effectively tied Ernst's hands. He was unable to call witnesses or submit supporting documents from the YMCA, from churches, or from distinguished public figures like the philosopher John Dewey or the sexologist Havelock Ellis. Instead, Ernst was left to state that the choice before the jury was learning about sex through endorsed publications such as "The Sex Side of Life," or getting information from the gutter.[81] Unable to weigh such evidence, the jury found Dennett guilty of sending obscene material through the mail and fined $3,000. Ernst then moved to have the conviction set aside, on the grounds that it was contrary to the weight of evidence and to the law. At that hearing, a journalist reported Ernst's emotional argument this way: "'Your honor should consider what it means to brand a woman such as this one as a felon,' [Ernst] pleaded in a husky voice. 'I am undertaking this case without a cent of pay, because I think it as important as the trial of Copernicus.'" The judge denied Ernst's motion; the *Brooklyn Citizen* reported that Ernst was "visibly upset" by the ruling.[82]

Soon afterward, Ernst and the American Civil Liberties Union worked to generate media outrage over the indictment; the public outcry over the verdict encouraged an appeal. Major popular periodicals wrote sympathetically about Dennett. The *Brooklyn Times* announced that "Mrs. Dennett's Sex Book" would be sent through the mail to President Hoover; affixed to the copy would be the signatures of "more than one hundred lawyers, ministers, physicians, and laymen" to challenge the verdict, and this "unique demonstration of sympathy and support" would take place the following day, simultaneously with the sentencing of Dennett.[83] In May 1929, the *Brooklyn Daily Eagle* highlighted Ernst and Broun in their coverage of a pro-Dennett rally. The newspaper reported that about 400 people gathered at the Civic Club in Manhattan "to condemn Brooklyn juries, New England judges, and Federal justice."[84] Broun set the tone for the evening, declaring that "I believe the thing that shocked the Brooklyn jury . . . was that Mary Ware Dennett said that sex might be fun. That was a very unfortunate thing to say to 12 married men in Brooklyn."[85] Ernst, and later Dennett herself, later took "pot shots at the morals of the Brooklyn jurymen, half in jest and half in irony." Ernst implied that the jurors were beyond the stage of being shocked by the facts of life, and Dennett—whom the unnamed reporter described as having "a certain gentleness and graciousness of manner"—titillated the crowd by declaring, "I'm just as lewd, filthy, and indecent now as I ever was. But apparently those words mean something different to Judge Burrows and the twelve 'peers' in Brooklyn than to most people."[86] The ACLU, for whom Ernst now worked as general counsel, also sponsored a Defense Committee for Dennett and held a rally at the New York City Town Hall on May 22, raising funds and public pressure for dismissal. Their cause was further boosted later that week, when reporters from the *New York Telegram* revealed that the prosecution had fabricated some key points in its story, and that "Miss Miles," the Virginia woman who purportedly received Dennett's pamphlet in the first place, did not exist. "Miss Miles," in fact, was a postal agent—and a man.[87] After Ernst and Dennett appeared at the U.S. Court of Appeals on January 15, 1930, Ernst made his final pitch to reporters: "The general mood of the pamphlet is one of idealism. It urges rational knowledge as an incentive to sexual decency. It contends that marriage is sacred by virtue of its being a reflection of human idealism rather than because it is a legalized institution."[88]

With the favorable publicity, new evidence, and expanded resources, Dennett won her appeal on March 3, 1930. One of Ernst's key arguments in that appeal explicitly referred to Victorianism. Ernst cited the precedent of the 1913 ruling by Judge Learned Hand in *United States v. Kennerley*, in which Judge Hand had dismissed the earlier obscenity precedent from *Regina v. Hicklin,* an 1868 British case. Hand's 1913 decision stated that the Hicklin rule, which judged obscenity on the basis of its ability "to deprave and corrupt those whose minds are open to such immoral influences,"[89] did not seem appropriate for the present-day understanding of morality, "however consonant it may be with Victorian morals."[90] It was a wise legal precedent to cite, as Learned Hand's cousin, Judge Augustus Hand, sat on the court of appeals for Dennett's case. Augustus Hand agreed with Ernst's argument, and the court of appeals decided that the case should never have gone to trial in the first place since the pamphlet was not obscene.[91] Ernst had successfully applied his understanding of Victorianism to his argument and persuaded the courts that the moral standards of the nineteenth century should not necessarily govern the twentieth century.

In *Dennett*, Ernst had not only liberated sexual education, he had sucked a certain amount of energy out of the Comstock Act. Prosecutors would now have to deal with the issue of context in obscenity cases.[92] Moreover, Victorian attitudes toward sex were dealt a blow. While the court did not take a position on whether masturbation was sinful or whether venereal disease really was curable, it did decide that such claims did not constitute obscenity. Dennett's pamphlet would continue to inform young readers that venereal disease could be cured, that masturbation was not sinful, and that the sexual act was a joyous part of life.

Ernst's successful appeal of the case was also an important step toward knocking out the legal manifestations of Victorian moral standards. According to Ernst himself, the benefits of the Dennett decision were that, "[f]rom this time on, honorable education of children had a chance. Parents could be informed; teachers were released from ancient legal fears (although not necessarily social fears) that sex was dirty and unmentionable."[93] In this sense, light was shed on Wilkinson's "darkened room." Sexual education, in other words, had gained some legal protection. It is true that the transformation from "unmentionable" to "honorable" did not occur as quickly as Ernst's comments proclaim; it is also true that non-monogamous, non-heterosexual, non-*traditional* relationships would be considered "dirty and unmentionable" for decades to come. But by 1940, Ernst could portray the Dennett appeal not only as a victory for free speech, but also as a victory for "sexual enlightenment."[94] Clearly, Ernst saw the need to push for more than just the technical freedom to mail sexual content from one state to another. Still, the Dennett case points to the fact that the law was gradually beginning to recognize the primacy of sexuality and the fact that long-held assumptions about masculinity and the nature of gender identity were slowly being recast.

Finally, the case was vindication of Ernst's exhibitionism, even if only indirectly. Ernst had defended a text that itself assumed that manliness was not necessarily synonymous with savagery, and had put himself out front at mass rallies in support of a modern conception of sexuality. His emotional performance at court had been noted, positively, by the local newspapers, which would become an important source of positive press for both him and his clients in the coming years. He had also defeated the government—not only the prosecution, but also the agencies which had published pamphlets that had propagated myths and inaccuracies about sexuality, masturbation, and even gender.

## NOTES

1. Samantha Barbas, *The Rise and Fall of Morris Ernst, Free Speech Renegade* (Chicago: University of Chicago Press, 2021), 51–56. Barbas provides an excellent overview of the origins of the ACLU and the American Fund for Public Service, popularly known as "The Garland Fund."
2. Ibid., 73.

3. Cited in Dudley Nichols, "Sex and Our Children," *The Nation*, Feb. 6, 1929, 154–155; emphasis in original.

4. Constance M. Chen, *"The Sex Side of Life": Mary Ware Dennett's Pioneering Battle for Birth Control and Sex Education* (New York: The New Press, 1996), 269–292. Chen's biography of Dennett includes a detailed description of the obscenity trial, as well as a reproduction of the 1928 edition of Dennett's pamphlet.

5. Robert A. Nye, "Locating Masculinity: Some Recent Work on Men," *Signs* 30, no. 3 (2005): 1937–1962, 1946; doi:10.1086/426799.

6. Barbara Dafoe Whitehead, "The End of Innocence (Review of Jeffrey P. Moran, *Teaching Sex: The Shaping of Adolescence in the Twentieth Century*)," *Commonweal*, June 2, 2000 (Vol. 127, Issue 11).

7. Ibid.

8. Allan M. Brandt, *No Magic Bullet: A Social History of Venereal Disease in the United States Since 1880* (New York: Oxford University Press, 1987), 28.

9. Paul Boyer, *Purity in Print: Book Censorship in America From the Gilded Age to the Computer Age*, second ed. (Madison: The University of Wisconsin Press, 2002), 3–4.

10. Ibid., 4–5.

11. Ibid., 31.

12. Brandt, *No Magic Bullet*, 30–31.

13. John D'Emilio and Estelle B. Freedman, *Intimate Matters: A History of Sexuality in America* (New York: Harper & Row, 1988), 155–156. See also Brandt, *No Magic Bullet; and Ruth Rosen, The Lost Sisterhood: Prostitutes in America, 1900–1918* (Baltimore: Johns Hopkins, 1982).

14. Arthur S. Link and Richard L. McCormick, *Progressivism* (Arlington Heights, IL: Harlan Davidson, 1983).

15. Brandt, *No Magic Bullet*, 14.

16. Ibid., 16, 26.

17. Prince A. Morrow, *Social Diseases and Marriage: Social Prophylaxis* (Philadelphia: Lea Brothers and Co., 1904).

18. Prince A. Morrow, "Health Department Control of Venereal Diseases," *New York Medical Journal* 94 (1911): 130. See also Amy L. Fairchild, James Colgrove, and Ronald Bayer, "The Myth of Exceptionalism: the History of Venereal Disease Reporting in the Twentieth Century (Emerging Issues in Population Health: National and Global Perspectives)," *Journal of Law, Medicine & Ethics* 31.4 (Winter 2003): 624 (15).

19. Mara L. Keire, "The Vice Trust: A Reinterpretation of The White Slavery Scare in The United States, 1907–1917," *Journal of Social History* 35.1 (Fall 2001): 5 n52. According to Keire, the American Social Hygiene Association was formed in 1913 when John D. Rockefeller arranged for the merger of his pet anti-vice organization, the American Vigilance Association, and the American Federation of Social Hygiene, thus linking the anti-vice and social hygiene movements. See also John C. Burnham, "The Progressive Era Revolution in American Attitudes Toward Sex," *Journal of American History* 59 (March 1973): 897–898. For more on Rockefeller

see Ron Chernow, *Titan: The Life of John D. Rockefeller, Sr.* (New York: Random House, 1998).

20. Boyer, *Purity*, 3.

21. Kermit L. Hall, *The Magic Mirror: Law in American History* (New York: Oxford University Press, 1989), 33.

22. Heywood Broun and Margaret Leech, *Anthony Comstock: Roundsman of the Lord* (New York: Boni, 1927), 81.

23. Craig L. LaMay, "America's Censor: Anthony Comstock and Free Speech," *Communications and the Law* 19.3 (September 1997): 1–59.

24. For more on the passage of the Comstock Act, see Nicola Beisel, *Imperiled Innocents: Anthony Comstock and Family Reproduction in Victorian America* (Princeton: Princeton University Press, 1997); and Boyer, *Purity*.

25. Jeffrey P. Moran, *Teaching Sex: The Shaping of Adolescence in the 20th Century* (Cambridge: Harvard University Press, 2000), 73.

26. D'Emilo and Friedman, *Intimate Matters*, 212–213.

27. Brandt, *No Magic Bullet*, 123–124.

28. Ibid., 125.

29. Cited in James H. Jones, *Alfred C. Kinsey: A Public/Private Life* (New York: W.W. Norton & Company, 1997), 67; Brandt, *No Magic Bullet*, 28.

30. Moran, *Teaching Sex*, 2.

31. Ibid., 10.

32. D'Emilio and Freedman, *Intimate Matters*, 209.

33. "Jewish Corruption in "Popular" Music Words of the Jazz Songs, Written and Published by a Jewish Monopoly, Filled With Disgusting, Vulgar, and Indecent Suggestions, Heightened With Idiotic, Sensuous "Music" of Jungle Type." *The American Standard*, 2.9, May 1, 1925; downloaded from *Understanding Hate in America: White Nationalism and the Press in the 1920s,* Reveal Digital, https://dwso.revealdigital.org/?a=d&d=BEIAIFJ19250501-01.2.15&srpos=13&e=.

34. Jones, *Alfred C. Kinsey*, 67.

35. E. Anthony Rotundo, *American Manhood: Transformations in Masculinity from the Revolution to the Modern Era* (New York: Basic Books, 1993), 227. For an analysis of the connection between masculinity and racism, see Gail Bederman, *Manliness and Civilization: A Cultural History of Gender and Race in the United States, 1880–1917* (Chicago: The University of Chicago Press, 1995).

36. Rotundo, *American Manhood*, 232.

37. Ibid., 246.

38. Estelle B. Freedman, "'Uncontrolled Desires': The Response to the Sexual Psychopath, 1920–1960," rept. in Kathy Peiss and Christina Simmons, eds., *Passion and Power: Sexuality in History* (Philadelphia: Temple University Press, 1989): 203.

39. For more on New York working women during this era, see Kathy Peiss, "'Charity Girls' and City Pleasures: Historical Notes on Working-Class Sexuality, 1880–1920," in *Passion and Power: Sexuality in History*, ed. Kathy Peiss and Christina Simmons (Philadelphia: Temple University Press, 1989), 57–69.

40. Freedman, "Uncontrolled," 204.

41. Freedman, "Uncontrolled," 203. For a terrific overview of feminism in the 1910s and 1920s, see Nancy F. Cott, *The Grounding of Modern Feminism* (New Haven: Yale University Press, 1987).

42. Morris L. Ernst and William Seagle, *To the Pure: A Study of Obscenity and the Censor* (New York: The Viking Press, 1928), 72–73.

43. Ernst and Seagle, *To the Pure*, 74.

44. Morris L. Ernst and David Loth, *American Sexual Behavior and the Kinsey Report* (New York: The Greystone Press, 1948).

45. Dennett, "Introduction for Elders," reprinted in *The Sex Side of Life*.

46. Moran, *Teaching Sex,* 5.

47. Although Dennett gained custody, she apparently did not spend much time with her children. According to Chen, once Dennett moved to New York City, she only saw her children every three weeks and, as she became more involved in various causes, saw them every six weeks. Both sons attended her 1929 trial, however, and were both referenced and cited in media accounts of the case.

48. Judith Schwarz, *The Radical Feminists of Heterodoxy* (Lebanon, NH: New Victoria Publishers, 1986). For the impact of one Heterodite on psychoanalysis and feminism, see Kate Wittenstein, "The Feminist Uses of Psychoanalysis: Beatrice M. Hinkle and the Foreshadowing of Modern Feminism in the United States," *Journal of Women's History* 10.2 (Summer 1998): 38(25). Wittenstein claims that Hinkle, and not Karen Horney, was the first feminist critic of Freud.

49. Chen, "*The Sex Side of Life,*" 81.

50. Robert S. Fogarty and H. Roger Grant. "Free Love in Ohio: Jacob Beilhart and the Spirit Fruit Colony," *Ohio History: The Scholarly Journal of the Ohio Historical Society*, Volume 89, (Spring 1980): 206–221.

51. Ibid., 219.

52. Chen, "*The Sex Side of Life,*" 83–85.

53. Ibid.

54. Cited in Nicola Beisel, *Imperiled Innocents: Anthony Comstock and Family Reproduction in Victorian America* (Princeton: Princeton University Press, 1997), 39.

55. Chen, "*The Sex Side of Life,*" 206.

56. For a superb case study of the way in which politics and sexuality can become conflated, see Richard Polenberg, *Fighting Faiths: The Abrams Case, the Supreme Court and Free Speech* (Ithaca: Cornell University Press, 1999).

57. Ernst and Seagle, *To the Pure*, 164–65.

58. Chen, "*The Sex Side of Life,*" 234.

59. Chen, "*The Sex Side of Life,*" 229.

60. The term "Victorianism" appears in *To The Pure* at least two dozen times, as Ernst used it to refer to beliefs he deemed to be antiquated.

61. Morris L. Ernst and Alexander Lindey, *The Censor Marches On: Recent Milestones in the Administration of the Obscenity Law in the United States* (New York: Doubleday, Doran & Company, Inc., 1940), 42.

62. "Heywood Broun, 51, Columnist, Is Dead," *New York Times*, December 19, 1939, 23; and "10,000 Pay Tribute To Heywood Broun," *New York Times*, February 13, 1940, 29.

63. Interview between Thomas Stix and Morris Ernst, January 23, 1935, Box 487.5, MLE. Cited in Laura Weinrib, "From Left to Rights: Civil Liberties Lawyering between the World Wars" (*University of Chicago Public Law & Legal Theory Working Paper* No. 571, 2016), 1.

64. Chen, "*The Sex Side of Life,*" 273.

65. Chen, "*The Sex Side of Life,*" 274.

66. "'Y' Sex Writer Is Indicted," *Detroit Free Press*, January 16, 1929, 1.

67. Chen, "*The Sex Side of Life,*" 273.

68. New York State Department of Health, "cooperating with United States Public Health Service," *Healthy Manhood* (J.B. Lyon Company, cir. 1920s), 13–14, Box 47, MLE.

69. Ibid., 14.

70. Appellant's Brief, *U.S. v. Mary Ware Dennett*, United States Circuit Court of Appeals, 5, Box 47, MLE.

71. "Manpower," United States Public Health Service, V.D. Pamphlet No. 6 (c. 1928) 13; Box 47, MLE.

72. "Manpower," 5–11. The pamphlet calls such women "charity girls" or "loose." Given Prince Morrow's findings earlier in the century, it is not surprising that the government pamphlet suggests that out-of-wedlock intercourse must lead to venereal disease.

73. "Manpower," 16.

74. Ernst and Seagle, *To the Pure*, 132.

75. Ernst and Seagle, *To the Pure*, 158–159.

76. Laura M. Weinrib, "The Sex Side of Civil Liberties: United States v. Dennett and the Changing Face of Free Speech," *University of Chicago Public Law & Legal Theory Working Paper* No. 385 (2012): 355.

77. Ibid.

78. Ibid., 354–5.

79. Chen, "*The Sex Side of Life,*" 273.

80. "Mrs. Dennett Found Guilty of Mailing Sex Pamphlets," *Brooklyn Daily Times,* April 24, 1929, 3, https://newscomwc.newspapers.com/image/559848836.

81. "Sex Pamphlet Author Guilty, Plans Appeal," *Brooklyn Citizen*, April 24, 1929, 2, https://www.newspapers.com/image/542655398.

82. "Mrs. Dennett Loses Composure Then Regains It at Sex Trial; Plans Appeals to High Courts." *Brooklyn Citizen,* April 26, 1929, 1, https://newscomwc.newspapers.com/image/542655547.

83. "Mrs. Dennett's Sex Book to Be Mailed to President," *Brooklyn Daily Times*, April 28, 1929, 2, https://newscomwc.newspapers.com/image/556458889.

84. "Brooklyn Jurors Rated Like Boston's and Dayton's By Mrs. Dennett's Friends," *Brooklyn Daily Eagle,* May 7, 1929, 22.

85. Ibid.

86. Ibid.

87. Chen, "The Sex Side of Life," 295–296. According to Chen, the newspapers covering the trial wrote that the prosecution had been guilty of entrapment by creating

a fictional complainant. Ernst also accused the prosecutor of entrapment. See Morris L. Ernst, *The Best is Yet . . .* (New York: Harper & Brothers, 1945), 143.

88. "Mrs. Dennett Asks Reversal of Ruling," *Brooklyn Daily Times,* January 16, 1930, 3A, https://newscomwc.newspapers.com/image/559591947.

89. Appellant's Brief, 10.

90. Appellant's Brief, 10.

91. Morris L. Ernst and Alan U. Schwartz, *Censorship: The Search for the Obscene* (New York: The Macmillan Company, 1964), 81.

92. Chen, *"The Sex Side of Life,"* 301.

93. Ernst and Schwartz, *Censorship*, 92.

94. Ernst and Lindey, *The Censor Marches On*, 43.

# Chapter 3

# "You Can't Forge a Womb"

## Defending Privacy

Morris Ernst's strategy of exhibitionism was already proving successful.[1] His 1928 book, *To the Pure*, a scathing critique of censors and vice societies, had received rave reviews and elevated his status among progressives. He quickly cemented his liberal bonafides, publishing article after article, and became a notable public lecturer and radio guest, as when he argued in the affirmative in a March 1928 debate, "Shall Jury Duty for Women Be Compulsory?" on WGL radio.[2] In January 1929, he was appointed general co-counsel of the ACLU, and by March 1929, he was already commanding healthy speaking fee minimum of $100, with out-of-town lectures starting at $200.[3] Mary Ware Dennett, recognizing Ernst's talents, had retained him to defend her in the "Sex Side of Life" case, and that timing had been fortuitous, for Ernst was honing his techniques as a popular lawyer and learning how to employ the media to promote his causes, his clients, and himself. A new kind of challenge for Ernst emerged on April 15, 1929, after police raided a birth control clinic and arrested two doctors and three nurses.[4] Margaret Sanger, the famous birth control advocate and the founder of Planned Parenthood, who had opened the Birth Control Clinical Research Bureau in 1923 and served as its director, thought first to hire Ernst, who had already amassed progressive credentials and whom she knew accepted such cases pro bono.

The resulting trial, known as *People v. Sideri,* offers a fascinating glimpse into the connection between early twentieth-century Americans' stances on contraception and their underlying assumptions about gender roles.[5] *Sideri* suggests that birth control opponents adhered to an antiquated, Victorian construction of masculinity, while those supporting contraception held more modern assumptions about gender identity. This case thus provides a helpful touchstone in the slow evolution of twentieth-century attitudes about sex. Specifically, *Sideri* illustrates the growing, if grudging, public acceptance of the idea that sexuality and sexual agency was not solely relegated to men.

Ernst's defense was built on a non-threatening case for the use of contraception—one based on public health—that reflected real changes in the public understanding of prescribed gender roles, wherein men could be envisioned as ceding some of their real and presumed sexual authority, and women might be granted greater sexual agency.

It was also an opportunity for Ernst to expand his growing celebrity. Ernst came to understand the courtroom as theater, and he delighted in performing the unlikely role of a dashing leading man in that venue. Unlike other cases, for which he anticipated the coming indictment of a controversial text and prepped in advance, the raid naturally took Sanger by surprise. Ernst had only days to prepare for the trial, and he was simultaneously defending the authors of "Sex Side of Life" and *The Well of Loneliness* in two other huge (and very public) cases.[6] Even so, based on the success of his own book and on the favorable public coverage he'd already received in the media, Ernst must have assumed that this case would be a slam-dunk. Just four days after the raid, and thanks in part to Ernst's skillful use of publicity, hundreds of people appeared to see him defend the birth clinic staff, and many more read about the case in articles published nationwide. In essentially untying the hands of New York City physicians, who gained the ability to legally distribute birth control, Ernst positioned himself as a progressive legal hero among some of the most influential members of the New York social set.

## MASCULINITY AND BIRTH CONTROL

If nineteenth-century masculinity was contingent on ideas of control and power, the very idea of birth control must have seemed quite threatening to many men and women at the beginning of the twentieth century. Certainly, male anxiety in the face of contraception reveals a great deal about the changing conception of masculinity during this era.[7] The Victorian conception of masculinity had, after all, assumed sex to be an unfortunate necessity for procreation, since male sexuality was a danger to the family and society.[8] Men who mastered self-control would presumably direct their energies toward non-sexual activities and thus would have no need for contraception. If men were inherently savage, had no autonomy, and were increasingly engaging women in the public sphere, then birth control might very well entice men into sinful practices—and could even put mankind at risk.

Following an era of increasing waves of immigration, these concerns took on a heightened importance. After *Harper's* published a series of articles defending birth control in 1915, one reader, Dr. R. C. Brannon, wrote a letter warning that birth control "is shortening the lives of the human race, making weaklings in mind and body the children of strong men, and wrecking the nerves and bodies of women who ought to be the proud and happy members of a dozen healthy children."[9] Exactly how birth control made men's children into "weaklings" isn't clear from the physician's comments, but anti-birth control activists frequently presented the Darwinian argument that birth control would dilute the white race and undermine white power, and the doctor's remarks fit this pattern. In any event, clearly Brannon saw a definite correlation between contraception and weakness. The implication is that the female control of sexuality could undermine the strength of the family. As Brannon's letter to *Harper's* suggests, racist and nativist fears were often intrinsically linked to perceived threats to masculinity. Those like Brannon who opposed birth control during this era often invoked fears of a watered-down race or even race suicide.[10]

In many cases, however, opposition to birth control was rooted in sincere religious conviction, and men weren't the only ones opposed. Roman Catholics, for instance, cited religious doctrine in their position on birth control and, accordingly, could easily interpret contraception as an affront to their devout interpretation of scripture. Ernst recognized this fact and discussed the Catholic take on birth control in his books.[11] It was in the best interest of Ernst's clients not to speak openly of their religious prejudices, of course, since doing so could easily alienate judge and jury. Ernst saw firsthand that the Church's position could evoke virulent anti-Catholic attacks, even from his own clients. The British author Marie Stopes, whom Ernst would later defend in the 1931 American obscenity trials of her books *Married Love* and *Enduring Passion*, betrayed her prejudice in a letter Ernst immediately marked "*Private not* to be used in any way" (*sic*; emphasis in the original):

> You will, of course, I expect, be up against Roman Catholics, and even if you are not you will find, or I may be able to find later, that Roman Catholics have advised, instructed, and generally "planted" your opponents with pseudo information . . . In the course of this trial my opponents, led by Sergeant Sullivan, a very foul mouthed Roman Catholic Counsel, did all they could to vilify me and my work.[12]

Stopes' disgust here is not with men per se; she associates the anti-birth control movement with a religious agenda, not a male agenda. Some men and women, in other words, opposed birth control because they believed it was an offense to God and family, and not necessarily because they associated birth control with an end to male hegemony.

Still, it is worthwhile to examine in greater depth the anxieties that birth control unleashed in certain men and women. A constant refrain heard from birth control opponents was that it threatened the size of families. It would be instructive, at this point, to discuss how the meaning of family changed during this era. In the Victorian period, Nancy Cott explains, families maintained separate spheres inhabited by males and females.[13] The home was the purview of the mother and wife, who was the manager and overseer of all domestic functions. The decor, the schedule, the meals, the cleaning, and the social events were her responsibility, and though presumably her husband could contribute to her decision-making process, or even overrule her, at least in theory, the home was her power base. She used this authority to discipline her children, to control their activities, and to keep her husband in line. As E. Anthony Rotundo concisely puts it, the nineteenth-century view was that the masculine sphere "depleted" virtue while the feminine sphere "renewed" it.[14] In this construction, and in the absence of women's supposed domesticating influence, men's worst masculine imposes might be unleashed. Jacqueline Moore demonstrates how one American icon, the cowboy, embodied masculine American savagery in the late nineteenth century, as he employed violence to regulate the behavior of women as well as minorities. Cowboy culture "involved conspicuous lack of control over passions."[15] "Respectable" women were not a presence at cowboy saloons and taverns, presumably because they would be both assumed to be prostitutes and at risk of sexual assault from the untamed cowboys.[16] As mentioned earlier, women in the Victorian era were widely considered chaste, pure, and sexually passionless creatures, and they were understood to be the civilizing force over both their boys and their husbands. Men were supposedly slaves to their own passions. The stability of the family, then, depended on the wife and mother, who must maintain a domestic environment that calms the savage beast and must slake the passion of her man by using her feminine virtue.

These assumptions about gender roles were increasingly being tested. First, though the vast majority of American wives continued to manage their homes, they were more active in the public sphere—driven, in part, by the marketplace. In her analysis of 1930s contraceptive advertising, Andrea Tone points out that twentieth century advertisers specifically targeted wives for all sorts of products, and that they portrayed the wives as the decision makers for the home. "In the 1920s," Tone writes, "the gendered dimensions of consumption were readily apparent. Hoping to influence women's buying behavior, advertisers shrewdly cast women's time-worn role as consumers in a flattering light."[17] While Tone's essay focuses on the marketing of birth control to women, contraceptives were one part of a larger trend of re-envisioning women as something other than vessels of purity. To the companies that used advertisements to target them, at least, twentieth-century women represented sources of revenue rather than purity. As Roland Marchand points out in his analysis of American advertising, during this era, advertisers believed that the modern woman was *the* source of income, since "everyone acknowledged that she made at least 80 percent of all consumer purchases."[18]

A second challenge to Victorian assumptions came from unmarried women. In the early twentieth century, single women were entering the work force in ever greater numbers.[19] The resulting daily social intercourse of men and single women posed a terrific threat to the Victorian family structure. Since men were considered creatures of passion, the "modern" single women they interacted with—women, that is, who supposedly lacked the self-control so vital in the maintenance of civilized manliness—this increase in exposure to the opposite sex troubled those who adhered to the traditional, Victorian-era concept of family.

The introduction of a widely available form of birth control could only heighten such tensions. Birth control promised to do away with at least some of the consequences of sexual intercourse, especially the most visible and tangible consequence: pregnancy. Men now spent more time outside the home and were increasingly interacting with women who were not their wives.[20] Women who had entered the labor force did not necessarily envision or value self-control in the way that Victorian mores prescribed. Indeed, some of these women were immigrants whose ideas about sexual morality differed greatly from the lingering moral influence of the Victorian era. Anxieties over sexual behavior did exist, to be sure. Such anxieties, as Jeffrey Moran argues, were "fueled by middle-class fear of a changing moral and social order. . . . Uneasiness over the new immigrants was thus bound up with concern for sexual morality, sometimes explicitly."[21] The anxiety was that women could indulge in sex without fear of repercussions, and that contraception could strain men's faithfulness as they were increasingly exposed to women who did not share the Victorian moral emphasis on self-control.

This perceived threat to the family was also a perceived threat to masculinity. bell hooks has pointed out that the American family structure of the twentieth century often unwittingly perpetuated sexism by teaching children the gendered roles that they must adapt.[22] For instance, boys and girls frequently learned that the father was the primary breadwinner while the mother cooked, cleaned, and managed the home. To repudiate these roles, hooks argues, so-called radical feminists proposed several alternatives to the traditional family, including "a utopian woman nation, separatist communities, and even the subjugation or extermination of all men."[23] Though hooks is analyzing the feminist politics of the late twentieth century, the connection she makes between the elimination of perceived gender stereotypes and the dissolution of the traditional family structure helps explain the anxiety some Americans felt about birth control in the early twentieth century. For if birth control eliminated the pregnancies that kept women home, more women could then work outside of the home, which in turn would allow women the sexual autonomy of earning power so threatening to traditional male privilege. Most importantly, the whole idea of contraception was anathema to the idolized image of women as passionless creatures. Birth control pulled back the veil on the scandalous fact that women could actually enjoy sex, since it would separate sexual intercourse from what was supposed to be its primary motive—namely, procreation.

But for men like Morris Ernst, who embraced birth control as a public health benefit, concerns about sexual morality were unfounded, based as they were on the assumption that men were inherently savage. Ernst, himself a son of immigrants, sympathized with the outsiders who provoked such anxieties. For those who did not agree with traditional assumptions about gender roles, the debate over birth control provided an opportunity to explore new conceptions of masculinity. After all, arguments against contraception seemed to assume that men were barely-contained savages whose self-control would be overcome by the temptation of consequence-free sexual intercourse that birth control granted. A less threatening construction of masculinity—one, that is, which was based on logic, reasoning, and scientific methodology—were intrinsic in Ernst's arguments in favor of birth control. Ernst demonstrated qualities of civility, education, and wit, and these same qualities enabled him to overcome his own sense of inferiority as a "small" son of Jewish immigrants.

## RAIDING THE REALM OF WOMEN

Though laws banning birth control were largely crafted, passed, and enforced by men, the raid of Margaret Sanger's New York clinic was facilitated by a woman who was initially identified in court records as Mrs. Tierney.[24] According to the trial transcript, on March 22, 1929, Tierney went to the Birth Control Clinical Research Bureau in Manhattan with a poignant story that revolved around her alcoholic husband, his low wages as a truck driver and their three children, aged one-, three-, and five-years old. Tierney first talked with a nurse, identified in court records as "Jane Doe"; she told Nurse Doe that after having birthed those three children in five years, she worried about the economic consequences of having more.[25] Her husband, Tierney said, only earned $40 per week.[26] After the nurse further questioned Tierney about her menstrual cycle and other medical history, she filled out a medical information card and told Tierney to make an appointment for a consultation.[27]

Tierney returned to the clinic on April 3 and, according to the *Herald Tribune*, received contraceptive advice, a tube of medicine, and a "device," for which she paid five dollars. A nurse told Tierney that the device was a rubber contraceptive which she was to "draw over your womb before sexual intercourse with your husband." The nurse explained that the tube of medicine was a jelly "which will kill every living germ that comes from your husband and prevent the pregnancy." After Tierney received the goods and paid her fee, the nurse instructed her, "Now go into the toilet and take your bloomers off and wait in the adjoining room until the doctor is through with other patients."[28] Tierney returned again by appointment on April 10, at which point the clinic's director, Dr. Hannah Stone, asked her how she was doing with the contraceptive. "Not very well," Tierney reportedly replied; she had experienced some difficulty in inserting the device. The doctor examined her, gave her further instructions, and told Tierney to come back to the clinic in six months.[29]

"Mrs. Tierney," however, would never again enter the Birth Control Clinical Research Bureau as a patient. Tierney's real name was Anna McNamara, and she was an undercover police officer. On the morning of April 15, 1929, based on McNamera's investigation, eight uniformed New York City police officers raided the clinic and arrested five of its employees for violating the New York State Obscenity Act.[30] Assistant District Attorney John Hogan charged Dr. Stone, as the clinic's medical director; Dr. Elizabeth Pissort; and three nurses, Antoinette Field, Sigrid Brestwell, and Marcella Sideri with violating the provisions of Section 1142 of the Penal Law of the State of New York. All five were accused of the "unlawful distribution of any instrument, article, or any recipe, drug or medicine for the prevention of conceptions."[31]

In addition to arresting the doctors and nurses, police seized hundreds of items and interrupted the examination of patients, some who were in various stages of undress. The list of seized objects, according to defense attorneys, included 249 pessaries, then used as a kind of diaphragm, and seven tubes of contraceptive jelly. But police also took speculums and "metal instruments" used for medical examination—items, in other words, that could be found in numerous doctors' offices. By confiscating legal, widely used medical equipment, which was indisputably used to examine patients, the police were challenging the authority of doctors everywhere. Even more importantly for the defense's case, the police seized 150 index cards, each of which contained private medical information about patients. The idea that the police could indiscriminately seize and view private medical records troubled doctors, nurses, and patients alike.[32] But it may ultimately have been the image of male policemen trying to barge into examination rooms containing naked women—there were reportedly more than 35 patients, most of them with babies, in the clinic at the time—that provoked the greatest outrage and excitement in the community and most damaged the prosecution's case.[33] One nurse told a reporter, "We had to work to keep [the police] out of the room in which a patient was undergoing an examination, but they finally consented to wait until she dressed before they entered."[34] Regardless of their position on birth control, many readers must have placed themselves in the position of that undressed patient, or else sympathized with her plight in the face of such savage masculinity.

Ernst met the aggressive police tactics with an aggressive media campaign and spoke to every reporter who would listen. His comments to the press placed his clients on the side of morality and justice, and newspapers quickly ratified that position. Ernst argued that the government's raid and seizure of clinic files was "illegal and unethical." He told the *New York Herald Tribune* that 40 doctors had volunteered to "aid" the clinic's case at court, a claim which suggested a level of support from the medical community that the prosecution lacked. The paper duly used Ernst's claim as its headline for the story, and if Ernst provided any verification for that assertion, the *Herald Tribune* does not mention it, and none appeared in Ernst's files on the case.[35] The *Telegram*, in turn, helpfully pointed out that Ernst was far from alone in his views, adding that "the raid drew down the wrath of physicians all over town."[36] Editorials highlighted privacy concerns and raised questions about limits to police and governmental authority. The *Herald Tribune* editorial was typical in this respect: "If police can seize doctors' and lawyers' general files without a specific warrant, and paw them over in search of possible evidence, the privileged relation of doctor or lawyer and client ceases to exist."[37] Many contemporary readers, particularly those in cities like New York, may have associated the police's actions with the curtailment of civil liberties during World War I. Years later, in a speech titled "The Law Catches Up With Science," Ernst would point to the fact that "policemen stole the records of the patients and would not give them back" as the "great break" for the birth control movement: "many a doctor who was giving birth control advice to his paying patients was outraged because private records were taken. Hundreds of women kept calling up and saying, 'Have they got my record?' The doctors were worried, and rose up in arms to help the birth control movement because they feared an attack on their confidential and privileged files."[38] At the time of the raid, Ernst also told the press that interest in the case went beyond physicians; "Wall Street men," he said, were putting up $300 for the clinic's defense.[39] Professional men of all kinds, it seemed, were opposed to the raid.

Finally, Ernst put Police Commissioner Grover Whalen on the defensive, suggesting that the raid was somehow related to the defeat of a birth control bill in the New York legislature. As the *New York World* reported, "The Remer bill, which would have allowed doctors to give contraceptive information to married persons, was killed in committee," and ten days after the bill died, McNamera made her first visit to the clinic. Whalen insisted there was no connection.[40] To raise further doubts about police motives, Ernst also claimed that "the raid . . . bore all the evidences of prearrangement, even the photographers being notified to be on hand."[41] While the raid was naturally planned (or "prearranged,"—for how could it have been executed otherwise?)

Ernst mentioned the photographers to imply that the police's motives were somehow tainted because they used the media to shame his clients. Of course, Ernst himself was attempting to shape public opinion even as he made such accusations; perhaps he believed that such a tactic seemed less suspect when employed by a defense lawyer than by a police force.[42] In any event, Ernst effectively persuaded reporters that his clients were victims of overzealous and overreaching officials.

Dr. Stone, one of the physicians arrested in the raid, also performed admirably before the media. Stone declared that the conditions in Jefferson County Court Jail, where the five accused women were held for almost a day until released on $300 bail, were "insanitary" and "inexcusable" and pledged to start a movement to improve conditions as soon as the *Sideri* case was closed.[43] Stone's rhetorical move, possibly orchestrated by Ernst, was impressive: In complaining about prison conditions, Stone raised further doubts about the integrity of the authorities who were, after all, the managers of the jail; in offering to help improve those conditions, she drew a contrast between herself as a caring citizen and the police, who presumably did not embrace the humanity of their fellow men and women as deeply. Finally, in suggesting that she would tackle prison conditions after the *Sideri* case, she presented the trial as an impediment to good works and her ability to help people.

## DOMESTICATING THE PUBLIC

In a strange way, Stone and Ernst were fulfilling some of the very same functions supposedly embraced by Victorian-era wives. The police represented savage masculinity and Ernst and Stone positioned themselves as the ones who could domesticate such men. The police had acted savagely in invading the privacy of women; Stone, like a late-nineteenth-century mother pledging to civilize her unruly boys and maintain the civility and cleanliness of her home, was now pledging to help clean up the space managed by the police. Ernst, in turn, was using his power to promote his client's cause in the media to rally public opinion against the police. Through the media and the courtroom, he could get the authorities to behave in a civilized manner. His idea of civilization, of course, was quite different than that of the Victorian moralists he was challenging.

The press was more than willing to help Ernst in his endeavor. Newspapers published sympathetic stories about the plight of the clinic's staff and patients. The *Herald Tribune* led the way with its initial coverage, pointing out that "small children" had accompanied their mothers to the clinic the day of the raid and thus witnessed the police storming in. Most of the patients remained outside the clinic after the raid, "and because of the excitement children began to cry, which added to the confusion."[44] The *New York World* recorded the anger of the patients, who were "hooting and jeering at the raiders."[45] The *Herald Tribune* appealed to its readers' sense of social justice, reporting Sanger's claim that in 1928, the clinic had treated 6,873 persons, "of whom 2600 were free patients."[46] The *World* similarly appealed to those readers who were sensitive to class inequality. The law invoked in the raid, the *World* editorialized, "is in effect class legislation of a peculiarly odious sort, because it can be enforced only upon those who are too helpless and too innocent of the ways of the world to circumvent the law."[47] In similar fashion, the *Herald Tribune's* editorial portrayed the authorities as overbearing thugs. Given that the clinic "(had) been in public operation, under distinguished medical direction, for five years," the editors asked why the clinic had been raided now. Doctors and nurses were "herded" into patrol cars, despite their offer to pay for taxicabs, and would have been fingerprinted "like common criminals" if an attorney had not arrived in time to protest. The actions of the state amounted to, "an arbitrary police invasion of medical privacy."[48] Ernst called the police action "unpardonable." "They ransacked the clinic and dumped all its private files, including case files, into a waste basket and carried them away. Communications between doctors and patients are supposed to be confidential and privileged. From such methods, blackmail could easily follow."[49]

## GENDER ROLES, AND SCIENCE, ON TRIAL

On the first day of the trial, some 500 women attempted to get one of the 86 seats in the tiny Jefferson Market courtroom.[50] The *Evening World* described the courtroom as "jammed": "Every seat in Jefferson Market Court was occupied this morning long before the hearing. . . . Standing room was not to be had when the hearing started, six rows of men and women having choked the space between the back of the rear row of seats and the wall."[51] By all accounts, women constituted the majority of those who tried to gain a seat at the spectacle. Some newspapers suggested that the women seeking a spot in the audience were well-positioned economically, if not socially. "Most of the crowd," reported the *Evening Sun*, "which so filled the room that many were standing around the wall, was made up of women. It was a more distinguished group than attends the average magistrate's Court hearing."[52] Also vying for seats: a "small army" of reporters and photographers.[53] The *New York Graphic*, while describing a more heterogeneous crowd, pointedly emphasized that professionals were on the scene: "Scientists, professors, students of medicine, doctors, laymen and women from all walks of life jammed the court to overflowing numbers crowding on the steps to devour each morsel of testimony as it was passed back in whispers."[54] The clear message was that most spectators had links to the upper stratum of society and that, despite the eagerness for "each morsel of testimony," the audience was not present simply for titillation.

In a 1961 unpublished interview, Ernst suggested that at least some of those in attendance were unwitting spectators to history:

> I recall trying this case in a courtroom crowded with men and young women in the back of the room. I asked the clerk, "What are they doing here? The subject of birth control is taboo. Shouldn't the courtroom be cleared if law is to be logical because no one should be allowed to listen to the story of contraceptives if it was illegal to spread it?" I recall the clerk telling me that the young people in the back of the courtroom were in luck, and when I asked why, he said, " . . . They've all been arrested on some picket line. They're in court, waiting for trial, and they're going to get their first real education in contraceptives."[55]

There are no newspaper accounts to corroborate Ernst's story, and it is possible that, three decades and dozens of trials later, Ernst may not have remembered exactly when (or if) he actually had such a conversation. It would not be unthinkable, either, that in his exhibitionist role, he embellished a memorable story for the sake of his presumed audience. Either way, his story suggests how important cases like *Sideri* were to his understanding of the courtroom as a theater. In other words, Ernst recognized that people yearned for the kind of "education" such a trial would provide, and would pay rapt attention, even from outside the courtroom, to someone like him, a legal actor who could simultaneously teach the public about science, law, and sexuality and still win his case. Ernst would be important to his contemporaries in the 1920s for many reasons, but one of the most important reasons was that he publicized facts and opinions about law, society, and sexuality that the lay public valued.

At trial, Ernst pointed out that while undercover, McNamara had told the clinic's staff that she had just weaned a child. He then cited statistics showing that infant mortality increased when only one year elapsed between births. There were 146 deaths per 1,000 births when only one year elapsed between births, Ernst said; that figure dropped to 96 deaths per 1,000 when two years elapsed between births. The clinical staff had thus given the fictional Tierney information that would have greatly reduced the chances that her next baby would die. This type of matter-of-fact scientific data challenged the prosecution's claim that the clinic's activities were obscene. Judge Abraham Rosenbluth would, in fact, later highlight this same evidence in his ruling. The media made much of the fact that "all the leading obstetricians are doing everything" to space babies three and four years apart. This fact, one paper stated, came as a surprise to the "young" Assistant District Attorney.[56]

But Ernst also exploited the behavior of the police by asking McNamara to discuss, in graphic terms, her physical examination in front of the mixed courtroom audience of some 200 women and men. "In one part of her testimony," the defendants' brief states, "the complainant admitted . . . that the doctor put her hand inside of the patient's vagina."[57] One journalist, referring to the prosecutor as "Young Assistant District Attorney Hogan," clearly took delight in reporting that Hogan "was a warm blushing pink throughout the time his star witness was on the stand," and that "the face of Magistrate Rosenbluth became a deep red and remained so, while the cops also blushed."[58] The *Daily News* reported that McNamara, whom the reporter identified as a "woman sleuth," herself blushed when questioned about her conversations and experiences at the clinic, and highlighted the blush in its headline to the story.[59] Her embarrassment at Ernst's frank discussion of her physical examination helped the defense make the case that authorities had violated patient confidentiality: if an undercover officer felt uncomfortable discussing the results of her investigation, how would the actual clinic patients have felt after the raid?

Once again, the media assisted Ernst in making his case. After the first day of the trial, most newspapers concluded that Ernst's team had already made a powerful case for birth control and come out ahead in the legal fight. The *New York World*'s April 20 headline, for instance, declared: "Birth Controllers Win First Skirmish." The *World* reported Ernst's revelation that the birth clinic staff had provided "Mrs. Tierney" with critical advice. *The Brooklyn Daily Eagle* reported that under cross examination of McNamara, "the very thing the two doctors had been arrested for doing, the law itself did in open court." The media consistently published sympathetic stories about the plight of the clinic's staff and patients. In the days following the raid the *New York World, New York Mirror, New York Graphic*, and *New York Sun* all included photographs of the accused doctors and nurses at court, posing together and smiling defiantly. Ernst's client and longtime friend, Heywood Broun, took a different tact and personalized the fight, belittling the prosecution in his column for the *New York Evening Telegram*: "Young Mr. Hogan, an Assistant District Attorney, is in charge of the case against Doctors Stone and Pissort," wrote Broun. "May I in all charity ask just what on earth young Mr. Hogan knows about the medical issues involved?"[60] Broun's acidic comments are especially revealing for two reasons. First, Broun suggests that Hogan is young, innocent, and ignorant of medical issues—and, by extension, sexual ones. The condescending tone places Hogan in a camp of less masculine men; someone like Hogan, as opposed to Broun himself, could not be a real man because he was sexually naive. To punctuate this point, Broun then attacked

Police Commissioner Grover Whalen, and imagined a future conversation in which "a great and gallant woman" like Margaret Sanger would be remembered while Whalen would be all but forgotten: "Don't you remember that little fellow that was Police Commissioner for a little while? Oh, you know, that fellow that wore a flower in his buttonhole and didn't solve the Rothstein case."[61] Broun dismisses Whalen as a "little fellow," an obvious slight which readers could interpret in multiple ways. In addition, Broun suggests that Whalen is less than manly by using Whalen's attire, ineffectiveness, and apparent lack of intelligence as evidence. Though Broun here does not mention Ernst by name, his column sets up a clear contrast between the masculine sexual incompetence of the prosecution and the worldly, science-based sexual aptitude of the defense.

The courtroom audience, too, was receptive to the scientific and public health grounds on which Ernst would defend his client. Science, after all, seemed like an objective and fair measure of reality, and data and statistics seemed to cut through superficial differences. Like Alfred Kinsey, the entomologist-turned-sexologist, Ernst believed that science held the key to demystifying sexuality. Kinsey, after studying thousands of gall wasps and identifying variations in each, applied this idea of variation to human sexuality.[62] While Kinsey's findings about human sexuality were published some 20 years after Ernst's use of scientific evidence during the *Sideri* trial, both men, to some extent, were employing science to liberate sexuality. When Kinsey published his findings about male sexual behavior in 1948, Ernst co-wrote a gushing book extolling the virtues of Kinsey's research. "The Kinsey Report has done for sex what Columbus did for geography," exclaimed Ernst and co-author David Loth. "It makes a successful scientific voyage to explore an unknown world which had been open only to speculation and suspicion—the sex life of human beings."[63] Though Ernst fully credits Kinsey's work, the fact that he used science and statistics in the courtroom perhaps helped him envision himself as a member of such a historic voyage, if not as a kind of modern courtroom Columbus himself. Ernst's book, titled *American Sexual Behavior and the Kinsey Report,* did more than simply report on the highlights of Kinsey's research. Ernst and Loth used the book to discount and discard what they considered antiquated notions about sexual morality. For instance, in discussing Kinsey's data on extramarital affairs, the authors cite Kinsey's findings that at least one-third of all married men commit adultery. After affirming that marriage is "our avowed ideal," they then apply these data in a radical way: "There are also those occasions when extramarital relations actually save a marriage," Ernst and Loth assert. "This is not supposed according to our customs to be admitted, but it happens. It may quench the man's curiosity or teach him that his wife is a better companion than he thought, or bring him wisdom. Certainly not every adulterous act ends the marriage."[64] With evident glee, the authors dismissed practically every Victorian assumption about sexuality with scientific data on homosexuality, the sexual behaviors of single men, divorce, and so forth.

Kinsey's work would later directly challenge some of the same assumptions about gender roles as Ernst was challenging indirectly in the courtroom; both did so by drawing from data and statistics. If Kinsey's findings normalized certain behaviors, to some extent they also normalized religious and ethnic backgrounds and physical attributes since, presumably, science knew no prejudice. By 1929, Ernst was already relying on the scientific method to make his arguments, both in the courtroom and in his many books. His clients benefited from this strategy, of course—Ernst won almost every case he ever argued—but by endorsing this vision of masculinity as based on rationality, rather than on savagery, Ernst himself earned respectability, popularity, and prestige as well.

In this sense, this scientific approach helped this once-insecure, cerebral Jewish man perceive himself as just as masculine as the nineteenth-century model of the athletic, Christian man. This intimate understanding of sex, together with Ernst's drive to be seen and heard, made Morris Ernst a new kind of man in the twentieth century, even if his contemporaries did not always envision him in masculine terms. Before completely selling the court on science, however, Ernst needed public support and sympathy for the accused, and this he easily secured. *Sideri* had all the ingredients of a spicy story: the testimony of a female police officer who had gone undercover and disrobed; the tales of undressed women; and the gritty details of the goings-on at a birth control clinic where, however clinically, women discussed sex. Thanks to newspaper reports and editorials, and due in part to Ernst's knack for generating publicity and shaping the news, the public was extremely interested in the story.

On the second day of the trial, several hundred people squeezed into the small courtroom.[65] "Society turned out in full force," one reporter wrote, and "[a]ll the 'best people in town' were in the tiny Mulberry street courthouse."[66] The prosecution tried to mitigate the gains the defense had made by drawing from the nineteenth-century sexual strategy of self-control. Yes, the prosecution conceded, there are "some cases where further conception may mean death or create invalidism for the mother." But birth control, the prosecution continued, is not a solution; "there is but one answer to this question," namely, abstinence.[67] A contemporary audience could find this approach to be reasonable. After all, it was absolutely true that refraining from intercourse was a surefire way of avoiding pregnancy. The prosecution's next comments, however, reveal how out-of-step the State was with contemporary attitudes about gender roles:

> Marital continence . . . is the only ethical course for a man when the life of the woman whom he has promised to love and cherish, the mother of his child, is placed in jeopardy. Of course, this is not easy, but to say that is impossible is to deny the heroic in every-day life. Maternity demands heroism, the daily struggle to support wife and children demands heroism. Honesty in business demands heroism. . . . What is needed is self-control, not birth control.[68]

The prosecution here focuses on the man as the responsible party; continence is his "ethical course," and not that of the couple. The long-held belief uncovered in the People's memorandum—namely, that sexuality was confined to men—had already been challenged throughout the 1920s, especially in New York City.[69] The very idea of self-control as a social mechanism, which had been popularized during the Victorian era (and which, again, generally attributed the sexual passion that necessitated such control solely to men), was also being challenged as new research emerged suggesting that masturbation was not harmful. If many doctors no longer considered masturbation to be dangerous, then perhaps sexual self-control itself was no longer necessary. Modern science had also produced birth control; many contemporaries must have wondered why birth control couldn't replace self-control. Birth control could presumably give women more of a say in the sexual decisions made in the home. In short, the assumptions inherent in the prosecution's brief—that it was the man who ultimately decided whether to impregnate his wife; that the resulting offspring was "his" child; that if the couple abstained from sex it would be the man who was heroic (because, presumably, the wife lacked sexual desire); and even that the man demonstrated heroism in supporting his family and being honest at work (couldn't wives also be heroic?)—were in tension with the changing realities of twentieth-century life.

Such attitudes clearly touched a nerve in many court spectators and contributed to a charged courtroom atmosphere. Those who had mobbed the courthouse to see or take part in court theater were not disappointed by the spectacle.[70] Given the fact that Ernst had openly discussed the vagina of a policewoman during prior testimony, one might have expected some nervous giggling or embarrassment. In fact, as one reporter described it, the proceedings devolved into "turmoil." The solemn atmosphere of the courtroom began to dissipate during the testimony of Dr. Foster Kennedy. Testifying that "too frequent pregnancies imperiled the mother's constitution" which endangered the unborn, Kennedy affirmed that patients who thus had given birth within a year should be given contraceptive advice.[71] The judge then suggested that some patients might try to deceive doctors to get such advice. "But what if the patient is lying?" the judge asked Kennedy. "Wouldn't it be better practice to check the official birth records to find out whether the patient is telling the truth?" Kennedy responded, "Judge, we doctors examine a patient before we prescribe. You can forge a birth certificate but you can't forge a womb."[72] The spectators "roared" with laughter, Ernst recalled, and the judge threatened to clear the courtroom if there were further outbursts. Ernst himself provoked the next outburst by gently mocking the judge, during the testimony of Dr. Lewis I. Harris, the former Health Commissioner of New York City. Harris proclaimed the clinic "beyond reproach" and gave his stamp of approval to the doctors' examination and treatment of McNamara, which he deemed "unusually thorough." "But," Judge Rosenbluth interrupted, "isn't it most important to find out whether the patient is married or not?" The audience laughed, nearly drowning out Harris's response that doctors were obliged to believe their patients. Then Ernst struck, asking the witness: "Do you know of any situation where a doctor sends out a detective to find out whether his patients are married?"[73] The resulting laughter and the judge's response led to a near riot, as the trial "waxed uproarious."[74] By illustrating the absurdity of the marriage requirement and, by extension, the silliness of the judge's question, Ernst enraged Rosenbluth. "Unless there is absolute silence I shall clear the courtroom," the annoyed judge warned. "On second thought, I shall clear it anyway. Out you go—all of you!"[75] As court attendants "herded" spectators out of the courtroom, Kitty Marion, a woman the *Herald Tribune* identified as a veteran birth control advocate, shouted: "Sweet land of liberty—land of dumb, driven cattle!"[76]

Immediately afterward, a coalition of "fur and gardenia adorned ladies" drafted a petition and presented it to Chief Magistrate William McAdoo, who reversed Rosenbluth, and the spectators were eventually allowed back into the courtroom.[77] The audience, thus emboldened, did not remain quiet once they returned to their places. On his cross examination of Pissort, the assistant district attorney's finger-wagging and line of questioning resulted in more laughter. After it emerged that McNamara actually had two children, and that her youngest child was seven years old, Hogan asked Pissort, "Couldn't you tell that this woman had not had a baby a year ago—that, in fact, her last child was seven years old?" all the while, in dramatic fashion, "leaning over the rail and shaking a finger in Dr. Pissort's face." She responded, "How could I?" resulting in another bout of laughter.[78] The humor here, at least, was at the expense of the prosecutor, not the judge, and the trial continued. Hogan's question suggested that, unlike Ernst, he was not well-versed in reproductive health. This interpretation did not go unnoticed by the press. Like Broun, the *New York World*'s Dudley Nichols teased Hogan, describing him as "a pleasant young man who had done a young man's best."[79] The implication was that Hogan was, at best, unsophisticated in matters relating to sexuality.

Ernst moved to dismiss the case, warning that if his clients were found guilty, doctors could face a future in which their every action would have to be justified before a court and every case would be subject to a rediagnosis by lawyers.[80] Despite his earlier outburst, or perhaps due in part to his embarrassment at being so publicly reversed by his boss, on May 14 Judge Rosenbluth ruled in favor of the defendants.[81] The judge framed his decision around the clinic's diagnosis of Tierney/McNamera. The prosecution, he said, had the burden of proof to demonstrate that the diagnosis was made in bad faith. Yet, in response to Ernst's statistics showing how the spacing of births could affect infant mortality, the prosecution failed to present evidence that challenged the clinic's diagnosis. Basing his decision on the precedent of *People v. Sanger,* the judge ruled that "[t]he law is plain that if the doctor in good faith believes that the patient is a married woman, and that her health requires prevention of conception, it is no crime to so advise and instruct therein."[82]

While the idea of birth control could be threatening to those who clung to traditional nineteenth-century attitudes about gender and masculinity, by stressing marriage and health in his ruling, the judge managed to uphold certain components of those constructs. First, since the ruling only applied to married women, single women would not be able to obtain contraceptives and, accordingly, their sexuality would presumably be kept under control. The great fear of vice societies and others who rallied against birth control was that contraception would lead to promiscuity. There were contemporary critics who warned against the sins of licentiousness which, they claimed, would in turn lead to unwanted children, disease, and race suicide. An underlying fear was that men might somehow lose power in the process. So long as women were constantly having and raising babies, they would not be members of the labor force, where they might compete with men (or, presumably, distract them with their feminine wiles). Birth control, as the argument went, might also allow women to take multiple partners without fear of getting pregnant. In short, unlimited birth control would burst apart the separate spheres beyond repair.

Second, the ruling focused on the health benefits of birth control, rather than the question of women's authority over their sexuality. Health policy, as Ernst quickly realized, could be quantified, and the data and statistics he cited in trials would bolster his defense by suggesting a degree of neutrality. Science, after all, was neutral, and how could one refute scientific facts that pointed to a healthier, safer society? Indeed, in this case, the prosecution did not challenge Ernst's data on the advisability of spacing births. And in fact, Ernst's approach actually helped to cement certain traditional gender assumptions. Why was it, after all, that infant mortality was higher for women who had births closer together? Under long-held conceptions of women, they were the "fairer sex," a gentle way of suggesting that women were weak—and, by extension, that men were powerful. By framing birth control this way, as a necessary medical treatment, rather than a woman's right, Ernst appealed to the public's sympathy and its assumptions about the relative weaknesses of women, and the judge codified that view.

Arguing this case enabled Ernst to polish his repertoire of citing scientific data, statistics, and health benefits in defense of his clients. It also placed men like Ernst, who could speak confidently and openly about sex, in stark contrast to men like Hogan, who fumbled nervously when broaching the subject of sexuality. Ernst's own popularity soared, and he moved happily onto other controversial cases, all the while solidifying his image as the modern man confident in his own masculinity. And the case itself helped add credence to the growing sense that Victorian sexual mores and assumptions about masculinity and gender were primitive, antiquated, and a threat to modern progress.

While Ernst had clearly won the case and had several other trials on his agenda, there were still two matters pending in *Sideri*. First, what had happened to the materials that the police had confiscated during the raid? And second, would anyone in the police department be punished for the abuse of power? Ernst had complained from the beginning that the police had left no receipt for the 150 patient records taken during the raid.[83] The police continued to insist that they had not taken any patient cards.[84] The same day the court released the five defendants, the police commissioner apologized for his officers' "tactics." He placed the blame on Officer Mary A. Sullivan, whom he said planned the raid, stated that the matter should have been referred to him and demoted Sullivan.[85]

Ernst was not satisfied with this demotion. In an unsigned letter to Ernst's nephew, DeWitt Stetten Jr., who was then president of the New York City Medical Society, his firm stated its intention to investigate the facts surrounding the issuance of the warrant and the raid. Although the magistrate and the police commissioner had announced that the case was closed, and a policewoman was demoted, "our own interest is primarily to have the matter thoroughly aired as a form of social protection for the medical profession in the future."[86] This was yet another opportunity, as well, for Ernst to keep the story alive, increase pressure on authorities, and boost his own celebrity. The commissioner, perhaps frustrated by Ernst's continuing questions into a matter that Whalen considered closed, challenged Ernst to fight it out in court.[87] Whalen's challenge was the twentieth-century version of a manly duel between two public figures. Rather than take the bait, Ernst focused on his other cases and let his associates battle over the demotion and the records. His office ultimately lost; the police continued to insist that no records were seized, and the cards never materialized. Ernst backed down but did not lose face.

After the trial, the Executive Secretary for the American Birth Control League, Penelope Huse, wrote to thank and praise Ernst for his work on Sanger's behalf:

> We all want to congratulate you upon the way you handled the case of Mrs. Sanger's Clinical Research Bureau. It certainly was masterly, and you made District Attorney Hogan look like an ape. The poor little creature stuttered around so in his cross examination and showed such a woeful lack of knowledge of anatomy and the sex functions that one might almost have pitied him, unless one realized, as a taxpayer, that he was being paid by all of us.[88]

The above letter from Huse, as well as the raid, the subsequent public outrage, and the raucous *Sideri* trial, illustrate how interpretations of gender and masculinity were changing during the first decades of the twentieth century. Ernst, who was "masterly" in his "knowledge of anatomy and the sex functions," represented modern manliness. Those who were ignorant of such matters, Huse suggests, were little better than apes. Ernst's decision to ignore the commissioner's challenge did nothing to diminish Ernst's popularity, and he moved happily onto other controversial cases, all the while fomenting his image as the modern man confident in his own identity and promoting his own celebrity among "society" and professional women and men and, increasingly, the general public.

Although the *Sideri* case took place over 90 years ago, it may help shed some light on the reasoning, motives, and values of United States policymakers and cultural spokesmen who continue to oppose contraception, even today. In 2012, after Sandra Fluke testified before Congress in support of insurance coverage for contraception, the conservative talk show host Rush Limbaugh called her a "slut" and a "whore."[89] American politicians embrace "personhood" legislative initiatives, which are ostensibly crafted with the professed intent to ban abortions, but which could also end access to certain types of contraception.[90] Modern-day opponents of contraception, and of the women who use it, may be recalling a romanticized era when masculinity was less a function of brainpower than "manpower," and when science took a backseat to idealized notions of self-control and abstinence. When men and women chose to support the idea and use of contraception in the early twentieth century, they inherently rejected the Victorian model of savage manliness. Today, with conservative critics and legislators attacking the legitimacy of contraception, the organizations that provide it, and the women who use it, the 1929 *Sideri* case remains startlingly relevant.

## NOTES

1. A version of this chapter was published in 2016; see Joel Matthew Silverman, "'You Can't Forge a Womb': The 1929 Birth Control Clinic Raid and Changing

Notions of Masculinity in Early 20th Century America," in *Masculinities: A Journal of Identity and Culture*, issue 5 (February 2016): 26–52.

2. "Radio Programs," *Brooklyn Daily Times*, March 15, 1928, 5A.

3. Sally Greene to Morris Ernst, March 15, 1929, in Box 11, MLE. The $100 minimum applied "only to those places which cannot pay more": the agency's commission was 25%. In 2021 dollars, $100 would be about $1,527, according to the U.S. Bureau of Labor Statistics' Consumer Price Index Inflation calculator (https://www.bls.gov/data/inflation_calculator.htm).

4."The Raid on the Birth-Control Clinic," (Editorial) *New York World*, April 18, 1929.

5. The case was initially named *People of the State of New York v. Marcella Sideri, Sigrid Brestwell, Antoinette Field, Elizabeth Pissort, and Hannah M. Stone*. The affidavit of policewoman Anna K. McNamera identified the case as *People v. Stone*, but other court documents and trial memoranda identified it as *People v. Sideri*. The case number is not reported.

6. To give a sense of both Ernst's schedule and the publicity around his clients, note that the front page of the April 19, 1929, edition of *The Brooklyn Daily Eagle* has stories about both the raid and about the *Well of Loneliness* trial.

7. See, for example, Andrea Tone, "Contraceptive Consumers: Gender and the Political Economy of Birth Control in the 1930s," *Journal of Social History* 29, no. 3.

8. Kevin White, *The First Sexual Revolution: The Emergence of Male Heterosexuality in Modern America* (New York: New York University Press, 1993), 3–4.

9. Cited in "The Battle Over Birth Control," *Current Opinion,* Nov. 1915, Vol. LIX., No. 5., 339. Dr. Brannon's letter originally appeared in the October 2, 1915 edition of *Harper's*.

10. For one case study on how eugenicists used such fears of "racial suicide" in Virginia to justify discrimination in the 1920s, see Lisa Lindquist Dorr, "Arm in Arm: Gender, Eugenics, and Virginia's Racial Integrity Acts of the 1920s," *Journal of Women's History,* 11, no. 1 (1999).

11. See, for example, Morris L. Ernst, *So Far So Good* (New York: Harper & Brothers, 1948), 72–77.

12. Marie Stopes to Morris Ernst, October 22, 1930, Box 360, MLE.

13. Nancy F. Cott, *The Bonds of Womanhood: "Woman's Sphere" in New England, 1780–1835* (New Haven: Yale University Press, 1977), 64–70.

14. E. Anthony Rotundo, *American Manhood: Transformations in Masculinity from the Revolution to the Modern Era* (New York: Basic Books, 1993), 23.

15. Jacqueline Moore, "'Them's Fighting Words': Violence, Masculinity, and the Texas Cowboy in the Late Nineteenth Century," *The Journal of the Gilded Age and Progressive Era* 13(01), 32. doi:doi:10.1017/S1537781413000479.

16. Ibid., 40.

17. Tone, "Contraceptive Consumers," para. 10.

18. Roland Marchand, *Advertising the American Dream: Making Way for Modernity, 1920–1940* (Berkeley: University of California Press, 1986), 167.

19. James R. McGovern, "The American Woman's Pre-World War I Freedom in Manners and Morals," in *History of Women in the United States, v.10: Sexuality and Sexual Behavior*, ed. Nancy F. Cott (New Providence: K.G. Saur, 1993), 386–388.

20. Rotundo, "Patriarchs," 71.

21. Jeffrey P. Moran, *Teaching Sex: The Shaping of Adolescence in the 20th Century* (Cambridge: Harvard University Press, 2000), 29.

22. bell hooks, *Feminist Theory: From Margin to Center*, second ed. (Cambridge: South End Press, 2000), 46–47.

23. Ibid, 43.

24. "Birth Control Backers Ready to Fight Case," *New York Telegram,* April 18, 1929.

25. "Birth Control and the Law" (Editorial), *New York Herald Tribune*, May 15, 1929.

26. "Court Frees 5 Taken in Birth Control Raid," *New York Herald Tribune*, May 15, 1929.

27. "Mrs. Sanger's Birth Control Clinic Raided," *New York Herald Tribune*, April 16, 1929, 1.

28. Affidavit of Anna K. McNamara, Police Officer of the 19th Division, *People v. Stone,* Box 358.4, MLE.

29. Ibid.

30. "Mrs. Sanger's," *Herald Tribune.* See also David J. Garrow, *Liberty and Sexuality: The Right to Privacy and the Making of* Roe v. Wade (New York: Macmillan Publishing Company, 1994), 23–24.

31. Affidavit of Anna K. McNamara.

32. Samuel J. Schur to Hon. Grover A. Whalen, Police Commissioner of the City of New York, June 11, 1929, Box 358.1, MLE.

33. "Mrs. Sanger's," *Herald Tribune*; "Birth Control Clinic Raided by N.Y. Police," *Catholic Advance*, April 27, 1929, 3.

34. Ibid.

35. "40 Physicians Volunteer to Aid Birth Control Clinic in Court," *New York Herald Tribune*, April 18, 1929.

36. "Birth Control Backers," *New York Telegram.*

37. "Police, Doctors and Birth Control" (Editorial), *New York Herald Tribune*, April 17, 1929.

38. Morris Ernst, "The Law Catches Up With Science," undated draft of speech, Box 877, MLE.

39. "40 Physicians Volunteer," *New York Herald Tribune.*

40. "Birth Clinic Raid Stirs Up Support for Mrs. Sanger," *New York World*, April 19, 1929.

41. Ibid.

42. Ibid.

43. Ibid.

44. "Mrs. Sanger's Birth Control Clinic Raided," *New York Herald Tribune*, April 16,1929, 1.

45. "Raid Birth Control Clinic, Arrest Five," *New York World*, April 16, 1929.

46. "Mrs. Sanger's," *Herald Tribune*.

47. "Birth Control" (Editorial), *New York World,* May 15, 1929.

48. "Police, Doctors and Birth Control," *New York Herald Tribune.*

49. "Pastors, Doctors Defend Birth Control Clinic at Trial, *Capital Times* (Wisconsin), April 20, 1929, 1.

50. Irene Kuhn, "500 Women Mob Court to Hear Story of Birth Control Raider. Woman Sleuth Blushes at Ruse to Snare Clinic," *New York Daily News*, April 20, 1929.

51. "Court is Jammed as Birth Control Hearing Starts," *Evening World*, April 19, 1929.

52. "Birth Control Hearing Ends," *Evening Sun*, April 24, 1929.

53. Marjorie Dorman, *Brooklyn Daily Eagle*, "Medical Men and Society Celebrities Jam Hearing on Birth Control Clinic," April 19, 1929, 1.

54. "Women Jam Birth Control Hearing," *New York Graphic*, April 20, 1929.

55. Transcript of unpublished interview with Morris Ernst (June 1, 1961), 18, Box 877, MLE.

56. *Brooklyn Daily Eagle,* "Women Hustled From Court For Applauding Doctor's Birth Control Testimony," April 24, 1929, 2.

57. Kuhn, "500 Women."

58. Dorman, "Medical Men."

59. Kuhn, "500 Women."

60. Heywood Broun, "It Seems to Me," *New York Evening Telegram*, April 18, 1929.

61. "Rothstein" was Arnold Rothstein, a Jewish gangster murdered in 1928 who was the inspiration for F. Scott Fitzgerald's character, Meyer Wolfsheim, in *The Great Gatsby.* For more on Rothstein's legacy as "the Moses of the underworld," see Rich Cohen, *Tough Jews* (New York: Simon & Schuster, 1998).

62. James H. Capshew, Matthew H. Adamson, Patricia A. Buchanan, Narisara Murray and Naoko Wake, "Kinsey's Biographers: A Historiographical Reconnaissance," *Journal of the History of Sexuality,* July 2003, v12 i3, p. 465(22).

63. Morris L. Ernst and David Loth, *American Sexual Behavior and the Kinsey Report* (New York: The Greystone Press, 1948), 11. Ernst would, at one point, serve as Kinsey's attorney.

64. Ibid., 87.

65. Dudley Nichols, "Whalen Promises Clinic Raid Inquiry," *New York World*, April 25, 1929. Nichols puts the number at about 200; the *Brooklyn Citizen* suggests double that number in its headline: "Birth Control Provides Fun for '400,'" *Brooklyn Citizen*, April 25, 1929, 2.

66. "Birth Control Provides Fun for '400,'" *Brooklyn Citizen.*

67. People's Memorandum of Facts and Law, *People of the State of New York vs. Marcella Sideri, Sigrid Brestwell, Antoinette Field, Elizabeth Pissort and Hannah M. Stone*, Undated, Box 358.7, MLE.

68. Ibid.

69. Christine Stansell, *American Moderns: Bohemian New York and the Creation of a New Century* (New York: Owl Books, 2001).

70. Ishbel Ross, "Birth Control Hearing Ends After Turmoil. Laughter Angers Magistrate, Who Clears Courtroom, Only to Be Overruled," *New York Herald Tribune*, April 25, 1929.

71. Morris L. Ernst and Alexander Lindey, *The Censor Marches On: Recent Milestones in the Administration of the Obscenity Law in the United States* (New York: Doubleday, Doran & Company, Inc. 1940), 156.

72. Ibid. Kennedy was Chief Neurologist at Cornell University and, interestingly, an enthusiastic supporter of eugenics.

73. Ross, "Birth Control Hearing Ends."

74. *Brooklyn Daily Eagle,* "Women Hustled From Court For Applauding Doctor's Birth Control Testimony," April 24, 1929, 2; Nichols, "Whalen Promises Clinic Raid Inquiry."

75. Ibid. The press reported that only the lawyers, the accused and the reporters were allowed to stay. Inexplicably, according to Ernst and Lindey, court attendants also allowed Carlo Tresca, "the well-known radical" to stay as well. Ernst had previously served as Tresca's lawyer.

76. Ibid. Kitty Marion was a fascinating figure: a German-born, British entertainer who became active in the suffragette movement who became known as one of Margaret Sanger's New York foot soldier for birth control. See Viv Gardner and Diane Atkinson, *Kitty Marion: Actor and Activist* (Manchester University Press, 2019), muse.jhu.edu/book/67219.

77. "Birth Curb Backers Ousted," *Daily Mirror*, April 25, 1929.

78. Ibid.

79. Nichols, "Whalen Promises Clinic Raid Inquiry."

80. "Uproar Interrupts Clinic Raid Hearing," *New York Times*, April 25, 1929, 24.

81. "Court Frees 5 Taken in Birth Control Raid," *New York Herald Tribune*, May 15, 1929.

82. Decision of *People v. Sideri et. al.*, Box 358.8., MLE. The case referenced by the judge in his ruling is *People v Sanger, 222 N Y 192.*

83. "40 Physicians Volunteer," *New York Herald Tribune.*

84. "Court Frees 5 Taken in Birth Control Raid," *New York Herald Tribune*, May 15, 1929.

85. Ibid.

86. Morris L. Ernst to DeWitt Stetten Jr., May 21, 1929, Box 358, MLE.

87. "Whalen Invites Birth Control Suit Over Raid, Challenges Ernst to File Charges Against Police Who Seized Records," *New York Herald Tribune*, May 16, 1929.

88. P.B.P (Penelope) Huse to M. L. Ernst, May, 20 1929, Box 358, MLE.

89. Brian Stelter, "Limbaugh Advertisers Flee Show Amid Storm," *New York Times*, March 5, 2012, B1.

90. Lori Robertson, "A Fight over Birth Control in Colorado," *FactCheck.Org, A project of the Annenberg Public Policy Center*, August 15, 2014, http://www.factcheck.org/2014/08/a-fight-over-birth-control-in-colorado/.

## *Chapter 4*

# Expanding Sexual Boundaries

As a newly minted Jewish lawyer considering job prospects in an era when anti-Semitism was an institutional reality, Ernst's only real option out of law school had been to join a Jewish firm or form one of his one. He chose the latter route, and he and his partners frequently defended causes that other, more traditional firms eschewed. When censors challenged unorthodox or sexually tinged books, their publishers often lacked the funds to finance their defense, and Ernst and his colleagues might accept such cases pro bono. But Ernst learned quickly that when a vice society condemned a text, that publication's sales would skyrocket, and the notoriety of the ensuing trial would guarantee Ernst a strong voice in the press. While working on *Dennett, Sideri,* and other causes, Ernst took on another such case: *The Well of Loneliness.* Radclyffe Hall's novel depicted a lesbian relationship, and John Sumner, director of the Society for the Suppression of Vice, deemed it "literary refuse."[1] Weeks after Sumner purchased a copy of the novel directly from the publisher, when the book was already in its sixth printing, the Manhattan police seized 800 copies.[2] Of all the texts Ernst had to defend against obscenity charges, Hall's was the least graphic. Her novel contains no words that could be labeled as "profanity," even by contemporary standards; there are no explicit depictions of sexual acts and no descriptions of sexual anatomy. Yet the fact that Hall's narrator was a lesbian had caused a stir in England, where the book would remain banned until 1949. Hoping that controversy would stimulate sales, Hall's American publishers, Covici-Friede, tapped Ernst to defend her novel before it had even been published in the United States. Part of Ernst's strategy was to argue that if one were to replace the female narrator with a male one, then no censor would have looked twice at the novel. Given that the narrator calls herself Stephen, this was an especially effective tactic, for judge and jury apparently made that substitution rather easily. It also helped Ernst that Radclyffe Hall went by the nickname "John," kept her hair short and dressed in masculine attire. During these years, notions of sexuality, to paraphrase Warren Hoffman, had less to do with whom one desired than with how one dressed and behaved.[3] Ernst's strategy, and the fact that he won the case in part by focusing on a rearrangement of gender identity, suggests that at least for a moment during the late 1920s, conceptions of masculine identity were in flux and the lines separating male and female identity were not quite so prominent.

## FEMALE MASCULINITY IN THE EARLY TWENTIETH CENTURY

To make sense of the changing conceptions of female masculinity during these years, this section provides an overview of female masculinity, how it is understood today, and what it seemed to signify in the years leading up to the *Well of Loneliness* case. Judith Halberstam suggests that masculinity is not necessarily a male construction, and that masculinity is not limited to male bodies. As Claudia Breger explains, Halberstam's overarching concern is to advance the premise that masculinities are not limited to white, middle-class males and to move beyond the binary classification of gender.[4] Halberstam has thus argued that female masculinity entails the enactment by women of the same masculine scripts as men.[5] He distinguishes between dominant or "heroic" masculinities, meaning those masculinities which are extolled, celebrated and rewarded by society, and "alternative" masculinities, such as female masculinities.[6] Halberstam's claim is that female masculinities have historically served as a frame of reference for the more dominant forms of masculinity. That is, "female masculinities are framed as the rejected scraps of dominant masculinity in order that male masculinity may appear to be the real thing."[7] Halberstam's point here is that modern female masculinity is conceived as a negative contrast to "real" masculinity; female masculinity, one might say, makes other men seem more manly.

During the first years of the twentieth century, men did not automatically reject female masculinity. As Laura Doan's analysis of women's attire in Britain demonstrates, during these years, and up until the time of Radclyffe Hall's American trial, many women embraced a clearly masculine fashion.[8] Even more interesting, women who sported short hair and boyish or mannish clothing were not identified with lesbianism, as they would be in the coming decades. Doan's study of fashions in the 1920s illustrates how women's so-called mannish attire, short-cropped hair and "manly strides" were simply accepted as the feminine style of the era since "[t]he meaning of clothing in the decade after World War I, a time of unprecedented cultural confusion over gender and sexual identity, was a good deal more fluid than fixed."[9] It was not until after 1928—the year of the British trial of Radclyffe Hall—that women began to return to the "feminine look" as a means "to assert their identity and individuality."[10] In the interim, women found it fun to dress and act like a man, and this behavior was by no means the exclusive domain of lesbians. While male cross-dressing never enjoyed the same acceptance, women's experimentations with masculine traits in the 1920s may have caused some men to at least call into question their assumptions about what constituted "masculine" and "feminine" identity.

Doan's findings, which hint at a slightly more permissive environment for lesbians in the first decades of the twentieth century, jibe with George Chauncey's groundbreaking analysis of male homosexuality in New York during the same era. Chauncey found that prior to the 1930s, there were actually fewer cultural constraints on gays and lesbians then the decades that followed.[11] No one could mistake either Doan's or Chauncey's analyses as evidence that homosexuality was *accepted*, but it is interesting to note that at the very moment Morris Ernst defended Radclyffe Hall, gay culture was on the cusp of being restricted and punished with far greater force than in preceding years.

This attitudinal sea-change toward female masculinity, on the one hand, and lesbianism, on the other, did not occur overnight. In the United States, as the right to vote seemed in reach, women who opted for the masculine look were appreciated less and ridiculed more frequently. In fact, anti-suffragettes increasingly identified politically active women with masculinity. Laura L. Behling's analysis of the American masculine woman during these years illustrates that the disparagement of so-called mannish women was a result of the fact that those women were associated with the suffragette movement—and not because they identified themselves as lesbian (or, as contemporaries would have it, "inverts"). From the late nineteenth-century until the mid-1930s, female masculinity actually seemed to be detached from sexuality. The real possibility of social and political independence for women, writes Behling, "was translated by a fearful society, in American literature and the popular press, into a movement of women whose assumption of the prerogative to vote was perceived to have altered them into 'masculine women' and female sexual inverts":

> In the Progressive and modern eras, when the difference between *sex* and *gender* was not as carefully defined as it is now, a seemingly paradoxical figure developed. Labeled a woman because of her female sex, she also was considered masculine because she dared to take on some of the behaviors of men—wearing bloomers, smoking, drinking, and, as this study emphasizes, demanding political enfranchisement.[12]

Though not all women who sought the vote were labeled as "masculine," Behling's analysis suggests that for many of their contemporaries, at least, female masculinity during the early twentieth century depended mainly on a woman's political activism, and not on her sexual partner.

Given that the novel was challenged because it was read as a *lesbian* novel, it will be helpful to explore the relationship between homosexuality and gender. According to Ernst's and Hall's early twentieth-century contemporaries, when it came to gender, people essentially fell under two categories: heterosexual or *not* heterosexual. One of the reasons the idea of malleable and fluid gender identity is today so valuable to scholars is that it eliminates that "either/or" binary construction of gender and moves away from the idea of normal and abnormal identity. At the turn of the twentieth century, however, homosexuality was subsumed under the category of "inversion," and not all inverts were necessarily considered to desire their own sex. Inversion, as George Chauncey explains, grew out of the analysis of sexologists Richard von Krafft-Ebing and Havelock Ellis, two writers who directly influenced Hall's novel.[13] Though Heike Baur argues that Krafft-Ebing's *Psychopathia Sexualis* owed its popularity among contemporary readers to the fact that it offered, in her words, "sexual kicks"—that is, that it was read for its eroticism—Krafft-Ebing was also noteworthy for presenting a relatively tolerant view of homosexuality.[14] In his analysis of turn-of-the-century medical journals on inversion, Chauncey rightfully warns this specialized discourse is not necessarily a true barometer of popular contemporary attitudes toward gender or sexuality.[15] Still, in the case of Radclyffe Hall, the names Ellis and Krafft-Ebing pop up repeatedly: Hall persuaded Ellis to write the preface to *The Well of Loneliness*, and several scholars have pointed to Krafft-Ebing's influence on Hall's construction of Stephen Gordon, her female protagonist in the novel. Moreover, after Stephen's father dies, we discover with Stephen that her father had been reading and annotating Krafft-Ebing as a means of understanding his daughter. Like Stephen's father, Ernst also did his homework by reading their contemporary theories about inversion and lesbianism; those readings may have ultimately persuaded him of the fluidity of gender.

## "JOHN," STEPHEN GORDON, AND GENDER FLUIDITY

Radclyffe Hall preferred to be known as "John," and her very existence might have hinted to contemporaries like Ernst that gender was not necessarily immutable. Hall was, after all, celebrated in the media for her masculine features and attire. She was also quite open about her sexuality and had been from the time her father died and left her a considerable trust fund. Born Marguerite Radclyffe-Hall in England in 1880, she was the product of a loveless marriage between a British man and an American widow, and she barely knew her father, who had separated from her mother when Hall was only three years old. The separation occurred after Hall's father, who was known for his indiscretions, contracted a venereal disease and gave it to his wife.[16] After her parents separated, Hall's mother aggressively pursued a settlement, but Hall's father stymied her by stipulating that almost all of his inheritance would go to their daughter.[17] Radclyffe Hall professed hatred for her mother, whom she believed had never loved her. Radclyffe's father contracted tuberculosis and died in 1898.[18] In 1901, after receiving her father's inheritance at the age of twenty-one, she was suddenly independent, eventually becoming confident enough to call herself "John," cut her hair short, and style herself as a hip British man. With encouragement from her partner, Una Troubridge, she devoted herself to her writing.

Before writing *The Well of Loneliness*, Hall had already enjoyed considerable critical acclaim and commercial success as a writer. Her career took off in 1924 when her first novel, *The Forge* was accepted. With a publisher, a literary agent, and a sizeable inheritance from her father, she had sufficient resources to consider herself a professional author. Each successive novel garnered more critical and popular success. In 1926, fresh off of a triumphant celebration of her prior novel, *Adam's Breed*, which won the prestigious James Tait Black prize award as the best literary novel of the year, Hall conceived of a novel in which the narrator, while named Stephen, would have a romantic relationship with a woman. *The Well of Loneliness*, her fifth novel, immediately became notorious in England. While other novels incorporated details from her life as a lesbian, only *The Well of Loneliness* presented a clear, unambiguous depiction of gay life. The novel begins with Sir Phillip Gordon and his American-born wife, Anna, both of whom sorely want to have a son—so much so that as soon as they learn that Anna is pregnant, they settle on the name "Stephen" for their child. When Anna gives birth, the parents are disappointed with a daughter rather than a son, yet the father insists on naming the daughter as planned. Stephen Gordon thus grows up with a boy's name and embraces masculine activities, such as hunting on horseback and fencing. Like Radclyffe Hall, Stephen Gordon is loved by her father but not by her mother, who feels nothing for her strange daughter. As Stephen matures, she realizes she is different, and even attempts to woo a married woman, but it is not until Stephen enlists in the war effort as an ambulance driver that she finds Mary, her true love. Like Hall, Stephen has the financial resources to dedicate herself to writing and becomes a celebrated author. The novel concludes in Paris, a city that Stephen finds more tolerant of homosexuality. Even so, Stephen knows that she will never be accepted as an "invert," and she is especially bitter about her mother's coldness and her refusal to recognize Mary as Stephen's partner. Because Stephen loves Mary and cannot stand seeing her exposed to such cruelty, Stephen distances herself from her lover. At the end of the story, Stephen Gordon assumes the role of a martyr, nudges Mary into the arms of a male friend and, now alone, prays to God to look after the inverts.

Hall's novel was an immediate hit with British readers, earning her accolades and positive reviews. The mood changed, however, when *Sunday Express* editor James Douglas wrote a five-column harangue against *The Well of Loneliness*. In the editorial, Douglas proclaimed that, due to its theme, the book was "moral poison" and that Hall's talent as a writer made her book even more dangerous, since "the adroitness and cleverness of the book intensifies its moral danger . . . we must banish their propaganda from our bookshops and libraries."[19] Douglas warned that the "flamboyant notoriety" of the "decadent apostles of the most hideous and most loathsome vices" were leading to a "pestilence" that wrecked young lives and defiled young souls.[20] In case his opposition to Hall and her novel was not yet clear, Douglas insisted, "I would rather give a healthy boy or a healthy girl a phial of prussic acid than this novel. Poison kills the body, but moral poison kills the soul."[21] The government followed suit, the book was challenged, and Hall was dragged into court to defend her work. Ultimately, her British publisher, Jonathan Cape, voluntarily withdrew the novel and the British government proclaimed it obscene. As a result, the *Well of Loneliness* would not be legally sold in England until 1949, even as it was published freely in the United States.[22]

One crucial element in the attack and censorship of Hall and her work, as suggested by Douglas's use of the word "flamboyant," is the subtle suggestion that displays of lesbianism—which really amounted to displays of female masculinity—were themselves dangerous. In both the British and American trials of the *Well of Loneliness*, the prosecution employed what Nancy J. Knauer has called "the contagion model" by arguing that Hall's novel would somehow recruit young innocents into lesbianism.[23] Since the novel contains no graphic descriptions of sexual relationships whatsoever, it follows that Douglas and other critics feared that Stephen Gordon's model of masculinity would prove most attractive to such potential converts. Following this homophobic logic, then, the public presentation of female masculinity was a critical aspect of lesbian "contagion," for without such flamboyant displays, how else would lesbians spread their propaganda?

Prior to the English obscenity trial, Blanche Knopf, the wife of American publisher Alfred Knopf, entered into talks with Radclyffe Hall and proposed that Knopf publish *The Well of Loneliness* in the United States. Once the British courts banned the novel, however, the publisher withdrew his offer, fearing that the U.S. courts would also conclude that it was obscene and, perhaps more importantly, that Knopf publishing produced pornography. "We didn't see anything heroic about publishing it here after what had happened in England," Knopf wrote.[24] One could argue that, in a very real sense, female masculinity scared off the American publisher.

## "UNCONSCIOUS HOMOS": THE PUBLICITY CAMPAIGN COMMENCES

Following the British trial and Knopf's decision not to publish *Well*, Donald Friede and Pascal Covici, seeing an incredible opportunity, obtained the American rights to Hall's novel and slated publication for the Christmas season of 1928.[25] Friede and Covici were part of what Edward de Grazia calls "the new breed" of publishing; much like Ernst's law firm, Covici-Friede approached controversial clients that the traditional, conservative Protestant firms ignored.[26] Perhaps more significantly, the two Jewish men "were the very personification of that young and 'alien' publishing generation so obnoxious to John Sumner."[27] As the head of New York's Society for the Suppression of Vice, Sumner had replaced the late Anthony Comstock in 1915. Sumner's contemporaries thought Sumner more reasonable and respectable than Comstock, but like his predecessor, Sumner aggressively enforced the obscenity statute.[28] Sumner wrote Covici-Friede in late 1928 to warn the publishers that they were under surveillance. "We have been advised," wrote Sumner, "that you contemplate publishing a book entitled 'Well of Loneliness' and in fact have noticed it for issue, December 10th."[29] Sumner urged Covici-Friede to reconsider because of the outcome of the trial in England and given that English law and its interpretation was "about the same" as that in America.[30]

In December 1928, in anticipation of a legal challenge, Ernst sent out copies of *The Well of Loneliness* to doctors, literary critics, newspaper columnists, and other notable members of the community with a view to getting positive comments to use for the inevitable trial. He also made use of his growing bond with newspaper columnists. He knew how to make his story salient. For instance, in a letter to Walter Lippmann, the famous political columnist for the *New York World* and a leading intellectual of his times, Ernst framed his information as if it were privileged. "Confidentially," Ernst wrote, "I am writing at this time that Sumner has referred the book to the District Attorney and that it is now being considered."[31] In return for this tidbit, Ernst hoped that he could get hold of the *World*'s book reviewer: "To me it is a stirring piece of writing in integrity. I would appreciate it greatly if, whoever of the *World* reads it, would get in touch with me so that I can get an additional opinion." In this pre-trial letter to Lippmann, Ernst also revealed part of his legal strategy. "It seems quite absurd to attack this book," Ernst wrote, "which would repel, rather than invite, readers to lead lives like the heroine."[32] On that same day, he sent a similar letter to Arthur Hays Sulzburger of the *New York Times*.[33] From these letters, it seemed that Ernst's plan was, first, to declare the artistic value of the novel; and second, to argue that the book actually turned off women who might otherwise be attracted to lesbianism.

Although he may have hoped for stirring words in defense of the literary merits of the novel, some initial responses were not wholly enthusiastic. "After very hard work, I finally finished 'The Well of Loneliness,'" wrote the noted psychoanalyst A. A. Brill. "I say hard work, because, had I known that the novel would be so long I surely would have refused to read it, and had I been aware that it would turn out to be so dry, I would have declined."[34] In *Well* Brill saw no harm to the "average man," found nothing in the book that "the perverts" could gain from it, but did conclude that "the great number of unconscious homos might even be harmed by it." Rather than elaborating on this potential harm, however, Brill returned to his exasperation over the quality of the book. "The idea that it is a great artistic production," he complained, "is sheer nonsense. . . . I had to force myself to continue reading the book, after I passed the first third of it."[35] Similarly, the writer and critic Carl Van Doren, then editor-in-chief of the Literary Guild of America, found the novel to be the opposite of stimulating. "I have read THE WELL OF LONELINESS and I am sorry not to like it so well as you do," Van Doren wrote to Ernst. "The copy which I am returning to you looks as if it has been slept with. Well, it has."[36]

Ernst's efforts to obtain community support for the novel weren't for naught. Before any action had even been taken against the novel in the United States, Ernst secured the promise of Dr. F. I. Wertham, from the Henry Phipps Psychiatric Clinic at Johns Hopkins Hospital, to appear as an expert in defense of the book at trial. Ernst made sure the press knew it, and tried to massage public sentiment about the book long before Sumner seized it. Accordingly, he fed information about the case to his friends in the media. "I thought you would be interested," Ernst wrote Lippmann, "in having in mind the fact that I just received word from one of the leading psychiatrists at Johns Hopkins University, who stated that he would be glad to appear as an expert to defend the book. . . . He will testify that the book will have no corrupting influence on normal adolescents or adults. That it might have a bad effect on perverts or abnormal people is, of course, entirely immaterial under the law."[37]

While Ernst was gathering resources for the fight ahead, Covici-Friede impatiently waited for censors to act. Despite the increasing media interest in the novel, authorities did not immediately seize the book, as Ernst and Covici-Friede had hoped. Friede finally contacted Sumner himself and personally sold him a copy of *Well* on December 15. At the same time, the *New York Telegram* publicized the availability of the novel. Ernst underlined and annotated the *Telegram*'s article in preparation for the seizure of the novel. Perhaps anticipating the appeal of the novel to those who did not consider themselves part of the status quo, Ernst underlined Hall's comment that, "I always write about misfits. I understand them better, perhaps." The *Telegram* made the novel seem more spectacular by focusing on Radclyffe Hall's masculinity: "She is Byronese in her appearance and her friends call her 'John,'" the reporter gushed. "Her jewels, large emeralds sunk in rings of platinum, are the only softening note in her mannish profile."[38]

Despite Sumner's warnings and such advanced publicity, Covici-Friede had to work to get the book seized. Finally, on January 11, 1929, police confiscated the books. By that time, the publishers had sold some 20,000 copies of the novel.[39] Three days later, the *Telegram*'s editorial mocked John Sumner. Thanks to Sumner, the editorial pointed out, "the book has been given columns of free first page press publicity. . . . If Sumner were not so entirely lacking in humor he would be suspected as an advertising agent skilled in increasing circulation of such books."[40] One writer, who identified himself as an "author of more than one dozen books," agreed with the *Telegram*'s sentiment and sent Ernst a letter to egg him on. "This person Sumner," he wrote to Ernst, "is certainly a fanatic, and he is equally certainly wild for publicity. Give him some."[41]

Ernst was gleefully aware of his well-deserved reputation as a publicity hound, and he revealed as much in his 1940 attack on censors, titled *The Censor Marches On,* which he co-wrote with his associate Alexander Lindey. In a section of the book dedicated to demonstrating how censors unwittingly increase sales of challenged texts, Ernst and Lindey describe the *Well of Loneliness* case in the context of publicity. At the beginning of the *Well* court proceedings, the "defense attorney"—meaning Ernst—asked for a week's adjournment "to enable him to prepare his case." According to Ernst and Lindey, the head of the vice society, John Sumner, complained that the defense attorney would only use that time "to whoop things up in the papers. He's after publicity." But Ernst and Lindey have their hero, whom they never identify, deny that charge: "We don't need any more publicity, Mr. Sumner," he says to the vice-secretary. "You've given us plenty."[42]

This scene is almost cinematic in its execution. This rebuke feels like a setup, a manipulation of the reader to side with the defense; the prosecutor looks foolish and the defense attorney appears witty. While the scene legitimizes Ernst's reputation as a publicity hound, it also justifies his use of publicity, since the defense attorney's response reminds readers that *any* controversial case results in press coverage. Even years later, Ernst would credit Sumner, not himself, in making *Well* "the lesbian Bible."[43] The question, then, might not be who instigated publicity but who would control the resulting image. During the 1920s and 1930s, it was Ernst's great talent, and a fundamental component of his masculine script, to capitalize on the media's constant yearning for controversy and direct and focus the resulting attention in a way that benefited his clients and himself.[44]

Certainly there was plenty of controversy to exploit over homosexuality. In 1964 Ernst and co-author Alan U. Schwartz recalled the *Well of Loneliness* case as a fleeting but shining moment during a dark era in which "all discussions of sexual relations other than those between male and female were illegal in the eyes of the State."[45] Indeed, the homophobic writing seemed to be on the wall. In 1927, New York had passed the Wales Act, which expressly prohibited "sex degeneracy or perversion" themes in the theater—a none-too-subtle reference to gay or lesbian topics.[46] According to Andrea Friedman, who has studied the use of the obscenity law in New York theaters during this era, this act amounted to "an absolute ban on a specified type of sexual speech, defining the discussion or portrayal of homosexuality on stage as inherently obscene."[47] Ernst and Lindey later recalled that the case was significant "because the prosecution sought to inject a new principle into the obscenity law. Up to that time only offensive words and expressions had been held criminal; no theme, as such, had been proscribed. Now an attempt was being made to suppress a book simply because it dealt with a questionable subject."[48] This attempt to suppress *The Well of Loneliness,* Ernst and Lindey suggest, was a slippery slope: if the judge had ruled against the book, in other words, there would have been a chilling effect on all unpopular speech, since "it would have been impossible to discuss a grave social problem in print."[49]

At the time he was preparing for trial, however, Ernst focused less on such pernicious consequences and more on a defense based on precedent and community standards. To this end, he had hoped for glowing reviews of the novel from community leaders. As if choreographed with Sumner's actions, positive reviews of the book now flooded into Ernst's office. Numerous literary icons, including Theodore Dreiser, Sinclair Lewis, Sherwood Anderson, and John Dos Passos, wrote letters in support of Hall's novel, and Ernst duly forwarded copies of such letters to the press.[50] While Ernst would continue to prize reviews from literary critics, who could depict challenged texts as artistic contributions to contemporary culture, he valued scientific commentary above all other. Accordingly, he sought positive evaluations of *Well* from doctors and scientists, which he could later cite as evidence that the novel was not harmful. One such response came, as promised, from Wertham. Ernst had gone to Baltimore to meet with Wertham to discuss the novel and lesbianism, and two days later Wertham sent a lengthy summation of their conference.[51] Although not a literary critic, Wertham did not hesitate to declare that *The Well of Loneliness* a "very well-written novel of considerable artistic merit." In making the case that the novel was not harmful, Wertham emphasized that Stephen was not anti-social but a victim of "obstructed development." "Despite her strong desire to fit harmoniously into the general consensus of her family and her social environment," he wrote Ernst, "she is somehow thwarted in the development of her emotional life." While Wertham claimed that "every description of emotional relationship between people and of their demonstrations of affection can of course arouse libidinous thoughts in almost everybody under certain circumstances," he assured Ernst that Hall's novel could have "no corrupting influence on the mind and morals of readers" and, in fact, "this book contains very much less of erotic suggestion than the average."[52] Other correspondents defended homosexuality itself. In a letter to Covici-Friede, one physician declared that "genuine homosexuality is neither a vice nor a disease. It is an endowment."[53]

In the meantime, as responses to his letters arrived, Ernst was educating himself about homosexuality. At the New York Public Library, he found other examples of lesbian literature and examined the works of sexologists such as Havelock Ellis, Richard von Krafft-Ebing, and Katherine Bement Davis.[54] Ernst also looked at medical and scientific journals, including *Mental Hygiene* and *The Journal of Social Hygiene*, and jotted down facts and statistics about homosexuality, such as *Mental Hygiene*'s 1925 claim that "163 out of 1000 married women indulged in homosexual relations *with* physical expression" (emphasis in the original).[55] Although contemporary medical sources ultimately concluded that homosexuality was an illness, Ernst valued whatever data might put Stephen Gordon and Radclyffe Hall in the most sympathetic light. According to Leslie A. Taylor, who has written about the American trial of *The Well of Loneliness*, "Ernst was more inclined toward a Freudian theory of homosexuality, that is, a theory that homosexuality was caused by an unsuccessful resolution of various developmental crises."[56] As evidence, Taylor cites Ernst's notes from his meeting with Wertham and focuses in particular on the fact that Ernst wrote down Wertham's comment that the novel was really "a story about a woman not fully developed; thwarted in life."[57] Indeed, when the case finally came to trial, Ernst would portray Stephen Gordon as a kind of victim, and in this sense Taylor's focus on a Freudian slant is appropriate. Ernst did not want to put homosexuality on trial; that was a case he could not win in 1929. For this reason, Ernst even tried to avoid the "L" word altogether and warned his associate, Alexander Lindey, "Don't use words like 'Lesbian.'"[58] Taylor points out that most of Ernst's research was left on the sidelines during the trial, and Ernst ultimately decided not to call any sexologists to the stand.[59] Instead, he would focus on the fact that other literature with lesbian themes had been cleared of obscenity charges.

One of Ernst's tactics, as Taylor has demonstrated, was to compare *The Well of Loneliness* with Theophile Gautier's *Mademoiselle de Maupin,* a French novel based on the life of an actual French woman who had sometimes dressed in men's clothes and who had sexual relationships with both men and women. The American courts had found that Gaultier's novel was not obscene. Ernst's decision to compare this novel to *Well* made sense; since the two novels included the similar theme of lesbianism, and the courts had ruled that Gautier's wasn't obscene, shouldn't they also allow Hall's novel to be published? Yet Ernst's defense went beyond that strategy. In the defense brief, he cited two passages from *Mademoiselle de Maupin* that were demonstrably more suggestive than *The Well of Loneliness*. In both passages, duplicated below, Gautier has his female protagonist discuss her less-than-feminine traits:

> Many women are more womanish than I. I have little of the woman, except her breast, a few rounder lines, and more delicate hands; the skirt is on my hip, and not in my disposition. It often happens that the sex of the soul does not at all correspond with that of the body, and this is a contradiction which cannot fail to produce great disorder.
>
> In truth, neither of the two sexes are mine; I have not the imbecile submission, the timidity or the littleness of women; I have not the vices, the disgusting intemperance, or the brutal propensities of men; *I belong to a third distinct sex, which as of yet has no name* . . . . I have the body and soul of a woman, the mind and power of a man, and I have too much or too little of both to be able to pair with either [italics added in the legal brief].[60]

Given that the *Well of Loneliness* did not have explicit descriptions of homosexual activity, it is clear why Ernst selected the above two passages from *Mademoiselle du Maupin.* Gaultier here focuses on masculine and feminine traits; the reader concludes that the narrator, like Stephen Gordon, is a woman who looks and behaves like a man. Since the censors' fear of lesbianism was predicated on the anxiety that lesbians would use female masculinity to recruit innocent girls into their tribe, Ernst uses these passages to demonstrate, first, that similar descriptions of female masculinities had been previously held to be not obscene; and second, that these passages are not attractive (or, as the prosecution would have it, "stimulating"). Furthermore, Gaultier's scenes, which suggest the existence of a woman who does not meet contemporary ideals of femininity, might have resonated with readers like Ernst himself, who seemed to understand from his early experiences as a young man (albeit on a much lesser basis) what it felt like to fail to meet the cultural ideals of gender.

Though Ernst surely realized that he could not win a 1929 censorship case by arguing in favor of lesbianism, his research files suggest that he may have been slightly more liberal in his views than his contemporaries. Among his legal documents for the *Well of Loneliness* case is a September 1928 *Psychology Magazine* article by Kenneth Swezey about Edward Carpenter, the British socialist poet and gay activist. It is probable that Hall or her barrister had sent Swezey's article to Ernst's office in an effort to help the American lawyers better understand homosexuality. While scholars disagree about which writers had the greatest influence on *The Well of Loneliness*, it seems that Carpenter's depiction of homosexuality was most appealing to Ernst.[61] For one thing, Carpenter's texts were much more accessible to laymen, a fact that Ernst, who often decried lawyers' use of jargon and who sought to reach a general audience with his own writings, would certainly appreciate.[62] In addition, as Swezey saw it, Carpenter was clearly improving the lives of others with his work, an achievement for which Ernst himself aimed. Swezey wrote that "thru five or six books and pamphlets, [Carpenter] has helped thousands who had been groping in darkness to walk straight again in the sunlight and lead full and beautiful lives."[63] The trope of sunlight itself may have appealed to Ernst since censors and prosecutors, such as the attorney in the *Sex Side of Life* case, associated darkness with sexual perversity. Moreover, Ernst may have personally identified with the act of emerging from an existence of insecurity to one of fulfillment and happiness. Ernst's own "darkness," especially his insecure childhood and the deaths of his mother and his first wife from tuberculosis, had given way to a sunny disposition (he now called himself a "glandular optimist"[64]) and a greater self-assurance.[65] Indeed, when one views the novel "from a Carpenteresque perspective," as Laura Doan does, one may frame *The Well of Loneliness* in optimistic terms.[66] The story ends "on a hopeful note as the narrative," which includes "a vivid depiction of Stephen's transition from 'outcast' to 'hero,' calls on all 'intermediate types' to fulfill their biological destiny in the evolutionary development of a new society."[67] Like Jacob Beilhart, who indirectly influenced Mary Ware Dennett, Carpenter suggested the potential superiority of such "intermediates"—that is, those who fell in between male and female gender roles, and thus were blessed with the dual perspective of both men and women—and while there is no evidence that Ernst himself adopted this view, given his background as an outsider, he may have also found this depiction appealing. Also like Beilhart and like Ernst himself as a young man, Carpenter was attracted to the potentiality of utopian, communal living. As a college student, before becoming a solid anti-communist, Ernst had admired the utopian philosophy of Robert Owen. Ernst was intrigued enough by the article to correspond with Swezey and even solicit his opinion on Ernst's draft of the brief. Swezey complimented Ernst on the brief and emphasized that Ellis and other experts in sexuality had argued that, "except in the rarest cases, sexual inversion cannot be acquired by suggestion."[68]

Even though he may have found Carpenter's ideas to be compelling, Ernst clearly saw that such an optimistic outlook on homosexuality would not fly in court. The prosecution in the case argued that the novel would intrigue innocent young girls and draw them into the world of lesbianism. Rather than rebut this claim, predicated as it was on contemporary anxieties about homosexuality, Ernst instead stressed Wertham's point about Stephen Gordon's stunted emotional and psychological growth, and argued that such a pitiful example as Stephen would actually repel would-be lesbians.

This approach failed to sway the judge to throw out the case. On February 21, 1929, Magistrate Hyman Bushel denied the defense's move to dismiss. Bushel supported the prosecution's claim that the book was obscene. "I am convinced," Bushel wrote in an opinion, "that *The Well of Loneliness* tends to debauch public morals."[69] Bushel's real problem with the book was what Taylor calls "the novel's plea for tolerance"; Bushel wrote that "the characters in this book who indulge in these vices are described in attractive terms" and that "the novel is calculated to corrupt and deprave minds open to its immoral influences."[70] Bushel employed the same imagery of predator and prey as the prosecutor had earlier that year in the *Sex Side of Life* case. "The book can have no moral value," declared Bushel, "since it seeks to justify the right of a pervert to prey upon normal members of a community, and to uphold such relationship as noble and lofty. Although it pleads for tolerance on the part of society of those possessed of and inflicted with perverted traits and tendencies, it does not argue for repression or moderation of insidious impulses."[71] Had the author imposed a punishment on her protagonist, Bushel may have dismissed the case, but since Hall did not do so, Bushel believed her novel could appeal to a certain segment of the population. Lawmakers, Bushel asserted, "[have] imposed upon the courts the duty of protecting the weaker members of society from corrupt, depraving and lecherous influence although exerted through the guise and medium of literature, drama or art."[72]

Ernst was undaunted by the ruling. Though, as he wrote to Hall's British attorney, H. F. Rubenstein, his defense team "got a first-class trimming today before the Magistrate," Ernst reassured Rubenstein that "this decision of the Magistrate is merely equivalent to a holding for trial. It acts in many ways like an indictment."[73] The next step was the Court of Special Sessions. In that trial, Ernst directly refuted Bushel's claim of guise.

> [T]here have been no elements of stealth or sly furtiveness, no suspicious or disreputable circumstances, no indicia such as customarily betray the spreaders of corrupt material. A sincere, serious, beautiful book has been fearlessly published and disseminated. The question is whether this Court will now renounce the enlightened policy expressed in our recent cases, brand it as obscene, and open the door henceforth to the wanton and undiscerning prosecution of legitimate literature.[74]

The defense then depicted the novel as a plea for tolerance based on a "profounder understanding of human nature, human shortcomings and human sufferings," thereby suggesting that Hall's call for sympathy for lesbians could be universalized and applied to all of mankind.[75] Continuing along this vein, Ernst argued that "if Stephen were a man and not a woman, the book would be merely a rather over-sentimental bit of Victorian romanticism."[76] This assertion, too, served to universalize Stephen's experience; the unstated assumption is that one could simply substitute a man's story for this woman's story. Admittedly, Ernst's strategy here was not an act of subversion or subterfuge; his goal was to win the case, and not at all to forward progressive ideas about the fluidity of gender. Still, it is interesting that he chose this route, since, to agree with Ernst's thought experiment, a judge would have to be capable of imagining the interchangeability of a lesbian woman and a heterosexual man.

Perhaps the judges who heard the appeal were better able to imagine this exchange of identities. As Ernst's brief claimed, "Times are moving so swiftly," and with them, the attitudes of the community were evolving:

> One-piece bathing suits for girls, if worn on the beaches ten years ago, would have occasioned immediate imprisonment for the wearers. The Federal Public Health Service and the State Department of Health are now yearly distributing to adolescents and adults millions of pamphlets discussing masturbation, venereal diseases and sexual intercourse with a frankness and a directness of detail that would have shocked us as recently as twenty years ago.[77]

Though Ernst was overly optimistic in his estimation of society's attitudes toward the "frankness" of gay and lesbian relationships, he won the case. On April 19, the Court ruled that *The Well of Loneliness* was not obscene.

Halberstam has commented that Radclyffe Hall, like her protagonist Stephen Gordon, rejected her "femaleness" and instead "fashioned it into a masculinity she could live with."[78] Though Ernst's situation was of course quite different, he too needed to fashion his maleness, which did not approach the tough or athletic physical models he'd held as ideals, into a masculine identity he could live with and live off. Cases like this one encouraged the exhibitionist in him to promote both his client and himself, getting his name in the press while allowing him to speak not only as an expert in the law, but as an expert on sexuality, thereby offering an attractive alternative to traditional conceptions of masculinity. For Ernst, the *Well of Loneliness* case contributed to his growing aura as the man to know. His decision to argue that readers could simply substitute a male character for a female character was an ingenious legal strategy, and it illustrates that Ernst was getting comfortable with the idea that gender roles were malleable. If there was enough flexibility in the understanding of gender to allow men and women to be interchanged in Radclyffe Hall's writings and in her life, surely there was enough flexibility to allow a man like Ernst to be accepted.

Though he may have contemplated the differences between male and female masculinity during his research for the *Well* trial, Ernst did not dare venture into the graphic realities of lesbian love in the courtroom. In 1948 he would maintain, on the evidence of Alfred Kinsey's research into male sexuality, the then-startling assertion that homosexual love was extremely common. He upheld that claim only in print, however, and not in the courtroom. Since Hall's novel, and not lesbianism, was on trial, Ernst sidestepped discussions about homosexuality. When the subject was *heterosexual* relations, Ernst had no such qualms, as demonstrated in *Sideri*, where Ernst used the courtroom to showcase his knowledge of female sexuality. The trial of *Well* exposed readers to the idea that masculinity was not simply limited to rugged men, and perhaps expanded the accepted gender space roles to modern men like Ernst. Yet Ernst's seemingly progressive attitudes toward homosexuality would not survive the Cold War, when, like many of his contemporary anti-communists, he would suggest that homosexuality was akin to duplicity.

## NOTES

1. Nancy J. Knauer, "Homosexuality as Contagion: From the Well of Loneliness to the Boy Scouts," *Hofstra Law Review* 29, no. 2 (2000): 440.
2. Ibid.
3. Warren Hoffman, "The Rise (and Fall) of David Levinsky: Performing Jewish American Heterosexuality," *Modern Fiction Studies*, Volume 51 number 2, Summer 2005, 397. Hoffman is referencing George Chauncey here; see also George Chauncey, *Gay New York* (New York: Basic Books, 1994), 65–66.
4. Claudia Breger, "Feminine Masculinities: Scientific and Literary Representations of 'Female Inversion' at the Turn of the Twentieth Century," *Journal of the History of Sexuality* 14, no. 1–2 (2005). Since the publication of this essay, the interview with Vicki Crowley, and the publication of "An Introduction to Female Masculinity," in which Halberstam was identified as "Judith," Halberstam now identifies as "Jack" and uses he/his pronouns.
5. Robert A. Nye, "Locating Masculinity: Some Recent Work on Men," *Signs* 3 (Spring 2005): 1937(26).
6. Vicki Crowley, "Within the New Moment—An Interview with Judith Halberstam," *Discourse* Vol. 25, no. 4 (2004).
7. Judith Halberstam, "An Introduction to Female Masculinity: Masculinity without Men," in *The Masculinity Studies Reader*, ed. Rachel Adams and David Savran (Malden: Blackwell Publishers Inc, 2002), 355.
8. Laura Doan, "Passing Fashions: Reading Female Masculinities in the 1920s," *Feminist Studies* 24, no. 3 (1998).
9. Ibid.
10. Ibid.

11. George Chauncey, *Gay New York: Gender, Urban Culture, and the Making of the Gay Male World 1890–1940* (New York: Basic Books, 1994), 2–5.

12. Laura L. Behling, *The Masculine Woman in America, 1890–1935* (Urbana: University of Illinois Press, 2001), 1–2, 16.

13. Chauncey, *Gay New York,* 283.

14. Heike Bauer, "Richard von Krafft-Ebing's Psychopathia Sexualis as Sexual Sourcebook for Radclyffe Hall's The Well of Loneliness," *Critical Survey* 15, no. 3 (2003): 23.

15. George Chauncey Jr., "From Sexual Inversion to Homosexuality: Medicine and the Changing Conceptualization of Female Deviance," in *History of Women in the United States, v. 10: Sexuality and Sexual Behavio*r, ed. Nancy F. Cott, *History of Women in the United States* (New Providence: K.G. Saur, 1993).

16. Michael Baker, *Our Three Selves: The Life of Radclyffe Hall* (New York: Morrow, 1985), 7.

17. Ibid., 12.

18. Ibid., 13.

19. Cited in Diana Souhami, *The Trials of Radclyffe Hall* (London: Weidenfeld & Nicolson, 1998), 178, 177.

20. Ibid., 177.

21. Cited in Laura Doan, "Sappho's Apotheosis? Radclyffe Hall's Queer Kinship With the Watchdogs of the Lord," *Sexuality & Culture 8*, no. 2 (Spring 2004): 91.

22. Knauer, "Homosexuality as Contagion," 404.

23. Ibid., 403.

24. Cited in Paul Boyer, *Purity in Print: Book Censorship in America From the Gilded Age to the Computer Age*, second ed. (Madison: The University of Wisconsin Press, 2002), 131.

25. For more on the British trial, see Souhami, *The Trials of Radclyffe Hall.*

26. Edward de Grazia, *Girls Lean Back Everywhere: The Law of Obscenity and the Assault on Genius* (New York: Vintage Books, 1993), 129.

27. Boyer, *Purity in Print*, 132.

28. Ibid., 30.

29. Ibid.

30. John Sumner to Covici-Friede, January 1, 1928, Box 383, MLE.

31. Morris L. Ernst to Walter Lippmann, December 7, 1928, Box 383, MLE.

32. Ibid.

33. Morris L. Ernst to Arthur Hays Sulzburger, December 7, 1928, Box 383, MLE.

34. A.A. Brill to DeWitt Stetten Jr., December 7, 1928, Box 383, MLE.

35. Ibid.

36. Carl Van Doren to Morris Ernst, December 6, 1928, Box 383, MLE.

37. Morris L. Ernst to Walter Lippmann, December 26, 1928, Box 383, MLE.

38. Mary Rennels, " 'Well of Loneliness' Now Republished Here," *New York Telegram*, December 15, 1928.

39. Taylor, 270.

40. Editorial, *New York Telegram,* January 14, 1929, Box 383, MLE.

41. Letter to Morris Ernst (correspondent's name unintelligible), February 2, 1929, Box 383, MLE.

42. Morris L. Ernst and Alexander Lindey, *The Censor Marches On: Recent Milestones in the Administration of the Obscenity Law in the United States* (New York: Doubleday, Doran & Company, Inc. 1940), 232.

43. Morris L. Ernst, "America's Three Periods of Sex" (undated draft of article), Box 877.2, MLE.

44. Ernst made the most of controversies and his prior successes. As early as 1929, he instructed his lecture agent to ask for $100 to $200 per engagement, and his files show that during this period, he was constantly in demand to lecture and to debate on the radio. Box 11, MLE.

45. Morris L. Ernst and Alan U. Schwartz, *Censorship: The Search for the Obscene* (New York: Macmillan, 1964) 72.

46. Andrea Friedman, *Prurient Interests: Gender, Democracy, and Obscenity in New York City, 1909–1945* (New York: Columbia University Press, 2000), 113.

47. Ibid.

48. Ernst and Lindey, *The Censor Marches On, 7.*

49. Ibid.

50. "Authors Protest Ban on Sex Novel," *New York World*, January 20, 1929.

51. Morris L. Ernst to Alexander Lindey, "Facts in regard to conference with Dr. Wertham in Baltimore-January 17, 1929" (Internal Memorandum), Box 383, MLE.

52. F.I. Wertham to Morris Ernst, January 19, 1929, Box 383, MLE.

53. Dr. Joseph Collins to Covici-Friede, January 16, 1929, Box 383, MLE.

54. Heike Bauer argues that Krafft-Ebing was an important inspiration for Hall's protagonist, Stephen Gordon. See Bauer, "Krafft-Ebing."

55. Morris Ernst, handwritten trial notes (n.d.), Box 383, MLE. The emphasis is Ernst's.

56. Leslie A. Taylor, "'I Made Up My Mind to Get It': The American Trial of *The Well of Loneliness,* New York City, 1928–1929," *Journal of the History of Sexuality* 10, no. 2 (April 2001): 264.

57. Ernst to Lindey, "Facts in regard to conference with Dr. Wertham."

58. Ibid.

59. Taylor, "'I Made Up My Mind to Get It'," 264–265.

60. Defendant's memorandum, 16–17; *People v. Friede,* Court of Special Sessions of the City of New York, Box 383, MLE. Ernst's legal brief cites page 276 of the Modern Library edition.

61. Laura Doan argues that by examining both Stephen Gordon and the secondary characters in the novel, one can see the influence of Carpenter's "powerful models." Laura Doan, "'The Outcast of One Age Is the Hero of Another': Radclyffe Hall, Edward Carpenter and the Intermediate Sex," in *Palatable Poison: Critical Perspectives on* The Well of Loneliness, ed. Laura Doan and Jay Prosser, *Gender & Culture* (New York: Columbia University Press, 2001), 166. Heike Bauer instead sees Krafft-Ebing's depiction of the masculine woman as informing Hall's construction of the text. See Bauer, "Krafft-Ebing."

62. Doan, "'Outcast'," 165. Doan suggests that Carpenter was resented by medical and scientific professionals because his writings were accessible, affordable, and popular.

63. Kenneth M. Swezey, "An Interview with Edward Carpenter–Apostle of Love and Democracy," *Psychology Magazine*, September 28, 1928: 66.

64. Interestingly, after Ernst died, at his memorial tribute a close friend wondered aloud whether Ernst meant for the phrase "glandular optimist" to have a "raunchy" meaning. Undated transcript of Morris Ernst memorial, SB.

65. There is another compelling (but unsubstantiated) motive for Ernst's liberal views about lesbianism. According to one Ernst relative, family lore has it that Ernst's wife, Margaret, may have had intimate relationships with other women, including Eleanor Roosevelt. Anonymous, personal interview by author, June 11, 2006.

66. Doan, "'Outcast'," 166.

67. Ibid.

68. Kenneth Swezey to Morris Ernst, February 22, 1929, Box 383, MLE. There is no record of Ernst's letters to Swezey.

69. Opinion, Magistrate's Court, City of New York, *People of the State of New York v. Donald Friede and Covici-Friede*, 133 Misc 611, 233 NYS 565 (1929), Box 383, MLE. Also cited in Taylor, page 281 (n151).

70. Taylor 281; Opinion, *People v. Friede*, 133 Misc 611, 233 NYS 565 (1929), Box 383, MLE.

71. Opinion, *People v. Friede.*

72. Ibid.

73. Morris L. Ernst to H.F. Rubenstein, February 21, 1929, Box 383, MLE.

74. Defendant's memorandum, 2; *People v. Friede*, Court of Special Sessions of the City of New York, Box 383, MLE.

75. Defendant's memorandum, 3; *People v. Friede.*

76. Defendant's memorandum, 10; *People v. Friede.*

77. Defendant's memorandum, 34; *People v. Friede.*

78. Judith Halberstam, "'A Writer of Misfits': 'John' Radclyffe Hall and the Discourse of Inversion," in *Palatable Poison*, 159.

# *Chapter 5*

# *Ulysses*, Ernst, and Literary Translation

In 1933, during the landmark *Ulysses* trial, Judge John Woolsey asked Morris Ernst whether he had actually read the epic novel. Ernst confessed that he had first tried and failed in the early 1920s, but added that, more recently and in preparation for the trial, he felt obligated to read the entire work. Ernst then seemingly went into a non sequitur: he told the judge that he was in Nantucket during this second attempt to read *Ulysses*; that he had been invited to speak at the Unitarian Church in Nantucket on banking issues; and that he gave a talk to about 400 people at that church.[1] Woolsey, understandably a bit perplexed, asked how any of these details related to his question. In Ernst's telling, he explained to the judge:

> "While talking about banks . . . I realized that I was thinking not only about the banks and the banking laws but also about the clock at the back of the hall, the gray-haired woman sitting in the front row, the tall shutters at the sides—and innumerable other physical objects. . . . Just as now"—I paused for a moment—"while I have been arguing about *Ulysses*, I must admit that at the same time I was thinking of my arguments I was also thinking of the gold ring around your tie, the picture of George Washington behind you, and the fact that your robe is slipping of your shoulders." . . . [W]hen the courtroom laughter had subsided, [Woolsey] said, "Now for the first time I understand the significance of this book. I have listened to you as intently as I know how . . . and still, I must confess that while listening to you I've also been thinking at the same time of the Hepplewhite furniture behind you." At that moment, I told Joyce, I knew the case was won. The double stream of consciousness had been acted out in the courtroom argument.[2]

In this way, Ernst powerfully helped translate a new literary technique, first for Woolsey, and later, whenever he retold the story. The modernist stream-of-consciousness technique Joyce popularized thus became crucial to Ernst's argument about the power and artistry of the novel, and Ernst's embrace of modernism seems to have been more than simply utilitarian. Ernst was in favor of certain principles he associated with modernism, insofar as they challenged the values he associated with Victorianism: granting women agency over their bodies; extending jury duty to women; open relationships; and so forth. But the very newness of modernism may have also suggested a world of possibility and opportunity, some of which had been partially or fully closed to Ernst, Jews and immigrants, and the Black Pullman Porters he'd defended earlier in his career. At the same, this proximity to literature would have, in turn, brought him closer to the ideal of the Pitching Professor, the Williams teacher he idealized.

The famed *Ulysses* case has been written about extensively—indeed, it is the case which rocketed Ernst to fame beyond the New York nightclub scene and helped him become a very wealthy man. This chapter will suggest how Ernst's background and experience informed his approach to the case, and it will illustrate the connections between Ernst's personality and life and Joyce's fiction. While it would be a stretch to liken Ernst to Joyce's Jewish protagonist, Leopold Bloom, as the Jewish son of an East European immigrant growing up in the 1900s and seeking opportunities in the 1910s, Ernst did have a sense of what it was like being an outsider. That understanding may have, in part, inspired his defense. Ernst not only could relate on a personal level with fictional outsiders; he also had learned to interpret otherness for a general audience. He'd done so in past trials, humanizing and evoking sympathy for birth control activists, for low-income women seeking birth control, for a lesbian protagonist, and for others. In other words, Ernst was uniquely positioned to make sense of *Ulysses* and to persuade a judge, and the public, of its artistic value.

After arguing several landmark cases, Ernst was on a seemingly unstoppable winning streak. Buoyed by his success, Viking Press, the publisher of *To The Pure*, brought out a new advertisement in 1929 for the book, playing off Ernst's understanding that controversy was good for sales. Under the title, "A Question for the Censors," the ad copy reminded censors of Ernst's prior success: "You have declared the Mary Ware Dennett pamphlet illegal, you have raided a Birth Control Clinic and seized its records . . . you have tried to suppress 'The Well of Loneliness' but failed." After this mocking list of failures, the advertisement asked its provocative question: "Why have you neglected TO THE PURE . . . Certainly it's far more dangerous to you than any of the books mentioned above. 'To the Pure' strikes at your very existence and shows up your absurdities and inconsistencies in a frank and daring manner." The ad then cited "paeans of praise" for the book, listing a dozen cultural and intellectual luminaries, including D. H. Lawrence, Aldous

Huxley, Bertrand Russell, Edna Ferber, and John Dewey. "According to your standards the public should be shielded from this book. According to liberal standards, every intelligent person should read it."[3]

The ad copy was pure Ernst: making a logical assertion (i.e., censors are never consistent in which texts they choose to attack) and then exaggerating that claim for effect (*To The Pure* must therefore be *more* dangerous than the works you censors want to ban!). It would be understandable if some readers bought the book hoping for titillation; it seems likely that Ernst and Viking, in reissuing the book and framing it this way, were hoping to attract just such customers. The advertisement speaks to Ernst's delight in provoking certain authorities and setting himself up as both the rebel—essentially daring censors to challenge his books, and as the "intelligent person" in touch with "liberal standards" and modern-day, current culture. And in this sense, it foreshadows Ernst's landmark defense of *Ulysses* and his use of exhibitionism to advance solid, worthy progressive concerns while simultaneously promoting his own reputation.

As early as 1933, at least one contemporary columnist had attributed Ernst's 1927 loss in his defense of the novel, *What Happens*—Ernst's only real censorship defeat, ever—as the impetus for his decision to write *To The Pure*. That columnist, Ernst's friend Lewis Gannett, wrote in the context of the *Ulysses* case that the "defeat aroused a crusading zeal in Morris Ernst" and led to Ernst immersing himself into the history of censorship and publishing his findings.[4] Gannett was insightful: through an artful use of wit, talent, networking, and self-promotion, Ernst was able to draw lessons from that loss—what he'd later call his "inadequacy"—and would thereafter dominate every courtroom he entered.[5] Much of this domination came not from grandstanding but from a clear understanding of the complexities of the legal system as well as the quirks of human nature. After 15 years of practicing law, Ernst had perfected a legal strategy for handling censors—one that invited his own participation/self-involvement to become the true face of the case. Arthur Joel Katz, Ernst's junior associate, recalled in a 2005 interview that Ernst was an "idea man" and that he left his partners and staff to take care of the nitty-gritty legal components. Katz recalled, for example, that Ernst would frequently ask his colleagues, "What do you lawyers think?" as if he were professionally separated from them.[6] Ernst relied on his talent for self-promotion to get his ideas out to the media and sway public opinion. In a 1932 article he published in *The Nation*, he referenced a number of the important cases he had won since 1928, including "The Sex Side of Life," *The Well of Loneliness,* and two books by Marie Stopes (*Married Love*, and *Contraception).* His conclusion: sex had triumphed in America. If Ernst could declare, as the title of that article stated, that "Sex Wins in America," it followed that Ernst was its champion.[7]

With *Ulysses,* Ernst was able to draw from his experiences in those cases and prepare well in advance of the actual trial. Joyce's novel had actually been challenged in the United States since 1919, after *The Little Review* began publishing *Ulysses* in installments, and the U.S. Post Office had seized and then destroyed copies on three different occasions.[8] When the magazine published the "Nausicaa" installment in 1920, its publishers, Margaret Anderson and Jane Heap, were convicted of publishing indecent matter.[9] The judges in the subsequent 1921 trial focused only on the "Nausicaa" text in isolation. In that episode, a young woman, Gerty McDowell, is aware that the protagonist, Leopold Bloom is eyeing her. As fireworks explode in the sky, Gerty leans back, exposing herself, leading to the older man's fully clothed ejaculation:

> she leaned back ever so far to see the fireworks . . . And she saw a long Roman candle going up over the trees, up, up, and, in the tense hush, they were all breathless with excitement as it went higher and higher and she had to lean back more and more to look up after it, high, high, almost out of sight, and her face was suffused with a divine, an entrancing blush from straining back and he could see her other things too, nainsook knickers, the fabric that caresses the skin . . . and she let him and she saw that he saw and then it went so high it went out of sight a moment and she was trembling in every limb from being bent so far back that he had a full view high up above her knee where no-one ever not even on the swing or wading and she wasn't ashamed and he wasn't either to look in that immodest way like that because he couldn't resist the sight of the wondrous revealment. . . . And then a rocket sprang and bang shot blind blank and O! then the Roman candle burst and it was like a sigh of O! and everyone cried O! O! in raptures and it gushed out of it a stream of rain gold hair threads and they shed and ah! they were all greeny dewy stars falling with golden, O so lovely, O, soft, sweet, soft![10]

A New York City lawyer who claimed that his daughter had been exposed to the Nausicaa installment complained to the Manhattan district attorney, who in turn sent that letter to John Sumner, the head of the New York Society for the Suppression of Vice. Sumner bought a copy, deemed it actionable, and set in motion a legal complaint.[11] Anderson and Heap were each fined $50, though the message of that penalty was chilling, as publishers and booksellers could be sentenced to a $1,000 fine and a year in prison.[12] The court had found *Ulysses* obscene, and publishing, purchasing, or importing it was thus inviting punishment.[13]

A little over a decade later, however, Ernst would bank on the strategy that, by submitting the entire book to the court, rather than isolated parts, he could make the case that Joyce's novel was literary, and thus not obscene. That strategy had already proven successful in his defense of *The Well of Loneliness.*

"Rather than declare the absence of obscenity," Molly Schwartzburg notes, Ernst instead argued "that the larger context of the work transcended specific instances of so-called obscenity."[14] This approach, however, challenged the dominant precedent in obscenity cases. Stephen Gillers explains that during this era, "the law . . . remained largely and thoughtlessly hostile to anything in print (or other medium) if 'the matter' had a 'tendency . . . to deprave and corrupt those whose minds are open to such immoral influences, and into whose hands a publication of this sort may fall.'"[15] This test for obscenity, known as the "Hicklin rule," stems from an 1868 British legal decision, which had largely been absorbed into the American legal system, and which, in Ernst and Seagle's view, gave "expression to the hypersensitiveness of Victorianism." [16] With that decision, they argue, "sanity was swept away, and Victorian literary prudery and the law made to coincide. Or rather law was swept aside to make room for hysteria."[17] *Hicklin*, Gillers writes, "had substantial influence on American obscenity law in the last third of the nineteenth and first third of the twentieth centuries and thereafter."[18] Gillers points out that the Nausicaa episode, which had cost Anderson and Heap in 1921, was "tame by comparison" to the "Penelope" episode, which presented "the erotic thoughts of a half-asleep Molly Bloom and contains a fair number of four-letter words."[19] If Nausicaa was enough to get *Ulysses* banned in 1921, the more graphic Penelope, isolated under the Hicklin rule, might have resulted in the same outcome, even under a more liberal judge. The key would thus be to get the court to view *Ulysses* as a complete entity and not as a specific scene or "dirty" word.

One year before being contracted to fight for *Ulysses,* Greenbaum, Wolff, and Ernst had already done some legwork on the case. Alexander Lindey, Ernst's associate and sometimes co-author, informed Ernst in an August 1931 memorandum that he had "just had quite a lengthy interview" with the sister of Sylvia Beach, the famed owner of the Shakespeare and Company bookshop in Paris. Lindey reported that Beach claimed to have the exclusive world rights to the novel and that she was "tremendously interested" in legalizing the novel "if a responsible American publisher could be found."[20] Bennett Cerf, Random House's publisher, recalled that one night in 1932, Ernst mused aloud that the U.S. ban on *Ulysses* was a "disgrace" and that "he'd like to wage a fight to legalize it."[21] Ernst and Cerf, whom Michael Chabon affectionately call "erudite, polished, and well-connected hustlers," saw an opportunity, and perhaps surmising that Joyce, who had watched helplessly from Paris as the notorious Samuel Roth and other underground publishers pirated his masterpiece, was willing to attempt publication in the United States with a legitimate publishing house.[22] Cerf subsequently had lunch with Ernst to offer a deal: Cerf would try to sign James Joyce to publish an American edition of *Ulysses* if Ernst would fight for Random House in the subsequent censorship battle. "Ernst said, 'Great, great,'" Cerf wrote, adding: "He loves publicity as much as I do!"[23] Cerf told Ernst that he could not afford to pay Ernst's "fancy prices," but offered to pay all court expenses and, should they win the case, Ernst would get a substantial payout.[24] Specifically, Random House would immediately pay a $500 retainer, and then, if the book was cleared for publication in the United States, Ernst would receive a 5 percent royalty on the hardcover copies, as well as on any net sum the publisher made from sales of the novel to book clubs, and a 2 percent royalty on all reprint editions sold for life.[25]

For Ernst, the stakes were low and the potential rewards almost limitless. He and his firm commonly took on "cause" cases pro bono, and even if he were to lose the case, he would still win, as his name would be even more strongly associated with civil liberties, progressive causes, and the fight to empower Americans to read whatever texts they chose. With Cerf's offer, Gillers writes, Ernst "must have realized that in winning the right to publish *Ulysses* he could achieve three goals simultaneously: support civil liberties, become more famous, and earn a lot of money."[26] In an earlier exchange with Ben Huebsch, the editor and vice president of Viking Press, Ernst—apparently attempting to entice his own publisher, Viking, into purchasing *Ulysses*—pointed out that if the novel were challenged in the courts, "[p]ossibly the controversy attending the proceedings will aid the sale."[27] Ernst had already witnessed this phenomenon firsthand; he and Lindey suggested that *The Well of Loneliness* might only have sold a few thousand copies had it not been challenged; instead, they wrote, over 250,000 copies were sold. "There was even a de luxe [*sic*] Victory edition in two volumes, boxed," they wrote, "at twenty-five dollars a set."[28] Cerf and Random House were also risking relatively little. Cerf and co-founder Donald Klopfer had founded the firm only five years earlier in 1927 and were both just in their early thirties. Whatever the outcome, it was sure to publicize the name of their young business.

Ernst strategy hinged on getting the text seized by customs agents under the Tariff Act, based on a clause in the Act which Ernst himself had helped draft.[29] "I had counseled with Senator Bronson Cutting to make the action . . . a case of the United States against a book rather than against the importer or addressee," Ernst later recalled.[30] The Act subsequently included a clause permitting the Secretary of the Treasury to "admit the so-called classics or books of recognized and established literary or scientific merit into the United States, when imported for noncommercial purposes."[31] Most importantly, under the Tariff Act, the court challenge would be against the book itself and not against Random House or the publishers. "Neither Joyce nor Random House's co-founder Bennett Cerf was the target of the litigation," Robert Spoo explains in his own analysis of the case. This would not be a criminal prosecution; rather, the defendant would be "a single copy of

*Ulysses,* seized at the Port of New York."[32] The potential gains of a test case were clear: it was an opportunity to get Random House's name in the press as well as on the minds of both the book-buying public and up-and-coming authors who might want the courageous Random House to publish their works. Americans had been smuggling in pirated copies of the novel since 1921, when Beach had first published it in its entirety in Paris.[33] The demand was clearly there. And so both the publishers and Ernst stood to boost their reputations and their bank accounts, with minimal risk to either party.

Cerf went to Paris and secured an agreement with Joyce, whereby Random House would pay the author $1,000 when he signed the book contract, $1,500 on publication day, 15 percent royalties on the trade edition up to 25,000 copies and 20 percent beyond that figure.[34] Meanwhile, Ernst and his associates encouraged Cerf to gather materials that would be helpful in a potential trial. Ernst had long recognized the increasing importance of the public opinion in censorship cases; it was the same flavor of testimonials that he had attempted to introduce in the first "Sex Side of Life" trial. These letters of support served to praise the text being challenged (in the case of *Ulysses*, establishing the novel's literary value) but also suggested that cultural values and social mores had dramatically changed; the assumption was that the law hadn't caught up with those changes. And because Ernst often solicited such testimony from leading cultural critics, authors, and scholars, the letters would provide the publisher the additional benefit of creating a buzz among cultural critics and the "influencers" of the day. In the case of *Ulysses*, Lindey recommended that Random House secure support from esteemed members of the community, such as critics, writers, medical professionals, librarians, and so on.[35] Robert Spoo points to the "Brandeis brief" as the likely model for Ernst's strategy of gathering letters from notable tastemakers. And it is true that Ernst idolized Louis Brandeis, treasuring his exchanges with the Supreme Court judge and keeping on his office desk an ugly goose-necked lamp that Brandeis once owned.[36] Spoo sees Ernst's "marshalling of educated opinion" as reflective of "[the] politics of top-down, administered progressivism."[37] This analysis rings true, especially given Ernst's own political associations at the time. He was a friend and close adviser of Franklin D. Roosevelt, whom he counseled when FDR was governor of New York, and again when FDR became president, and Ernst strenuously supported the New Deal. But Ernst also wanted to impress the court with sheer data. Lindey had already asked Cerf to contact at least 100 colleges to find out if they taught Joyce's works and whether *Ulysses* itself had been assigned.[38] Ernst then directed Lindey to have Random House send 500 letters to "eminent people" to solicit their opinions on the novel, and then to contact 100 libraries to learn, first, if they carried *Ulysses;* and, if so, whether the book was available to the general public.[39]

Since *Ulysses* could not be legally published in the United States, the plan was to ship a very clearly marked-up copy of the novel from Paris to New York across the ocean, and to alert the New York customs agency in advance so that the book did not slip through. First, Ernst had Cerf ask Paul Léon, Joyce's friend, champion, sometimes secretary, and Paris agent, to paste positive French reviews into the physical copy of the novel they were sending, knowing that the court would have to consider any such materials when evaluating the book itself.[40] Once the book was shipped, Léon alerted Ernst's firm that the book was on its way, and Lindey wrote to the New York Customs House to let the Collector of Customs know that the ship was expected to arrive at the Port of New York on May 2.[41]

Just two days after the U.S. Customs Service officially confirmed that their office had detained the book, the *Brooklyn Daily Eagle* printed a piece in its Sunday "Of the Making of Books . . ." section. Under the subhead "Crusade," the paper reported that Cerf had hired Ernst "to wage war on the ban against James Joyce's *Ulysses*" and were "enlisting editors, critics, authors, clergymen, members of the Bar, sociologists, psychologists, teachers, and librarians."[42] This would have been Ernst's handiwork. The book was not even in the district attorney's hands—the government wouldn't formally act for months—but Ernst was already getting the case out in front of the public. And he must have known that his own name had a certain cachet; otherwise, why include his name and not his firm's (or Lindey's, as Lindey was doing a great deal of the legwork)? The *Daily Eagle* also previewed part of Ernst's strategy by amplifying the idea that *Ulysses* was hugely important: "It has done more to alter modern rhetoric than any other single thing." At the same time, the article continued, the novel was so complicated that most people wouldn't read it anyway. "All this department can say," the *Daily Eagle* declared, "is that anyone with enough patience to wade through 'Ulysses' just to find the naughty words will do it anyway, and might as well be allowed to do it legally . . . . 'Ulysses' is in a fair way of becoming a classic and, like most classics, a book nobody ever reads."[43] Two days later, *Variety* included a brief notice in its "Literati" section, identifying Ernst as "a leader in frequent agitation against book censorship" who was "said to be the best versed person on the matter in this country."[44] While there is apparently not documentation of Ernst's fingerprints on this story, three months later, in an office memorandum, Ernst directed Lindey to call Ernst's contact at the *World-Telegram* should there be any action taken against the book.[45] Ernst was friendly with many newspaper writers, and clearly knew the importance of cultivating his relationships with the press.

The U.S. Customs Service, at Lindey's request, sent the book to the U.S. Attorney, as the Customs Court did not have jurisdiction in this case.[46] And then some 17 months passed before the book finally appeared in court. Some of that delay was due to the density and length of the text itself. When the book reached the U.S. District Attorney's office, the Assistant D.A., Sam Coleman, struggled to read the novel. When Coleman finally finished it at end of July—just before going on vacation—he told Lindey that while he thought it was a "literary masterpiece," it was still obscene under federal law.[47] Coleman gave the book to George Medalie, the U.S. Attorney for the Southern District of New York, saying that Medalie would make the final decision on whether to prosecute.[48] Medalie told Ernst a few weeks later that he thought *Ulysses* was "a very important book."[49] He was troubled by the novel, but at the same time, wanted to see Ernst's quickly growing file of comments on the novel—from libraries and universities especially.[50] After months of review, in December 1932, Medalie began the proceedings. Random House and the government agreed to waive a jury trial. "Both parties knew how unmanageable and potentially unfair a jury trial could be," Spoo writes. "Had a jury been empaneled, the U.S. Attorneys, following *Hicklin*, would have read out selected passages of alleged indecency—words, sentences, large samplings of Molly Bloom's monologue. Then, Ernst and Lindey, contending that the proper test was the entire book, would have read another seven-hundred-odd pages into the record."[51] But Joyce's challenging text also helped dictate which judge would ultimately determine whether it could be legally permitted into the country. The rotating schedule of judges included a number before whom Ernst did not wish to appear. They included, for instance, a judge whom Lindey identified as "a strait-laced Catholic" and whom colleagues in the U.S. Attorney's office thought to be "about the worst man on the bench for us."[52] Another judge was recovering from pneumonia and had a very sick child.[53] Still another judge simply refused to read the book.[54]

In any event, Ernst's top choice was the Honorable John J. Woolsey, and Ernst worked to ensure that it would be Woolsey before whom he would argue his case. Delays meant that Random House would not be able to latch onto the public interest that the media had drummed up, and they could result in unscrupulous publishers selling unauthorized copies of the novel. But Ernst knew that delaying until Woolsey appeared on the rotating schedule would give the novel its best chance of being deemed not obscene. In 1931, Ernst had successfully argued two cases before Woolsey on behalf of the British author and birth control advocate Marie Stopes, freeing both *Married Love* and *Contraception.* Woolsey concluded that *Married Love,* a sex manual, would do for adults what "The Sex Side of Life" did for adolescents, and added: "To one who had read Havelock Ellis, as I have, the subject-matter of Dr. Stope's book is not wholly new, but it emphasizes the woman's side of sex questions. It makes also some apparently justified criticisms of the inopportune exercise by the man in the marriage relation of what are often referred to as his conjugal or marital rights, and it pleads with seriousness, and not without some eloquence, for a better understanding by husbands of the physical and emotional side of the sex life of their wives."[55] Woolsey's reference to the sexologist Havelock Ellis, a modernist, along with the suggestion that female sexuality existed (as opposed to the Victorian assumption about passionless vessels), were right in line with Ernst's.[56] And Ernst genuinely admired and respected the judge. Woolsey himself cut a figure not unlike Ernst's college mentor, the Pitching Professor: Erudite, worldly, and progressive. Ernst later recalled Woolsey as "one of those rare jurists who was a rounded, physically as well as spiritually, human being who, unlike many members of the bench and bar, read widely in fields remote from his professional interests."[57] Like Brandeis, another Ernst hero, Woolsey was incredibly well-read and prided himself on being cultured and modern. Thus Ernst waited; as Chabon states, "the delay was largely—but not entirely—due to skillful manipulation on the part of Ernst, as he maneuvered to ensure that the case landed on the docket of Judge John Woolsey, known to be an obscenity skeptic with literary pretentions."[58]

In the meantime, Ernst had had a second copy of *Ulysses* sent to his own office.[59] After it arrived, Lindey, again writing on behalf of the firm, wrote to the Customs House asking whether the fact that the novel had made it through Customs, and that their agents had not seized it, meant that *Ulysses* could now be legally admitted into the U.S.[60] The Assistant Collector denied that there had been any change in policy or regulation. In response, the law firm would be sending their copy of the novel *back* to the Customs office, with the expectation that this time, it would be seized. Upon getting official notice of the seizure, Lindey continued, the firm would apply to the Secretary of the Treasury for admission of *Ulysses* under the "classics" clause of Section 305 that Ernst had helped write.[61] Ernst's drafting of Section 305, was, in Chabon's words, a "handy bit of foresight, part of Ernst's long game on behalf of artistic freedom."[62] So was Lindey's wording of their petition; even as Ernst and Lindey were petitioning to admit the book under the clause of the Tariff Act that exempted classic books from forfeiture, he was not conceding that the book itself was obscene in the first place. Lindey's petition included Ernstian inflated claims, including:

- No other book in the history of letters "has been accorded such remarkable eulogies";
- Some say that *Ulysses* is "the most important book that has ever been written";
- No other work "has had such a profound and far-reaching influence"; and
- Joyce was the only author in all of English literature "worthy of a place beside Shakespeare."[63]

In support of this definitional argument that *Ulysses* was a "classic," the petition's exhibits included some of the same documentation Ernst and Random House had been collecting: raves by librarians; critical reviews; books and magazine articles on Joyce and/or on *Ulysses.* There were also letters of praise for the novel from "representative men," some 50 authors, columnists, editors, publishers, psychologists, and others. Among them were the philosopher, John Dewey; the publisher, Alfred A. Knopf; the critic Edmund Wilson; the editors and writers H. L. Mencken and Malcolm Cowley, and the writers Theodore Dreiser, Louis Untermeyer, F. Scott Fitzgerald, and John Dos Passos.[64] Ernst's firm thus presented in support of their petition what amounted to a collection of rave reviews scribed by some of the best loved, most talented, and most influential writers of the early twentieth century. Beyond the understanding that *Ulysses* was a challenging read—indeed, Ernst would later count on that fact in his own deliberations—it would have been exciting to many contemporaries to see such an impressive portfolio of praise. Seven years earlier, in *To The Pure,* Ernst had pointed out that "[j]ury antagonism is easily aroused by boredom . . . and the first duty of the defense is entertainment."[65] Ernst had figured out that it wasn't just juries who could get frustrated and take it out on his clients and knew to appeal to his audience, whether that was a judge or a federal official. In this instance, the treasury secretary might have found these exaggerations, together with the pages and pages of commendations from literary and journalistic celebrities, to be much more entertaining than Joyce's novel; Hardiman, for one, suspects the secretary never read the book.[66]

And in fact, just two weeks later, the petition was approved. Writing on the secretary's behalf, the acting commissioner of customs confirmed that this decision was based on the facts that *Ulysses* was "of sufficient literary merit" and that Lindey's copy was not being imported for commercial purposes.[67] Soon after the collector of customs acknowledged the secretary's decision, the *New York Times* reported that a copy of *Ulysses* had been admitted into the United States as a "classic," which the newspaper described as "a preliminary victory" for Cerf. The *Times* added that bootlegged copies had sold for as much as $50 some years earlier. This decision would raise the stakes for the prosecution. Now that the government's own official had allowed the book in under the "classics" clause, it was no longer possible to argue that *Ulysses* had no societal value. The court might still rule it to be obscene, but it would not be able to dismiss the book as worthless smut.

After months of postponements, some of which were products of Ernst's deliberations and design, the case was set to be heard by Woolsey. When the case finally was assigned to Woolsey's court, however, there was a further delay, as Woolsey still needed to read the dense, long, and unconventional novel. Wire services, keeping the story alive in the press, had fun with Woolsey's response. Under the headline "He'll Find Out," the *Seattle Daily Times* reported: "Customs inspectors told Judge John. M. Woolsey that 'Ulysses,' by James Joyce, was obscene. Randon [*sic*] House, publishers, said it wasn't. 'I'm going on my vacation,' said the judge. 'I'll find out.' He took the volume with him."[68] Woolsey needed a few months to fully digest the novel. Ernst helpfully sent Woolsey some supplemental reading, including *The Key to the Ulysses of James Joyce*, that scholars had written to make sense of *Ulysses,* but it seems clear that Woolsey took no shortcuts: he had the full, unadulterated reading experience.[69]

On November 25, 1933, the trial finally took place. Ernst's brief made six major points:

I. that obscenity had to be judged by contemporary mores;
II. that the courts had spoken: with past rulings on obscenity as the measure, *Ulysses* simply did not meet those criteria;
III. that the government itself had declared the novel to be a classic and therefore cannot be obscene;
IV. that features of *Ulysses* (and connected with it) negated any implication that it was obscene;
V. that it had been generally accepted by the community; and
VI. that the work had to be judged as a whole.

To buttress his arguments about the Ernst again included the written support of respected and respectable community members. This strategy had proven successful in past obscenity cases. Gillers explains why: "By providing judges (and therefore the public) with the favorable views of those whose positions gave them special standing to identify literary value, it became respectable and safe for judges to permit publication."[70] Doing so also gave Ernst to argue that the only "true" test of obscenity was provided by public opinion.[71] Finally, the fact that Ernst and his firm had amassed such substantial support surely reflected well on them, as well.

In addition to successfully demonstrating that there was considerable public approval for *Ulysses*, Ernst worked to demystify some of the words that censors would find especially troubling. He analyzed the words with his wife, Margaret, who was an etymologist, and who would publish a best-selling book about word origins at the end of the decade titled *In a Word.* Ernst explained to the judge that one possible derivation of the word *fuck* was "to plant," suggesting that it was an Anglo-Saxon agricultural term, and gave the example, "The farmer fucked the seed into the ground."[72] When Ernst pointed out that *fuck* had "more honesty" than other phrases authors used to denote sexual congress, Woolsey asked for an example of such a phrase. "Oh—'they slept together,'" Ernst said. Woolsey, according to Ernst, then smiled, saying, "That isn't even usually the truth." "At that moment," Ernst later recalled, "I knew that the case was half won."[73]

The case was likely already won after Ernst's brilliant lesson in stream of consciousness, where he "taught" Woolsey how stream of consciousness worked by referencing his Nantucket church speech on banking and Woolsey's gold tie ring and robe, thereby demonstrating just how groundbreaking and artistically modern Joyce's text was. There is no transcript of the 1933 case against *Ulysses*; most of what is known comes from newspaper accounts and from those involved in the defense. Gillers, however, put together his own valuable "transcript" (quotation marks in the original) culled from press reports.[74] That account has Samuel Coleman, arguing for the government, focusing on the effect that *Ulysses* might have on readers, as the contemporary concern, oft voiced by censors, was that obscene works could corrupt innocent children and the so-called feeble-minded. "I do not think that obscenity necessarily should be limited to exciting sexual feeling," Coleman argued. "I should say a thing is obscene by the ordinary language used and by what it does to the average reader. It need not necessarily be what the author intended." Coleman stated that he liked *Ulysses*, and acknowledged its literary value, but argued that "obscenity is in the very texture of Ulysses and could not be eradicated without destroying essential values of the book."[75] Ernst countered with the point that *Ulysses* was already considered a classic and that the court should follow the will of the public. Referencing *To The Pure*, Ernst noted that he'd studied how language affects ordinary readers but could not find "one single instance where it could be proved that the reading of any book led to the commission of a crime of passion." He also reiterated the importance of audience. *Ulysses* was adult literature and "[t]he law does not require that adult literature be reduced to mush for infants."[76] When Woolsey, after pronouncing that he was against all censorship, and after noting that censorship often just resulted in bootlegging, with profits going to those acting illegally, mentioned that "[t]he book left me bothered, stirred, and troubled," Ernst replied, "I think that is exactly the effect of *Ulysses*. You have not used the adjectives 'shocked' or 'revolted.' You have used the adjectives 'bothered,' 'troubled.'"[77] Judge Woolsey was persuaded.

After Woolsey ruled in favor of *Ulysses* on December 6, 1933, Ernst released an appropriately triumphant statement to the press. He contrasted the culture of the past, when those who circulated the novel could be imprisoned, with the new reality that the text could freely enter the United States. "The victory of *Ulysses,*" he concluded, "is a fitting climax to the salutary forward march of our courts."[78] The newspapers, drawing from this statement, lavishly praised Ernst. In the *New York Herald Tribune*'s "Books and Things" column, Gannett hailed Ernst as a "Crusader Against Censorship." After describing Ernst's early (and, as it would turn out, only) loss in court, Gannett described how that loss motivated Ernst to make himself an expert on the subject. "He dug into the history of censorship," Gannett wrote, "published his books exposing its absurdities and contradictions, and emerge as the logical and fearless defender of frank honest literature." Gannett then recounted some of Ernst's greatest hits: *The Well of Loneliness,* "The Sex Side of Life," *Married Love, Contraception,* and several others were cleared, "all with Mr. Ernst defending them . . . . An amazing series of amazing victories for Morris Ernst."[79] Gannett's serialized column was published in newspapers across the country, as were many of the articles saluting Ernst. The Associated Press, in an article again printed throughout the nation, presented Ernst at his rhetorically clever best: "Ernst . . . saluted the opinion as one that banishes 'squeamishness and circumlocution' from literature. 'The first week of December, 1933, will go down in history for two repeals,' Ernest [*sic*] said, 'that of prohibition and that of squeamishness in literature. We may now imbibe freely of the contents of bottles and forthright books.'"[80]

Cerf wanted to include a version of Ernst's statement as the foreword to the soon-to-be-printed Random House editions of *Ulysses*, and Ernst complied. In typical Ernstian fashion, he hailed the victory as the "New Deal in the law of letters."[81] Woolsey's opinion, he proclaimed, would become "a major event in the history of the struggle for free expression." Interestingly, Ernst posed the challenges by censors as an effort to "emasculate literature." The phrase sets a nice contrast between modern, twentieth-century values, which Ernst himself was defending; and Victorian mores, with which Ernst and others had associated censors, and which harbored very different assumptions about gender roles. What was more manly than defending the right for one to express oneself? He continued, in aggressive terms: "The *Ulysses* case . . . is a body-blow for the censors." Ernst suggested that Woolsey's precedent "would rescue the mental pabulum from the censors" who wanted to "convert it into treacle," and would instead "help to make it the strong, provocative fare it ought to be." Ernst, who could be extremely witty—he had to know during the trial that Woolsey would find the sentence "The farmer fucked the seed into the ground" funny—then called the victory "a fitting climax to the salutary forward march of our censors."[82] After a manly battle with the censors, who wanted only to emasculate and weaken the public, Ernst had given them a body blow, helping to make the public discourse appropriately strong and provocative resulting, then, in climax.

With the election of Franklin D. Roosevelt in 1933, Medalie was replaced as U.S. Attorney by Martin Conboy, who had been an officer of the New York Society for the Suppression of Vice.[83] Medalie had not sought to appeal Woolsey's decision. Yet Conboy, perhaps emboldened by John Sumner, who dismissed Woolsey's ruling as "a literary review trying to explain away the appearance of admitted obscenity and filth" pursued the case and secured permission for the appeal.[84] Conboy and Ernst appeared before judges Martin T. Manton, Learned Hand, and Learned's cousin, Augustus Hand. To demonstrate that the novel was obscene, Conboy read some twenty-five passages from *Ulysses* aloud.[85] Learned Hand interrupted him to ask Conboy if he was going to read the entire work; Conboy reportedly said he'd provide a "generous sampling."[86] Conboy continued but seemed genuinely flummoxed by the text; as the *New York World-Telegram* reported, he blushed, stammered, and rocked nervously on his heels.[87] As he read, he was unable, according to the *Herald Tribune*, to "keep a shocked note from creening into this voice."[88] Ernst's response was not complicated. He again praised both Joyce and *Ulysses;* again pointed to the sheer number of critics who acknowledged the genius of the author and the art of the novel; and argued that the work needed to be considered as a whole, and not through excerpts.[89] With Manton dissenting, the Hand cousins affirmed Woolsey's ruling and the continued legality of *Ulysses* in the United States.[90]

* * *

How was Ernst able to make sense of *Ulysses* and, to a lesser extent, modernism for Woolsey, for the media, and ultimately for the general public? It may have helped that Ernst could relate to characters who were outsiders. Ernst was working within a network that frequently excluded Jews; white shoe legal firms wouldn't hire Jewish lawyers when Ernst got started in 1915. It was no accident that Ernst's firm, founded by three Jewish men, gravitated toward newer, more daring clients like Random House. Cerf and his business partner, Donald Klopfer, as well as many of those who published less traditional, edgier literature were themselves Jewish. This support and mutual respect between avant-garde publishers and Ernst wasn't simply out of fellowship, although that certainly was a point of connection. Instead, the attraction was more likely forged partly out of their shared experience of being part of a sometimes-ostracized ethnic group. And while it's hard to imagine that Ernst felt much affinity with Joyce, given their very different backgrounds, he might have identified with the *idea* of Joyce, and especially the idea of Joyce one could draw from the text and characters of *Ulysses.* The novel shows Joyce's mastery of so many different lines of inquiry; he knew of mythology, languages, cultures. Ernst may have fancied himself a kind of renaissance man, too: he learned what he could about many different types of law and not just freedom of speech; he wrote not just about censorship, but government, sexual matters, marriage and divorce, communism, futurism, and much more. In addition, Ernst reveled in humor, enjoying witticisms with clients and friends like Groucho Marx, Edna Ferber, E. B. White, and James Thurber. Joyce, according to the scholar Hugh Kenner, lamented the fact that readers didn't appreciate the humor he'd injected into *Ulysses.*[91] Ernst, along with the overwhelming majority of readers, past and present, may not have completely understood all of the many arcane references in the book; recall that he could not finish it when he first tried to read it in 1922. But he would have appreciated its witticisms.

And though his memoirs, unlike his brilliant *To The Pure* and other co-written books, cry out for editing, they do sometimes read like stream of consciousness. Here for instance, is Ernst, writing in his published 1961 untitled diary:

> Why do toe nails and hair grow more quickly and longer on males when very young and when very old? I do observe. Whether precise or not it's a good observation. And what a mass of unobserved I live in. I remember the first time I observed the details of a horse's eye. Not all horse eyes are identical—Titian's father licked him if, after a stroll, he could not describe, always as unique, each and every horse he looked at. All are different, or each is different from all.[92]

And here is Joyce's protagonist, Bloom, jumping from topic to topic:

> Dedalus' daughter there still outside Dillon's auctionrooms. Must be selling off some old furniture. Knew her eyes at once from the father. Lobbing about waiting for him. Home always breaks up when the mother goes. Fifteen children he had. Birth every year almost. That's in their theology or the priest won't give the poor woman the confession, the absolution. Increase and multiply. Did you ever hear such an idea? Eat you out of house and home. No families themselves to feed. Living on the fat of the land. Their butteries and larders. I'd like to see them do the black fast Yom Kippur. Crossbuns. One meal and a collation for fear he'd collapse on the altar. A housekeeper of one of those fellows if you could pick it out of her. Never pick it out of her.[93]

In other words, there was enough within the novel, as distant as it was from Ernst's own education and experience, to enable him to connect with it and make sense of it for a contemporary audience.

While the fruits of Ernst's success were sweet and abundant, not everyone was as impressed with Ernst or his triumphant declarations. One critic zeroed in on what Ernst called his exhibitionism. Francis Talbot, S.J., the literary editor of *America* magazine, described Ernst as "the legal protagonist of literary sexuality," and though some might wear such a description as a badge of honor, Talbot did not intend it to be a compliment. Talbot called out

Ernst's claims about "Ulysses the Dirty," dismissing Ernst's attempt to liken the *Ulysses* trial to a "New Deal in the law of letters," Ernst's comparison of Woolsey to Oliver Wendell Holmes, "and other Oriental exaggerations."[94] The *Herald Tribune*, too, reported that Ernst had overstated the case.[95]

Still, most contemporaries rightly recognized Ernst's brilliance in this case, as do a good number of twenty-first-century critics. In a recent essay written in support of the ACLU, Michael Chabon hails Ernst's work: "I now see that my gratitude has been somewhat misplaced. With no disrespect to Judge Woolsey . . . we owe the *Ulysses* decision less to the judge in the case than to counsel for the defense. What an incredible feat of lawyering!"[96] Marisa Anne Pagnattaro has argued that Ernst and Lindey "strategically used *Ulysses* to change the obscenity standard of all literature. The intellectual significance of *Ulysses* was the catalyst for what has essentially become an exception to obscenity laws for literary works."[97] *Ulysses,* to again reference Spoo, brought Ernst international celebrity, wide respect both in and beyond the legal fields, and a lot of money. Ernst's deal with Cerf paid off handsomely, as he'd always anticipated. In Ernst's 1976 obituary, the *New York Times* stated that sales of *Ulysses* alone had brought Ernst "several hundred thousand dollars."[98] He deservedly entered the history books as a brilliant attorney. And though he would successfully defend every future client he represented in the courtroom, he increasingly sought new excitements, new challenges, and new heroes. The choice to move beyond censorship to other subjects of interest, and his continued quest to prove his worth to others, would ultimately undermine his brilliant defense of *Ulysses.*

## NOTES

1. Morris L. Ernst, *The Best Is Yet . . .* (New York: Harper & Brothers, 1945), 116.
2. Morris L. Ernst, *A Love Affair With the Law: A Legal Sampler* (New York: The MacMillan Company, 1968), 99–100.
3. Display Advertisement for *To The Pure*, published in the *New York Times*, June 2, 1929, BR14, ProQuest Historical Newspapers, June 5, 2021.
4. Lewis Gannett, "Books and Things," *New York Herald Tribune*, December 9, 1933, 11. Gannett was the newspaper's book critic.
5. Paul Boyer, *Purity in Print: Book Censorship in America From the Gilded Age to the Computer Age*, second ed. (Madison: The University of Wisconsin Press, 2002), 147.
6. Arthur Joel Katz, email message to the author, July 20, 2005.
7. Morris L. Ernst, "Sex Wins in America," *Nation*, August 10, 1932.
8. Richard Ellman, "Introduction," in Michael Moscato and Leslie LeBlanc, eds., *The United States of America v. One Book Entitled Ulysses By James Joyce:*

*Documents and Commentary: a 50-Year Retrospective* (Frederick, MD: University Publications of America, Inc.), xvii.

9. Marisa Anne Pagnattaro, "Carving a Literary Exception: The Obscenity Standard and *Ulysses,*" *Twentieth-Century Literature* (Summer 2001): 47.2, 217–218.

10. James Joyce, *Ulysses* (New York: Vintage Books, 1961), 366–367. Part of this passage was also cited in Gillers; see note 11, below.

11. Stephen Gillers, "A Tendency to Deprave and Corrupt: The Transformation of American Obscenity Law from Hicklin to Ulysses II," *Washington University Law Review* 85, no. 2 (2007): 251–252.

12. Ibid.

13. Michael Chabon, "United States v. One Book Called 'Ulysses' (1933)," in Michael Chabon and Ayelet Waldmen, eds., *Fight of the Century: Writers Reflect on 100 Years of Landmark ACLU Cases* (New York: Avid Reader Press, 2020), 14.

14. Molly Schwartzburg, "The Writer and His Lawyer: James Joyce, Morris Ernst, and *Ulysses,*" 176–177; in Susan F. Rossen, Ed., *Other People's Books: Association Copies and the Stories They Tell* (Chicago: Caxton Club, 2011), 175–179.

15. Gillers, "A Tendency to Deprave and Corrupt," 218.

16.Morris L. Ernst and William Seagle, *To The Pure . . . A Study of Obscenity and the Censor* (New York: Viking Press, 1928) 107.

17. Ibid., 129–130.

18. Ibid., 218–219.

19. Ibid., 252–253.

20. Office Memorandum, Alexander Lindey to Morris L. Ernst, August 6, 1931. Reprinted in Moscato and LeBlanc, *The United States of America,* 77. Lindey also recognized what an amazing opportunity this could be, writing in that same memo that "this would be the grandest obscenity case in the history of law and literature, and I am ready to do anything in the world to get it started."

21. Assuming this exchange actually occurred, it would have taken place in 1931, as Cerf wrote to Ernst in December 1931 hoping to meet "to talk further about *Ulysses.*" Bennett A. Cert to Morris Ernst, reprinted in Moscato and LeBlanc, *The United States of America,* 101.

22. Chabon, "United States v. One Book," 15

23. Bennett Cerf, *At Random: The Reminiscences of Bennett Cerf* (New York: Random House, 1977), 90. Gillers disputes this narrative, citing Cerf's earlier 1934 recollection of events. In that account, Cerf had written that he "was 'summoned' to the brokerage firm of Sartorius & Smith in December 1931 by Robert Kastor, a wealthy businessman, but more importantly, the brother of Helen Joyce, wife of Georgio Joyce, James Joyce's son. . . . Cerf recalled that Kastor had asked him if Random House was interested in publishing Ulysses. After consulting Klopfer, Cerf said yes. By April, Random House had a contract giving it the United States rights to the book." Gillers, "A Tendency," 275.

24. Ibid.

25. Adrian Hardiman, "The Trial of Ulysses, 1933," *Dublin University Law Journal* 33 (2011): 50. Ellman states that Ernst would receive a 5 percent royalty on

the first 10,000 copies sold, and then "2 percent for life" on subsequent reprintings; see Ellman, "Introduction," xx.

26. Gillers, "A Tendency to Deprave and Corrupt," 275–276.

27. Morris L. Ernst to B. W. Huebsch, October 21, 1931. Reprinted in Moscato and LeBlanc, *The United States of America,* 98. Huebsch was also an ACLU member. Ultimately, Huebsch decided not to pursue a contract with Joyce, wrote to Cerf to let him know "we cannot object if you should now determine to try to get the book," and even promised Cerf that he would share all related correspondence he'd had on *Ulysses.* See letter from Huebsch to Cerf, December 17, 1931; and letter from Cerf to Ernst, December 22, 1931; reprinted in Moscato and LeBlanc, 100–101.

28. Morris L. Ernst and Alexander Lindey, *The Censor Marches On: Recent Milestones in the Administration of the Obscenity Law in the United States* (New York: Doubleday, Doran & Company, Inc., 1940) 233. This would be the equivalent to about $380 in 2021–and in the early 1930s, during the Great Depression. The very existence of the "Victory" edition speaks to the perceived demand following Ernst's successful defense of the book. https://www.saving.org/inflation/inflation.php?amount=25&year=1930.

29. Chabon highlights the fact that Ernst was making use of the very legislation that he had helped craft: "Ernst was more than a little familiar with the classics exemption, having written it himself, with the connivance of a powerful friend in Washington, who saw that it was inserted into the Tariff Act." See Chabon, "United States v. One Book," 19.

30. Morris L. Ernst, "Recollections on the 'Ulysses' Trial and Censorship," *James Joyce Quarterly*, Fall 1965, Vol. 3, No. 1, 6, https://www.jstor.org/stable/25486535.

31. Hardiman, "Trial of Ulysses," 54.

32. Robert Spoo, "Judging Woolsey Judging Obscenity: Elitism, Aestheticism, and the Reasonable Libido in the "Ulysses" Customs Case," *James Joyce Quarterly*, Summer 2013, Vol. 50, No. 4, 1027.

33. Edward de Grazia, *Girls Lean Back Everywhere: The Law of Obscenity and the Assault on Genius* (New York: Vintage Books, 1993), 25–27.

34. Memorandum of Agreement between James Joyce Esq and Messrs. Random House Incorporated, 1932, in Moscato and LeBlanc, *The United States of America,* 105.

35. Alexander Lindey to Bennet Cerf, March 29, 1932, in Moscato and LeBlanc, *The United States of America*, 112.

36. Ernst, *The Best is Yet,* 13.

37. Spoo, "Judging Woolsey," 1034. Spoo defines the Brandeis brief as "a collection of economic or sociological data presented to the court, not as proof of the facts in controversy . . . but as an aid to judicial policymaking," 1030.

38. Lindey to Cerf, March 29, 1932, in Moscato and LeBlanc, *The United States of America*, 112.

39. Office Memorandum from Morris L. Ernst to Alexander Lindey, April 30, 1932, in Moscato and LeBlanc, *The United States of America*, 120.

40. Paul Léon's wife described her husband's role somewhat differently: "He very much resented being called—as he often was—Joyce's 'paid secretary,' Joyce's 'lawyer,' Joyce's 'manager,' or Joyce's 'agent.' But since it was often impossible to

reach Joyce without going through Paul, those titles were bound to arise in people's minds." Cited in Michael Patrick Gillespie, "'Prying into the Family Life of a Great Man': A Survey of the Joyce/Léon Papers at the National Library of Ireland," *James Joyce Quarterly*, Vol. 30, No. 2 (Winter, 1993), 277–294, https://www.jstor.org/stable/25485376.

41. Letter from Alexander Lindey to Collector of Customs, May 2, 1932, in Moscato and LeBlanc, *The United States of America*, 133–134.

42. Jerome Coignard, "Of the Making of Books . . ." *Brooklyn Daily Eagle*, May 15, 1932, E 7, https://newscomwc.newspapers.com/image/59987380.

43. Ibid.

44. "To Free 'Ulysses,'" *Variety*, May 17, 1932, 47.

45. Office Memorandum, Mr. Ernst to Mr. Lindey, September 27, 1932, in Moscato and LeBlanc, *The United States of America*, 160.

46. Alexander Lindey to H. C. Stewart, May 17, 1932, in Moscato and LeBlanc, *The United States of America*, 146.

47. According to Lindey, Coleman told him that he planned to pass *Ulysses* around in the office: "He said that that was the only way his staff could get a literary education." Office Memorandum from Alexander Lindey to Morris Ernst, July 30, 1932, in Moscato and LeBlanc, *The United States of America*, 157.

48. Ibid.

49. Office Memorandum from Morris L. Ernst to Alexander Lindey, August 12, 1932, in Moscato and LeBlanc, *The United States of America*, 158.

50. Office Memorandum from Morris L. Ernst to Alexander Lindey, September 27, 1932, in Moscato and LeBlanc, *The United States of America*, 160.

51. Spoo, "Judging Woolsey," 1036.

52. Office Memorandum from Morris L. Ernst to Alexander Lindey, June 6, 1933, in Moscato and LeBlanc, *The United States of America*, 102.

53. Office Memorandum from Alexander Lindey to Morris L. Ernst, July 25, 1933, in Moscato and LeBlanc, *The United States of America*, 212.

54. Bennett Cerf to Paul Léon, July 26, 1933, in Moscato and LeBlanc, *The United States of America*, 213.

55. Decision in *United States v. One Obscene Book Entitled "Married Love,"* April 6, 1931; 48 F.2d 821 (S.D.N.Y. 1931); Decision in *United States v. One Book, Entitled "Contraception,"* July 16, 1931; 51 F.2d 525 (S.D.N.Y. 1931).

56. Ellis was a popular and internationally respected sexologist. He was also a eugenicist. See Kate Atkinson, "Ellis, Havelock (1859–1939)," in *Routledge Encyclopedia of Modernism*, Taylor and Francis, doi:10.4324/9781135000356-REM1610–1.

57. Ernst, "Recollections," 3.

58. Chabon, "United States v. One Book," 20.

59. Ibid., 19. Though Chabon states that the copy of the book was sent to Random House, Lindey's letter of May 3, 1933, states that it was sent to him. It's possible that the law firm, acting on behalf of Random House, was also receiving packages and mailings directly related to the case on their behalf.

60. Alexander Lindey to H. C. Stewart, May 5, 1933, in Moscato and LeBlanc, *The United States of America*, 177.

61. Alexander Lindey to H. C. Stewart, May 13, 1933, in Moscato and LeBlanc, *The United States of America,* 179.

62. Chabon, "The United States v. One Book," 19.

63. PETITION FOR RELEASE AND ADMISSION OF BOOK INTO THE UNITED STATES ON THE GROUND THAT IT IS A CLASSIC, June 2, 1933, in Moscato and LeBlanc, *The United States of America,* 187.

64. Ibid., 190–192.

65. Ernst and Seagle, *To The Pure,* 6.

66. Hardiman, "The Trial of *Ulysses,"* 55.

67. Frank Dow (Acting Commissioner of Customs) to the Collector of Customs, June 16, 1933, in Moscato and LeBlanc, *The United States of America*, 203–204.

68. "He'll Find Out," *Seattle Daily Times,* August 30, 1933, 21.

69. Morris L. Ernst to Hon. John M. Woolsey, September 12, 1933, in Moscato and LeBlanc, *The United States of America*, 225.

70. Gillers, "A Tendency to Deprave and Corrupt," 281.

71. Preliminary Memorandum Submitted On Behalf of Claimant, With Exhibits, United States of America–against—1 book entitled *Ulysses* by James Joyce, in Moscato and LeBlanc, *The United States of America*, 227–229.

72. Ernst, *The Best is Yet*, 116.

73. Ibid.

74. Gillers, 282.

75. Ibid.

76. Ibid.

77. Ibid., 282–283.

78. "Statement of Morris L. Ernst, of the Firm of Greenbaum, Wolff & Ernst, Upon the Handing Down of Judge Woolsey's Opinion in the *Ulysses* Case," undated, in Moscato and LeBlanc, *The United States of America*, 317–318.

79. Lewis Gannett, "Books and Things," *New York Herald Tribune,* December 9, 1933, 11.

80. "'Ulysses' Ban Dropped as Judge Rules for Volume," *The San Bernardino County Sun* (San Bernardino, California), December 8, 1933, 4, https://newscomwc.newspapers.com/image/49359373.

81. Morris L. Ernst, foreword to James Joyce, *Ulysses* (New York: Vintage Press: 1961), v–vi.

82. Ibid.

83. Joseph M. Hassett, *The Ulysses Trials: Beauty and Truth Meet the Law* (Dublin: The Lilliput Press, 2016), 143.

84. Ibid., 143–144. Sumner's remarks were originally cited in Ernst and Lindey, *The Censor Marches On*, 22.

85. Paul Vanderham, *James Joyce and Censorship: The Trials of Ulysses* (London: Macmillan Press Ltd., 1998) 138.

86. Ibid.

87. Cited in Hassett, *The Ulysses Trials*, 145.

88. "Convoy Opens U. S. Appeal to Bar 'Ulysses'," *New York Herald Tribune*, May 17, 1934, 19.

89. Vanderham, *James Joyce*, 140.

90. Hassett, *Ulysses Trials,* 146.

91. Michael J. O'Shea, Review of Zack Bowen, *"Ulysses" as a Comic Novel*, *James Joyce Quarterly*, Vol. 29, No. 2 (Winter, 1992): 421. O'Shea's full quotation: "To quote Hugh Kenner quoting Ezra Pound quoting Joyce, 'in old age [Pound] liked to recall how Joyce had responded to reviews and explications: 'If only someone would say [Ulysses] was so damn funny!'"

92. Morris L. Ernst, *Untitled: The Diary of My 72nd Year* (New York: Robert B. Luce, Inc, 1962) 103.

93. Joyce, *Ulysses,* 151–152.

94. Francis Talbot, S.J., "Ulysses the Dirty," *America,* September 1, 1934, in Moscato and LeBlanc, *The United States of America*, 15.

95. Moscato and LeBlanc, *The United States of America*, 68.

96. Chabon, "United States v. One Book," 22.

97. Pagnattaro, "Carving a Literary Exception," 218.

98. Alden Whitman, "Morris Ernst, 'Ulysses' Case Lawyer, Dies," *New York Times,* May 23, 1976, 40.

# Chapter 6

# Promoting Birth and *Life*

In 1938, *Life* magazine published a photo essay, titled "The Birth of a Baby," which prompted police and vice societies to raid newsstands in cities across the United States. The issue's photos were not at all graphic, but they drew from an instructional film of the same name that had itself faced some resistance from the censors. In New York, in addition to confiscating the offending issues of *Life*, police officers arrested several news dealers for violating the obscenity statute. This aggressive response shocked and puzzled many contemporary readers. *Life*'s issue contained no nudity or depictions of sexual activity and, prior to the arrests, had been sent to the homes of its 650,000 subscribers with little objection. At the resulting trial, Morris Ernst handily won the case for *Life* and, in doing so, helped to destigmatize public representations of pregnancy and birth and further the goals of public health advocates. The case eventually bought Ernst a sizeable *Life* article about his career. But the case reads as a performance, whereby the powerful publisher, risking little, enlisted the country's top censorship lawyer to promote his magazine through a controversy largely of their own making. "The Birth of a Baby" trial marked the beginning of the end of Ernst's progressive fights, and with the challenge and excitement of censorship battles waning, Ernst would soon seek other forms of stimulation.

> If a child . . . has never indulged with his comrades in, let us say, the language of the street, he wouldn't know any more when he gets through looking at those pictures than when he started. If [he] has indulged in the language of the streets, and if he does entertain erroneous ideas, he will be assisted upon the path of truth and verity. That hurts no man, be he eight or eighty. . . . We are born this way, every one of us. Why should we be ashamed to tell our children so? Aren't they entitled to know it? [1]—Testimony of Dr. Nelson A. Ludington, *State v. Samuel Matloff*

No man, Dr. Nelson Ludington argues above, is injured by the truth. Dr. Ludington's testimony came during the trial of *State v. Samuel Matloff*, a

New Haven, Connecticut, case brought to court after authorities seized *Life* magazine's "Birth of a Baby" issue in 1938. Ludington's point—that information about sexuality isn't injurious—serves as a useful barometer for the changing conceptions of gender and masculinity Ernst had witnessed even since his successful defense in the cases of "The Sex Side of Life," *The Well of Loneliness*, and the raid of Margaret Sanger's birth control clinic only a decade earlier. In stating that sexual information "hurts no man" Ludington likely meant to include women in his diagnosis; still, his statement is revealing for its underlying assertion that, contrary to the suppositions of vice societies some 10 years earlier, men were not inherently savages who would respond to sexual information by pouncing on women or girls.

The fact that *Life* was seized across the country, and that some news dealers were arrested, demonstrates that Ludington's view was not shared by everyone. But the trial of *People v. Larsen*, in which Morris Ernst successfully defended *Life*'s publisher against obscenity charges, does illustrate how much currency Victorian-era concerns about depictions of reproduction had lost among the larger society by the late 1930s. And the case, which was Ernst's last great victory in obscenity law, demonstrates the extent to which Ernst had seemingly mastered his strategy of exhibitionism. By 1938, Ernst was so practiced in representing challenged texts that he could practically defend *Life* on autopilot. The basic outline of his strategy was the same: push the case in the press, send out a letter to dozens of influential citizens calling for their support of the cause, publicize the favorable responses and assemble past "greatest hits"—including many of the landmark cases that Ernst himself had won—to promote the position that the prosecution's argument was antiquated. Given his track record, and his ability to read public opinion, Ernst knew he would prevail. "We haven't any doubt we'll win the case," he told reporters. "The arrests were silly and stupid. Why if those pictures were obscene, some 800 books in general circulation, many of which can be secured by anyone at any public library, are obscene."[2]

Unlike most of Ernst's other censorship clients however, the motives behind *Life*'s decision to publish "The Birth of a Baby" came under scrutiny. Whereas Dennett originally published her sexual education pamphlet for her sons; and Radclyffe Hall created art for, by, and about lesbians; and the nurses and doctors in *Sideri* helped low-income women gain sovereignty over their sexuality, some of Ernst's friends and contemporaries doubted the purity behind *Life*'s heavily publicized actions. Ernst took on the case anyway. He once mentioned that his firm accepted clients who could pay handsomely so that it could also represent clients who could not pay at all. (Indeed, in the case of *Sideri*, Ernst and his firm had donated their time.) The *Life* case, however, would additionally compensate Ernst with celebrity, and the legal exhibitionist could not have resisted such a possibility. He would win, easily, thus further whittling away the censorship of sexuality. Moreover, he would be associated with (and, later, promoted in) the era's most popular magazine. If any doubts about his authority and influence lingered, they would surely be dashed now.

As in many past cases, Ernst once again became the face of reason against aggressive police and prosecution tactics. In this drama, police officials acted as expected. When the controversial "Birth of a Baby" issue hit newsstands on April 8, 1938, authorities were ready. Police and vice societies raided newsstands in several cities across the United States and seized copies of the offending issue. Not content to simply seize the goods, Bronx police arrested news dealers who were selling the issue. In addition to seizing their magazines, police in New York arrested several men who sold *Life* for violating Section 1141 of the Penal Code, better known as the obscenity clause. "The photographs and drawings in the magazine," the prosecution charged in its trial memorandum, "are disgusting, obscene, indecent and unlawful."[3] The raids and arrests surprised many across the nation. After all, *Life*'s issue contained no nudity, nor depictions of sexual activity and, prior to the arrests, it had been sent to the homes of its 650,000 subscribers with little objection.[4] From a modern perspective, as in the *Sideri* case, the authorities' swift and forceful action seems to have been a physical reincarnation of the Victorian matron who would use moral suasion to purify her home and domesticate her family.

From a contemporary point of view, however, Goliath seemed to be picking on David, and the police grossly miscalculated the public response to their actions. Unlike the prior cases Ernst had defended, where traditional views on issues important to women were still widely held, in the "Birth of a Baby" trial, the general public seemed to believe, mistakenly, that prosecutors were claiming that birth itself was obscene. That perception, along with the popularity of *Life*, doomed the prosecution's case from the start. Though Dr. Nelson Ludington's above testimony was cited at the famous New York "Birth of a Baby" trial, he had actually given it three days earlier in the New Haven, Connecticut, trial of *State v. Matloff*, where the judge subsequently lifted Connecticut's ban on the issue. Other cities soon followed suit, and prosecutors in the most scrutinized trial held in New York were placed in the unenviable position of fighting what was clearly becoming a losing cause.[5] In New York, where Ernst successfully defended the article, the decision in favor of *Life* helped to destigmatize public representations of pregnancy and birth and to further the goals of public health advocates. Once again, Ernst seemed to be acting as a pro-feminist, doing the work of feminism by arguing down restrictions on female reproductive health. More importantly, the case reveals, yet again, how Ernst took a controversial issue important to women, argued it in a legal atmosphere almost completely closed to women, and in the process promoted his own career and social currency.

The controversy began a year earlier in 1937, when the American Committee on Maternal Welfare (ACMW) first presented the original "Birth of a Baby" as a medical film. The ACMW was a loose confederation of doctors, medical professionals, and educators with the stated purpose of promoting "the welfare of mothers and their unborn and newborn babies."[6] According to *Child* magazine, the objective of the 72-minute film was "to educate the public to the need for maternal care and the value of the physician's services."[7] When the film was released, it was met with some resistance, mostly from vice societies and censors, who argued that its graphic nature made it inappropriate for many audiences. Such arguments were countered by newspapers such as the *New York Times,* which editorialized that the assertion that the film was indecent "is hard to take . . . seriously," given that so many prominent medical authorities and agencies had approved of the film.[8]

*Life* capitalized on this controversy. During the first week of April 1938, *Life* sent its subscribers an unusual letter in the mail. The letter, signed by publisher Roy Larsen, warned readers that the upcoming April 11 issue of *Life* would include an illustrated article about childbirth. The article in question, the publisher explained, was an adaptation of a highly praised movie titled *The Birth of a Baby. Life* readers would see a photo spread containing stills from the movie along with captions that would explain what was taking place in each frame. Given the graphic nature of the subject, the publisher concluded, some readers might deem the photo spread inappropriate for their children.[9]

At first glance, the motive behind *Life*'s letter seems fairly straightforward. It is generally not in the best interest of publishers to alienate their readers (or their advertisers, for that matter), and one could certainly understand *Life*'s cautionary note to subscribers in this light. Although controversy can sell magazines, *Life*'s target audience was the American family, and so one might conclude that Larsen sent out the letter in an effort preserve that readership. In other words, by alerting families beforehand, *Life* would be seen as a considerate, responsible publication that empowered parents by letting them make their own decision about the contents of the issue. Had this been the motive, however, then *Life* carelessly overlooked a high percentage of its readers, because no such letter was attached to the cover of the *newsstand* editions, and some 1,350,000 *Life* readers—more than double the number of subscribers—bought their copy at the newsstand.[10] A copy of Larsen's letter did appear in the issue itself, but not on the cover or even on the first pages; rather, the letter was printed on the page that preceded the story's photos. Any readers who arbitrarily flipped through the magazine (or who innocently gave it to their children) might be in for a shock. In short, it made no sense for *Life* to go to such efforts to retain their subscribers while ignoring their newsstand audience.

Some contemporaries seemed to read this cautionary letter as an element of an orchestrated publicity stunt, which allowed *Life* to garner national headlines while burnishing its image as an altruistic educational resource and a defender of free speech. When *Life*'s publisher went to trial in defense of the article, Ernst petitioned influential people to testify on behalf of *Life*. The responses he received were not always favorable. For instance, the historian James Truslow Adams wrote Ernst, "I cannot help but feel that the use of the material was more or less a stunt on the part of *Life* to increase circulation . . . The material is so commonplace from the standpoint of physiological text books and seems to me to contribute little to public welfare in connection with childbirth that I do not see the necessity for publishing it."[11] Brooks Atkinson, the drama critic at the *New York Times*, was similarly unwilling to provide his support. "I don't think the publisher of Life needs me to help him pull his chestnuts out of the fire," he wrote. "My liberalism does not extend to the business offices of successful publications that know how to handle their business affairs far more competently than I."[12] Even Ernst's close friend, Edna Ferber, the famous novelist and playwright, was also dubious about *Life*'s motives for taking on this particular fight: "I don't think LIFE is the ideal medium for the presentation of those BIRTH OF A BABY pictures," she wrote. "I think LIFE's reason for publishing them was not humanitarian. The notoriety which now follows the attempt to suppress the pictures will, of course, make the pictures seem dirty and LIFE seem courageous, neither of which is true."[13] Ferber, as it would turn out, was quite prescient in this regard.

By modern standards "The Birth of a Baby" seems quaint in its modesty. In fact, compared to Mary Ware Dennett's "Sex Side of Life," which Ernst had freed from the obscenity clause years earlier, the *Life* magazine article is not very revealing at all. What was it about the issue, then, that led authorities to order police to seize it and arrest those who sold it? To understand why it raised concern among authorities, it will be instructive to describe the controversial article in detail. In its introduction to the article, *Life* began by citing maternal mortality statistics, and claimed that modern medicine could cut that rate by at least 75 percent, "but at every turn it is hindered by public indifference and social taboos."[14] The movie, *Life* suggests, could overcome those obstacles. *Life* then lists the doctors, "all recognized leaders in obstetrics and gynecology," who supervised the making of the movie.[15] After including statements of praise from various leader and experts, like Surgeon General Thomas Parran Jr. (who had been the chief of the Venereal Disease Division of the Public Health Service in the 1920s) and Minneapolis Mayor George E.

Leach, each of whom has their photograph inserted in the introduction, *Life* states that film's audiences "are impressed by the unfailing dignity and taste with which it is handled and its altogether wholesome spirit," and promises that the magazine has made every effort to preserve that spirit in its "Birth of a Baby" article.[16] The story itself consisted of 35 panels of stills taken from the film with brief text summaries below each still panel. The first three panels simply show the title and credits of the film and allow *Life* the opportunity to emphasize that "from the title on, *The Birth of a Baby* is presented with uniform good taste."[17] The credits include a list of eight medical organizations; beneath this panel, *Life* states that the information in the film and in the article "is endorsed by the best medical authorities."[18]

The movie itself, at first blush, appears only to promote traditional gender stereotypes and thus hardly seems threatening. "Birth of a Baby" tells the fictional story of Mary, a married woman who becomes pregnant and then learns, along with readers, about the major stages of pregnancy and birth. At the beginning of the story, Mary is ignorant of the facts of life, and learns about menstruation by shyly sitting next to her mother-in-law, Mrs. Burgess, as Mrs. Burgess reads a book about menstruation to her own young daughter. Afterward, Mary asks Mrs. Burgess if many women die in childbirth and then "admits" she has missed her period.[19] Her mother-in-law reassures her and advises her to see the doctor. Before doing so, Mary first tells her husband John in a roundabout way that she might be pregnant: John had been planning an exotic vacation in Canada, and is surprised to hear his wife say, "I don't like vacation trips." Then she tells John that he might be a father.[20]

The only thing for Mary to do is go to a professional man who can fulfill the role her husband cannot and who will provide her with information about her reproductive system. We see here that, as far as women's reproduction goes, the only one who has the answers is a medical professional, in particular a man of science, who will certainly not get aroused in the exercise of his duties. At the doctor's office, Dr. Wilson tells Mary about the process of fertilization and sanctions what he calls "marital relations," as well as short car rides, up to the sixth month of pregnancy.[21] We also learn at this time that "The wide-hipped female figure is naturally designed for childbearing," and that's good news for Mary.[22] Dr. Wilson also shows Mary drawings that show the different stages of pregnancy, with details of the fetus's growth.[23] When Mary goes into labor, we see Dr. Wilson and his nurse arriving at John and Mary's house, where John is "put to work" boiling water to sterilize the medical equipment.[24] From the information given in the story, it seems that this is the husband's only role in the pregnancy or birth. Later, as a happy conclusion to the happy event, we see John embracing Mary six weeks after the birth, excitedly telling her, "Why, you're just as slim as you used to be, and more beautiful!"[25] This last frame shows the couple kissing. Marital relations, and John's manly function, may resume.

What, then, could have been deemed objectionable about this story? For one thing, *Life* was considered a family magazine. Perhaps the idea of a mother reading a scientific book about menstruation to her daughter was not threatening, but the idea that boys and young men might be voyeurs of that scene would have disturbed those readers who embraced the nineteenth-century ideal of separate spheres for men and women. And there are other such voyeuristic moments in the story. Unlike John, who is not present when Dr. Wilson shows Mary diagrams of her reproductive system, male readers of *Life*, including boys, would see the forbidden diagrams as well. So even if the discussions of reproduction are handled properly within the magazine from the standpoint of traditional gender roles, the gaze of male readers may have made censors uncomfortable.

The greatest stated concern of censors was the article's illustrations, particularly the diagrams displaying the development of the fetus and the stages of growth and birth of the baby. The article also included a photograph of an actual baby's head emerging from the birth canal. The area around the baby's head, however, is so thoroughly enveloped in white sheets that there is no evidence, save the textual commentary, that a baby is actually emerging from a woman's body.[26] The prosecution later argued that these images would plant impure thoughts in young minds. Some censors also suggested that there was a subversive element to the article. Although there is no mention of birth control, explicit or otherwise, authorities believed that there was some correlation between the article and the birth control movement. On April 7, 1938, the night before the issue hit the newsstands, WNEW radio in New York reported that police chiefs throughout New England viewed the article as "muffled propaganda for birth control" and that these authorities therefore believed that the article "would be detrimental to the morals of youth."[27]

By suggesting that birth control was somehow embedded in a story about childbirth, these police chiefs were either reading between the lines or were being completely disingenuous. *Life* makes no reference whatsoever, direct or indirect, to birth control. One suspects that, if authorities truly viewed the issue as birth control propaganda, then they must have interpreted the birth as a handicap upon the personal relationship between John and Mary. In other words, one would have to maintain that the article subversively promoted birth control because it showed pregnancy as debilitating—for the husband. For instance, one could argue that John's romantic plans for a vacation in Canada are derailed when Mary gets pregnant. According to this interpretation, John's ultimate act of heterosexual masculinity, the impregnation of his wife, has thus undermined his plans for leisure. Unprotected sex, it would appear, may destroy extracurricular activities. Additionally, marital relations, as the doctor calls it, must cease after the sixth month and won't continue until six weeks after the birth. And John has all but been supplanted by Dr. Wilson during this time: John literally exits the picture until Mary goes into labor, at which point the only function assigned to John is the apparently emasculating work of boiling water. This interpretation may seem curious to a modern reader, in an era in which fathers were not invited into hospital delivery rooms and birth control was legally deemed obscene for single women, and it is at best a weak explanation of the police force's use of birth control as a justification for seizing the article. Or one might assume that at the end of the story, John remains in the dark about female reproduction; in this reading, John's function is that of the breadwinner, and that role must fulfill whatever manly needs he has until Mary recovers from the birth of their child, at which time husband and wife can resume their recreational activities. Or one could even read "The Birth of a Baby" as a cautionary tale: unless men learn about reproduction and can find some way to prevent pregnancy—say, birth control—their manly function will be disabled for several months. Whatever dastardly subtext authorities might have read into the photo essay, in reality, there's not a hint of contraceptive propaganda anywhere to be found.

Despite the concerns of censors, *Life*'s subscribers did not find the magazine threatening. When the anticipated issue arrived in the mail, the reaction of subscribers was generally positive. Few readers canceled their subscriptions, and many sent enthusiastic letters to the magazine in praise of their photo spread. But when that same issue hit the newsstands, police in numerous cities claimed that it was obscene and seized the offensive issue. The day before the issue was delivered to newsstands, several cities, including Pittsfield, Boston, Worcester, Holyoke, and Springfield, Massachusetts; Providence, Rhode Island; and Bridgeport, Connecticut announced that copies of the magazine would be banned unless the four "Birth of a Baby" pages were removed. (They weren't.) Bans were also announced in Northampton, Fall River, and Lawrence, Massachusetts. The next day, copies of *Life* were seized in Merrick, Long Island, Jersey City, Newark, Elizabeth, and Trenton, New Jersey, and elsewhere. It was no secret that many of these cities had large Catholic populations or that the local authorities were responding to the wishes of their constituency. "My ideas are Catholic ideas and American ideas," declared Bronx District Attorney Samuel J. Foley. "I try to live as a Catholic and administer my job as a Catholic." People who disagreed with him or with the authorities who had suppressed the magazine, he said, were "sneering at God."[28]

Although the confiscations momentarily dug into *Life*'s profits, they had not yet paved the way for *Life*'s public relations coup, since in those raids, police had only seized the magazines; there was not yet a human face or a clear victim. While issues of *Life* piled up in police stations, the tone began to change as police arrested newsstand vendors. In the Bronx, in addition to seizing one-thousand copies of *Life*, police arrested Benjamin Zaresky on April 8, and Harry Mish, Morris Weinstein, and Joseph Horowitz on April 9. Each man was charged with violating the obscenity clause. Morris Ernst, understandably, portrayed them as victims of an overzealous prosecutor, and most New York City newspapers agreed.

The arrests opened the door for a test case to decide who was ultimately responsibility for the distribution of printed matter. In Ernst's 1945 memoir, *The Best Is Yet*, he recalls his visit to Roy Larsen's office after police arrested the newsstand owners. Larsen presumably called Ernst, the censorship expert, for advice on how to use free speech arguments to stop police from confiscating the controversial issue of *Life*. As Ernst recalls it, the meeting took a surprising turn when Ernst told the publisher that he was "damned weary" of watching relatively powerless people like those vendors "take the rap" for powerful publishers. To begin with, Ernst said, news dealers generally didn't know what they were selling. How could they read through the dozens and dozens of magazines and newspapers dumped in front of their stands? Even if they were somehow able to do so, were the dealers equipped to determine which of those periodicals were legally obscene when the courts had such difficulty doing so? These news dealers, who frequently lacked the financial means to pay for their own defense, were more often than not the target of prosecutors. Once arrested, the retailers understandably caved and chose to plead guilty in return for a smaller fine. In front of Larsen, Ernst wished aloud that *someone*—some brave publisher—would "dig his heals in the ground and stand back of his material."[29] Ernst thus appealed to Larsen's sense of himself as a powerful man who had the ability to improve the lot of the literal man on the street. The news dealers were Jewish and poor, two sources of prejudice and limitations on power that Ernst intimately understood, and he was thus able to relate to their predicament. More importantly for him, he was able to depict their pathetic status in terms that Roy Larsen could understand. According to Ernst, upon hearing Ernst's lamentation, Larsen immediately volunteered to surrender himself for arrest, effectively taking the rap for the poor vendors.[30]

Ernst then arranged for an April 11 meeting with Bronx District Attorney Samuel J. Foley at Foley's office. There, Foley agreed to try Larsen as a test case and hold a trial on April 19; in the meantime, the news dealers' cases would be held in abeyance.[31] To set the test case in motion, Larsen sold a copy of the April 11 issue of *Life* to a detective in the presence of Ernst and Foley, and the next day surrendered himself to the detective. Larsen pled not guilty and was released into Ernst's custody.[32] All of these events were well-publicized, in large part due to Ernst's efforts. The same day that Bronx police arrested Zaresky, Ernst orchestrated a rapid-response media campaign.

The April 9 edition of the *New York Herald Tribune* reported not only that Zaresky had been arrested on April 8, but that Larsen would surrender himself that very morning with the intention of making himself the defendant in a test case. The story also cited Ernst, who had wasted no time in presenting his argument to the public. Foley's attempt to suppress the issue, Ernst said, was an attack on both the freedom of the press and on public health and welfare.[33]

The prosecution, led by Foley, argued that the article would cheapen sex or even increase illness and mortality by encouraging sexual activity among the innocent. At court, the prosecution pointed out that the issue was sold in candy stores and could be "sold in the rack with . . . magazines such as *Boy's Life*, Boy Scout magazines and other periodicals intended for persons of tender and immature years."[34] Foley then cited the 1868 English case of *Regina v. Hicklin,* the same legal precedent cited by prosecutors in Ernst's prior censorship trials, in which Lord Chief Justice Cockburn defined "obscenity" as material which tends "to deprave and corrupt those whose minds are open to immoral influences and into whose hands a publication of this sort may fall."[35] The prosecution believed that "The Birth of a Baby" "would suggest impure and libidinous thoughts in the young and inexperienced," and therefore should be banned.[36] It was indeed appropriate for Foley to cite this 70-year old precedent, as prosecutors routinely did in obscenity cases, for it in fact reflected nineteenth-century assumptions about the way in which men and boys responded to sexual material. In addition, Foley's focus on reading material designed for boys, such as *Boy's Life* and scouting magazines, reveals that the "young and inexperienced" minds he was most concerned with belonged to boys. The fear was that "The Birth of a Baby" might incite boys to have sex, with the underlying assumption that boys, upon mere exposure to the theme of female sexuality, would be unable to control themselves.

This assumption—that boys were on some level "animals"—harkened back to the nineteenth century. As E. Anthony Rotundo has illustrated, in the Victorian era boys were frequently portrayed as "wild," and as "primitive savages."[37] The nineteenth-century belief was that, away from the civilizing effect of the domestic world, where women and girls resided, boys could be animalistic. If one pictures boys this way, as savage, wild animals, the idea of introducing them to sexually charged material might indeed be worrisome. And the worries didn't cease when boys grew into young men. According to Rotundo, during the nineteenth century, "sexual desire was seen as a powerful force in a young man, distracting him from his work, blinding him to his future duties as a breadwinner, and leading him even to disease and insanity."[38] With this nineteenth-century specter haunting twentieth-century censors, it is clear why even the discussion of birth could be seen as threatening.

Ernst countered the prosecution's use of *Regina v. Hicklin* with the recent ruling of *United States v. Levine*, a case Ernst successfully defended in 1936. In that trial, Judge Learned Hand dismissed the applicability of *Hicklin* by stating: "No civilized community not fanatically puritanical would tolerate such an imposition, and we do not believe that the courts that have declared it, would ever have applied it consistently."[39] Even if *Hicklin* were applicable, the defense continued, the "Birth of a Baby" pictures did not tend to corrupt, since the matter was presented in a "coldly scientific" and dignified manner. Ernst then presented the testimony of numerous experts, including psychologists, doctors, educators, and clergymen, who concluded that the *Life* article was actually beneficial to children.[40] In essence, Ernst's defense asked the court to listen to professionals who actually studied children instead of accepting outdated and unscientific assumptions about how children think and act.

Ernst's emphasis on professionalism was a wise strategy for two reasons. First, by focusing on the article's "coldly scientific" and, therefore, *professional* approach to sexuality, Ernst was attempting to reassure any judge who might cling to the assumption that discussions of intimate matters could unleash the unbridled passions of boys and men. His approach exploited the inherent contradiction in obscenity cases, which was that judges, juries, and lawyers involved were never themselves harmed by the indecent materials they examined firsthand during obscenity trials. In addition, medical journals and legal writings were routinely ignored by censors, even though they often contained much more graphic descriptions of sexuality then the texts that were challenged in the courtroom. In other words, in the hands of professionals, sex seemed safe. Ernst knew about this double standard from his own experience as a lawyer. When "The Sex Side of Life" was initially published in the *Medical Review of Reviews,* it hadn't ruffled any feathers; it was only years later, when the pamphlet was in the hands of the public that its author was indicted on obscenity charges. Ernst thus knew that science and professionalism offered a certain protection to texts dealing with sexuality. In addition, the scientific, medical, and professional man presented a reassuring image of controlled, passionless masculinity at odds with the savage animalistic assumption Rotundo describes above. Ernst therefore argued that a "coldly scientific" examination of pregnancy would not incite boys; in fact, it would support twentieth-century reformers' goal to instill sexual self-control.

The other benefit of this approach was personal. Although he wasn't a scientist, Ernst was an avid aficionado of the sciences and by 1938, was widely read in sexual matters. In promoting the scientific method, he was indirectly promoting himself. Accordingly, he continued to advance this approach for years, and when Alfred Kinsey published his mammoth *The Sexual Behavior of Men*, Ernst focused his efforts on championing Kinsey's work and relating it to the law. "I now say," Ernst would declare in 1949, "that the Kinsey Report is the single greatest contribution of science to the rule-making part of the law in my lifetime."[41] Kinsey's report, after all, gave scientific clout to Ernst's long-held stance that sexuality could be studied and understood, and that the findings would reverse or eliminate long-held prejudices about the nature of sex. One such prejudice involved masculinity. In *American Sexual Behavior and the Kinsey Report*, Ernst and co-author David Loth dismissed the Lewis Terman "test" on the "masculinity" and "femininity" of men and women.[42] Terman claimed that masculinity and femininity were quantifiable attributes and gave men and women masculine and feminine points based on answers to questions about likes and dislikes.[43] For instance, one gained masculinity points for disliking foreigners; one gained femininity points if they disliked playing with snakes.[44] Ernst and Loth argued that "there is no proof that the characteristics labeled by them 'masculine' or 'feminine' are in truth exclusively or even predominately the property of one sex or the other," and suggested that more scientific methodology was needed to understand gender.[45] In *American Sexual Behavior*, as in the *Life* case and his other defenses of causes relating to women's sexuality, Ernst's promotion of a more liberal and flexible understanding of sexuality and gender invariably promoted his own standing as a man by expanding the boundaries of what features of gender identity—and, therefore, whom—was accepted by the general public.

Accordingly, Ernst and his defense team continued to highlight observable facts and scientific evidence and emphasized the film's public health bona fides. *The Birth of a Baby* was depicted as a wild success in Minneapolis where, according to the defense, about 70,000 people saw it.[46] The audiences, the brief continued, "represented a cross-section of every social class and religious denomination of the population."[47] Along with the mayor of Minneapolis, whose support was highlighted in *Life*'s introduction to the article, the public school authorities, the PTA, churches, social welfare organizations, and the press all approved of the film. But *Life*'s lawyers had to contend with the fact that the New York State censors had refused to give the film a permit, a fact that *Life* openly acknowledged in its introduction to "Birth of a Baby." There, *Life* reported that there had been "a storm of protest" from the media and from doctors after the censors' decision, and as a result, that ruling was up for reconsideration. *Life* then cited an editorial in the *New York Times*, "whose editor is conservative Dr. John H. Finley," as evidence.[48] Indeed, in July of 1937, the ACMW had applied for a license to display *Birth of a Baby* publicly in New York State, and Irwin Esmond, the director of the Motion Picture Division in the Education Department had rejected the application, labeling the film "Indecent."[49] In November, 1937 the committee screened the film before Dr. Frank P. Graves, the commissioner of the New York State of

Education, who agreed with Director Esmond that the film was "Indecent"—and added that the film was also "Immoral" and "Would Tend to Corrupt Morals."[50] It seems likely that this decision was a largely political nod to New York's large and influential Catholic community. As *Life* had claimed, *The Birth of a Baby* was up for reconsideration, but on April 14, six days after the article went on sale and five days before Ernst's trial, the Board of Regents of the University of the State of New York affirmed Director Esmond's decision to refuse to license the film to be shown in places of amusement.

If the defense team planned to tie its wagon to the fortunes of the film, then, it needed to address this recent decision. Fortunately for *Life*, the Board of Regents' decision contained praise of the film as well as language that Ernst could exploit. The board stated that the film had been prepared "under careful scientific supervision" and that it undoubtedly had high educational value. Most importantly, the board had not rejected the film outright; it allowed the exhibition of the film for educational purposes. Ernst argued that if the film were truly obscene, then no permit whatsoever would have been issued. Yet the obstacle for the board would also be Ernst's obstacle to overcome; namely, Ernst had to address the contention that the film, while educational for an adult audience, could harm children or other, less sophisticated audiences. "As motion picture theaters are attended by children of all ages in large numbers and by people of all creeds, colors and races," the board stated, "this picture is not licensed to be shown in places of amusement."[51] The underlying assumption here is that certain audiences must not be exposed to the images and information in the film. Interestingly, the board lumped together children and "people of all creeds, colors and races," a coded reference to immigrants and non-whites. The board's message was clear: whatever the film's benefits, they were counterbalanced by the potential damage the film could do to weak, innocent minds. If the film was potentially harmful, then it followed that *Life*'s adaptation carried the same risks.

Given the prevailing prejudices about race and ethnicity, and the fact that the kind of savage masculinity no longer so frequently applied to white children was still very much a part of the popular perception of non-whites and immigrants, the board's racist response to the film is not surprising. As Gail Bederman has shown in her telling of the Jack Johnson story, the black prizefighter was feared for more than his muscles. Some whites believed—or so claimed—that Johnson's sexual relationships with white women threatened their communities, as evidenced by negative media coverage and hate mail.[52] Though Johnson was ultimately imprisoned for transporting a minor across state lines, the conviction was a stretch, since the "illicit purposes" were never corroborated. Still, the fear of non-white masculinity led to laws which ultimately served the secondary purpose of punishing white women for succumbing to such apparent savagery.[53] In Lisa Lindquist Dorr's article on the racial integrity acts passed in Virginia during this era, she demonstrates how anti-miscegenation laws ultimately served as a means by which the society could ostracize white women who had sex with black men.[54] And as Jeffrey Moran argues, sexual mores of immigrants differed from those of native-born Americans in important ways, a fact which increased the anxieties of established white Americans about the possibility of "race suicide":

> The sense of race consciousness and racial superiority grew sharper in the United States toward the end of the nineteenth century as hundreds of thousands of "new" immigrants arrived yearly from eastern and southern Europe, threatening the "old stock" Americans with their sheer numbers and their unfamiliar habits. Many "old stock" Americans commented with disdain on the distance between what they saw as the newcomers' degraded sexual habits and the native Anglo-Saxon's sexual purity. Thus the moral code that originated as a highly personal response among middle-class whites to the disorder of American life in the early to mid-nineteenth century gradually came to be thought of as a group characteristic, even a racial trait.[55]

Under this racist theory, immigrants and non-whites would not only be more susceptible to the kinds of sexual suggestion left by a film like "Birth of a Baby," but would also be more apt to reproduce, thereby decreasing the native-born white stock.

Ernst's defense team attacked the board's assumption about the vulnerability of children head on. In the first place, Ernst suggested, the legality of "Birth of a Baby" shouldn't be based on the potential effects the article might have on children. Ernst knew from experience, however, that judges and juries preferred some assurance that, in fact, the material in question didn't pose a threat to children, and he accordingly addressed that concern. Children are more intelligent and have more "moral stamina" than adults think, the defense claimed.[56] That said, one cannot "look into the mind of a child and ascertain, as a matter of scientific fact, the effect of anything the child has seen or heard."[57] If one is intent on getting the best analysis of a child's mind, though, one must ask experts in medicine, psychology, and public health—in other words, "persons who have dealt with children for many years, have observed and studied them, and can therefore be reasonably counted upon to appraise the possible influence of any given material on the juvenile or adolescent mind."[58] The brief offered a list of "the foremost psychiatrists" who thought that the film was "not likely to have an undesirable effect on those viewing it."[59] It would follow that if the film was harmless, then the article would be as well.

Another strategy for the defense was to suggest that *Life* was a major contributor to the health and welfare of the general public. *Life*, the defense pointed out, had published a number of public health articles in the past. With series on topics like tuberculosis, epilepsy, and cancer, *Life* had helped educate the public on health issues. Here, the implication was that "The Birth of a Baby" article also fell into that category. To help support its claim that these types of articles could truly have an impact on readers, the defense included a footnote that detailed the commendations from public health officials on *Life*'s work in this area. In addition, the brief told of one female reader who wrote to *Life*'s editor claiming that the *Life* series on cancer had provided her with medical information that helped save her life.[60]

Having established its argument that both the *Life* article and the movie it was derived from were beneficial to the general public, Ernst now focused on the specific charge of obscenity. To counter the prosecution's "tendency to corrupt" standard, the defense brief asked:

> Is it criminal to present, in a restrained, dignified and scientific manner, the basic facts concerning human embryology, pregnancy and delivery? Is it criminal to cooperate with federal and state authorities, social hygiene groups and welfare agencies in a campaign to reduce our childbirth death-rate through public education? If it is, then *Life*'s picture-story may be condemned. But if we believe in the soundness of the principle that maternal and infant mortality thrives on ignorance, that the spread of knowledge is an invaluable weapon in the campaign for public health, if we are to work toward the creation of an informed and intelligent community, the information must be dismissed.[61]

Ultimately, then, Ernst used the trial as a referendum on sexual education and public health. Prior to the trial he had labeled the attempted suppression of the magazine "an attack on public health and welfare."[62] At court he argued that "maternal and infant mortality thrives on ignorance," and piled on statistics—again, favoring science over passion—to support the need for sexual education.[63] In the defendant's memorandum, the defense cited 1936 data on mortality rates of mothers and babies. Ernst's data showed that 12,000 mothers died of childbirth; 30,000 babies died within 24 hours after birth and 40,000 more died before they were one month old. In all, the defense claimed, 150,000 lives were lost each year.[64] The none-too-subtle claim was that articles like "Birth of a Baby" helped lower the mortality rate. "Physicians are almost unanimous in their opinion," Ernst argued, "that a large percentage of these deaths of mothers and babies can be prevented if expectant mothers realize the importance of good medical attention, and seek it. The obvious remedy for the high death-rate is a program of education."[65] Ernst summed up his argument by making a direct connection between actual birth and *Life* magazine, proclaiming: "*Life* is not obscene unless human birth is."[66]

*Life*—and birth—were ultimately ruled not obscene. In defending the article, Ernst helped to destigmatize public representations of pregnancy and birth and furthered the goals of public health advocates. Here was a progressive man doing the work of feminism by arguing down restrictions on female reproductive health. Ernst had taken a controversial issue important to women, argued it in a legal atmosphere almost completely closed to women, and in doing so, had promoted his own career and standing in male society. Ernst's defense of birth and pregnancy reaffirmed his celebrity: for his efforts, Ernst was ultimately rewarded several years later with a portrait of his work and his life, in the pages of none other than *Life* magazine. But Ernst increasingly dedicated his considerable intellect, talent, and energy to supporting first, the director of the FBI, and later, the dictator of the Dominican Republic. These choices contributed to his diminished stature and influence and, ultimately, to the darkening of the public image he had worked so hard to establish.

## NOTES

1. Cited in Defendant's Trial Memorandum, 50, *People of the State of New York-against-Roy E. Larsen,* 5 N.Y.S. (2d) 55, Box 91, MLE.
2. "'Life' Ban Spreads to Pennsylvania," *New York Times*, April 10, 1938, 21.
3. Memorandum on Behalf of the People, 19, *People of the State of New York-against-Roy E. Larsen,* Box 91, MLE.
4. Defendant's Trial Memorandum, 6, *People of the State of New York-against-Roy E. Larsen.*
5. "Wide Ban On 'Life' For Birth Pictures," *New York Times*, April 9, 1938, 15; "'Life' Ban Spreads To Pennsylvania," *New York Times*, April 10, 1938, 21. The article was also banned or seized throughout Pennsylvania; in Essex, Bergen, Hudson, Union and Mercer Counties in New Jersey; and in Nassau County, L.I.; as well as in the following cities: Boston, the Bronx, Atlantic City, Chicago, St. Louis, and Newport News, VA.
6. Fred L. Adair, "Maternal, Infant and Child Health," *Child*, May 1937, 5–7. Adair, the chairman of the ACMW, emphasized in this article that his group "is not to be confused with the American Committee on Maternal Health, which was a later development and which has an entirely different purpose, namely, birth control."
7. "Motion Picture on 'The Birth Of A Baby,'" *Child*, December 1937, 134.
8. "Immoral or Educational?" *New York Times*, March 17, 1938, 20.
9. Case materials, *People of the State of New York-against-Roy E. Larsen*, Box 91, MLE.
10. Ibid. The data on readership came from the testimony of Charles D. Jackson, the General Manager of Life, in the New Haven case of *State of Connecticut v. Samuel Matloff* (which was cited in *People v. Larsen*). According to Jackson, paid circulation

was 2 million. *Life*'s surveys suggested that there were nine readers per copy, or 18 million readers in 1938.

11. James Truslow Adams to Morris L. Ernst, April 15, 1938, Box 92, MLE.

12. Brook Atkinson to Morris Ernst, April 13, 1938, Box 92, MLE.

13. Edna Ferber to Morris L. Ernst, April 11, 1938, Box 92, MLE.

14. "'The Birth of a Baby' Aims to Reduce Maternal and Infant Mortality Rates," *Life*, April 11, 1938, 33.

15. Ibid.

16. Ibid.

17. Ibid.

18. Ibid.

19. Ibid.

20. Ibid.

21. Ibid., 34.

22. Ibid.

23. Ibid.

24. Ibid., 35.

25. Ibid., 36.

26. Ibid., 35.

27. Richard Brooks, "The Little Things in Life," April 7, 1938, WNEW radio broadcast, Box 91, MLE. Brooks was probably citing Pittsfield, Massachusetts Police Chief John L. Sullivan, who was quoted in the April 8 edition of the *Cleveland Plain Dealer*. Interestingly, that article can also be found in Ernst's files. It is possible that Ernst fed Sullivan's quotation to both WNEW and the *Plain Dealer.* "'Life' Banned in East For Photo of Birth," *Cleveland Plain Dealer*, April 8, 1938, Box 271.9, MLE.

28. "Foley Condemns 'Sneering at God'," *New York Times*, April 25, 1938, 9.

29. Morris L. Ernst, *The Best Is Yet . . .* (New York: Harper & Brothers, 1945), 140. This strategy, in which Ernst proclaims before a desired client his wish that *someone* would fight for the little guy, is similar to his declaration before Bennet Cerf, six years earlier that the U.S. ban on *Ulysses* was a "disgrace" and that "he'd like to wage a fight to legalize it."

30. Ibid.

31. Summary of Facts, *People of the State of New York-against-Roy E. Larsen.*, Box 91, MLE.

32. Ibid.

33. *New York Herald Tribune*, April 9, 1938, Box 91, MLE.

34. Case materials, *People of the State of New York-against-Roy E. Larsen.*

35. Ibid.

36. Memorandum on Behalf of the People, *People of the State of New York-against-Roy E. Larsen.*

37. E. Anthony Rotundo, *American Manhood: Transformations in Masculinity from the Revolution to the Modern Era* (New York: Basic Books, 1993), 31.

38. Ibid., 72.

39. Decision in the case of *United States v. Levine*. No. 252, Circuit Court of Appeals, Second Circuit, April 6, 1936, 85 Fed. (2d) 156 (1936). Cited in Defendant's

Reply Memorandum, *People of the State of New York-against-Roy E. Larsen.*, Box 91, MLE.

40. Defendant's Reply Memorandum, *People of the State of New York-against-Roy E. Larsen.*

41. Morris L. Ernst, "The Kinsey Report and the Law," *Scientific Monthly,* Vol. 70, No. 5 (May, 1950), 279–282, https://www.jstor.org/stable/19936.

42. Lewis Terman was a student of the psychologist G. Stanley Hall and invented the Stanford-Binet IQ test.

43. Nancy F. Cott, *The Grounding of Modern Feminism* (New Haven: Yale University Press, 1987), 153–154.

44. Ibid.

45. Morris L. Ernst and David Loth, *American Sexual Behavior and the Kinsey Report* (New York: The Greystone Press, 1948), 17–18.

46. Defendant's Trial Memorandum, 4, *People of the State of New York-against-Roy E. Larsen.*

47. Ibid.

48. "Birth of a Baby," 33.

49. "Proceedings in Connection with the Motion Picture, "The Birth of a Baby," Box 91, MLE.

50. Ibid.

51. Ibid.

52. Gail Bederman, *Manliness and Civilization: A Cultural History of Gender and Race in the United States,1880–1917* (Chicago: The University of Chicago Press, 1995), 8–10.

53. Ibid.

54. Lisa Lindquist Dorr, "Arm in Arm: Gender, Eugenics, and Virginia's Racial Integrity Acts of the 1920s," *Journal of Women's History* 11, no. 1 (1999).

55. Jeffrey P. Moran, *Teaching Sex: The Shaping of Adolescence in the 20th Century* (Cambridge: Harvard University Press, 2000), 16–17.

56. Defendant's Memorandum, 41–42, *People of the State of New York-against-Roy E. Larsen.*

57. Ibid.

58. Ibid.

59. Ibid.

60. Ibid., 6.

61. Ibid., 51.

62. Morris Ernst, form letter, April 9, 1938, Box 91, MLE. Ernst's letter was sent to hundreds of prominent members of the community. His list of recipients included authors such as Sherwood Anderson, Floyd Dell, Theodore Dreiser, Fanny Hurst, Freda Kirchwey, John Dos Passos, Lewis Mumford, and E. B. White; clergymen such as Harry Emerson Fosdick and Reinhold Neibuhr; columnists and critics like Walter Lippmann, H. L. Mencken, Westbrook Pegler, Dorothy Thompson, Carl and Mark Van Doren, and Walter Winchell; educators such as Charles and Mary Beard, and John Dewey; physicians, playwrights, doctors and social hygiene authorities—and a

"miscellaneous" group of recipients including Aline Davis Hayes, who is identified as the President of the "League of Women Shoppers."

63. Defendant's Memorandum, Conclusion, *People of the State of New York-against-Roy E. Larsen,* Box 91, MLE.

64. Defendant's Memorandum, "Supplemental Materials and Exhibits," *People of the State of New York-against-Roy E. Larsen*, Box 91, MLE. The brief credits a *New York Times* article from March 17, 1938 for these data.

65. Defendant's Memorandum, Conclusion, *People of the State of New York-against-Roy E. Larsen.*

66. Defendant's Memorandum, 3, *People of the State of New York-against-Roy E. Larsen.*

# Chapter 7

# From Court Giant to "Court Jester"

A good portion of Morris Ernst's success stems from his eagerness to tackle cases that advanced his feminist clients' agendas, which were steeped in the proposition that American laws hadn't caught up to modern assumptions and values. His public stances had put him on the side of doctors and nurses who had been jailed due to police overreach, of authors whose texts had been challenged, of those authors' readers, and of so many others who felt like legal institutions, politicians, and corporations were "rackets" working against them. And yet the more famous Ernst became, the further he strayed from that initial proposition. This chapter examines some of the choices Ernst made during the latter half of his legal career. With his expertise and experience in fighting for the rights of the less powerful, his potential to inspire real and lasting change in areas he deeply cared about, such as civil rights and civil liberties, was enormous. But he instead opted to embrace J. Edgar Hoover and the FBI. He may well have feared being tarred as a communist: though he'd been labeled as such prior to the Cold War, by the 1950s he knew that such accusations could end careers. It is just as likely, however, that his desire for excitement and recognition spurred him to change course. Censorship and free speech cases no longer held the same allure, and with the death of FDR, Ernst longed for another powerful man with whom he could associate. Though his career would continue for another quarter-century—he turned 60 in 1950—his choices likely disappointed many of those whose interests he had defended prior to the start of the Cold War, as Ernst's acts of exhibitionism, which his fans had found so endearing in the past, began to wear thin.

## *LIFE*, LOYALTY, AND WOMEN'S BOTTOMS

While Ernst's work on women's issues was critical to his public persona, since it enabled him to define and present himself as a modern man with a superior knowledge of female sexuality, in the 1930s and 1940s he also defended—and publicized—many other causes. Three years after sealing his credentials as a free speech champion by freeing *Ulysses,* Ernst joined his friend Heywood Broun, who had founded the American Newspaper Guild, in helping establish the right of reporters to organize. Ernst represented the Guild after the Associated Press fired a reporter for taking part in union activities. The case, *Watson v. Associated Press*, went all the way to the U.S. Supreme Court. Ernst's work further strengthened his solid reputation with journalists, though it also may have indirectly inflamed Ernst's hatred of communists. During the course of the trial, Ernst later recalled, "I had a drink at the Carleton Hotel in Washington with John W. Davis, who had argued the case for the Associated Press. This casual and pleasant meeting was interpreted by the Communist leaders who had infiltrated the Guild as a betrayal of my client. I was offended and hurt, but not surprised, when, eventually, I was replaced as counsel for the Guild by a Communist sympathizer."[1] Davis, after all, was a staunch Democrat, Ernst continued, who promoted state's rights and opposed women's and civil rights, and who was therefore a clear foe to communists.

Though the journalist Harrison Salisbury placed a good amount of importance on this painful experience in increasing Ernst's antipathy toward communists, Ernst's ire did not prevent him from representing the Congress of Industrial Organizations (CIO) at the Supreme Court two years later in its fight against an autocratic politician. Mayor Frank Hague ran a traditional political machine in Jersey City and forbade dissent; he accused those who opposed him of being communists. Ernst knew that some communists did belong to the CIO, but nonetheless eagerly threw himself into the cause. Hague repeatedly accused the CIO, the ACLU, and Ernst himself of being a communist.[2] Ultimately, Ernst's successful and very public repudiation of "Boss" Hague in the 1939 Supreme Court decision, *Hague v. Committee for Industrial Organization*, helped establish the right to public freedom of assembly.[3] In newspapers articles with headings such as, "Ernst vs. Hague," the media personalized the fight, making a dispute over civil liberties into a battle between two men, thereby helping ensure that Ernst was yet again the protagonist and the very public face of another protracted court case.[4] As always, Ernst made trials into events by courting the journalists and enlisting friends and clients to give public support to each cause, thus ensuring ample publicity.

With so many high-profile cases to his name, by the 1930s Ernst had become one of the world's most famous and successful lawyers. The artist Peggy Bacon immortalized Ernst in her 1934 collection of portraits titled *Off With Their Heads!* which included other contemporary luminaries, such as President Franklin D. Roosevelt, New York Mayor Fiorello LaGuardia; authors such as Dorothy Parker, Sinclair Lewis, and Djuna Barnes; and artists like Diego Rivera and Georgia O'Keefe. In 1935, Phillip Wylie included "Morris Ernst" as a character in his murder mystery spoof, *The Smiling Corpse*. In Wylie's novel, Ernst joined other celebrities like the pianist George Gershwin, *New Yorker* editor Harold Ross, authors Dashiell Hammett and G. K. Chesterton, and many more in solving the mystery.[5] Ernst's name appeared regularly in the news and in the columns of Walter Lippmann, Broun, and Leonard Lyons. He wrote many articles himself in which he often alluded to the cases he had successfully argued and to the latest books he had published. Ernst maintained his connections with opinion-makers and power brokers by holding parties at his Greenwich Village home and by regularly prowling the late-night club and restaurant scene at 21, Lindy's, Sardi's, the Stork Club, and other New York hot spots. He was even a peripheral member of the Algonquin Club—the famous group of writers and artists who gathered at the Algonquin Hotel.[6] His celebrity only grew during the 1930s. Harold Ross, the founder of *The New Yorker*, underscored Ernst's fame in a facetious note to Ernst from a Florida hotel where, presumably, Ross was on vacation. Attaching page one of the *Herald Tribune,* which cited Ernst's announcement that the New York City taxi strike he had mediated was over, Ross's note speaks to Ernst's omnipresence: "Christ, stop haunting me."[7]

But the apex of Ernst's fame came in 1944, when *Life* magazine published a long article on Ernst, complete with photographs of Ernst and his family. Ernst was initially delighted when *Life* approached him, and in his breezy way, feigned modesty. "I know that your boys are out around town getting the dirt on Ernst," he wrote to publisher Roy Larsen. "Can't I persuade you that there is no story in that guy?" Ernst then hinted, not so subtly, that he hoped *Life* would provide favorable coverage—if not for him, then for the sake of Ernst's causes: "You must know that I am thick-skinned and can dish it out and can take it. I am immodest enough, however, to feel that the little I can do toward my kind of a better world can be thwarted by glaring publicity. As far as I am personally concerned, disclosure of my worst follies—and they are legion—won't bother me."[8] Larsen duly flattered Ernst. "How can you expect to be important and, at the same time, anonymous? . . . how can you believe that you are not a most interesting person for the press to tell readers about?"[9] Ernst might have expected favorable coverage, given that he had defended Larsen in 1938 for the *Birth of a Baby* case and helped provide his magazine with the reputation of a staunch defender both of free speech and of promoting public health issues. Still, even given any expectation of loyalty, Ernst's concern about "glaring publicity" shows him to be unusually jittery, despite his unquestionable love of the limelight. Yale law professor Fred Rodell, whom *Life* had hired to write the article, reassured Ernst that "since most of what I know of you is decidedly all to the good, most of what I write of you will conform to that judgment."[10]

**Figure 7.1. Morris Ernst with Morris Watson after the Supreme Court ruled in favor of** *Watson v. Associated Press.*

Rodell was likely telling the truth. On paper, after all, the two men seemed to have plenty in common. To begin, both men were Jewish. Born Alfred M. Roedelheim in 1907 in Philadelphia, Rodell changed his name in 1928.[11] Both Rodell and Ernst were raised in assimilated households, and both families enjoyed periods of financial security. Rodell's parents divorced when he was four years old and he avoided his father once he turned sixteen; like Ernst, his relationship with his father was strained.[12] After attending Haverford College, Rodell studied abroad in England—a country Ernst adored and visited frequently. In 1928, Rodell entered law school at Yale, where he studied under the future Supreme Court judge Felix Frankfurter, with whom Ernst was a regular correspondent. Once he earned his law degree, Rodell worked as a special advisor to the governor of Pennsylvania, Gifford Pinchot; this was the same type of role that Ernst himself had played so frequently in New York politics.[13] As a Yale professor, Rodell eventually became a younger member of the Legal Realist movement. Ernst's former associate, Jerome Frank, was one of the prime players in this movement, and Ernst himself was a proponent of this philosophy in action, if not in words. In 1933 he famously worked to delay the trial of *Ulysses* to ensure that a specific judge, whom he knew would be swayed by critics' praise of the novel, would hear his case.[14] In other words, Ernst and Rodell agreed, as Frank had once written, that cases could be decided by what a particular judge had for breakfast that morning.[15]

As a legal realist, and a nonconformist, Rodell even discussed the law in similar terms as Ernst. In his 1938 work, *Woe Unto You, Lawyers!*, Rodell called the law "a racket," called lawyers "hocus-pocus artists" and argued that the country should "do away entirely with both the magicians and their magic."[16] Three years earlier, Ernst too had called the law "a racket" during a radio broadcast. He had taken lessons as a magician in the 1920s and discussed the similarities between magicians and lawyers in his 1968 memoir, *A Love Affair With the Law*. Both men were thus liberal, Jewish lawyers who presented themselves as insiders who were eager to demonstrate to the world that the legal profession, like the fabled emperor, had no clothes. Was Rodell's article on Ernst flattering? For Rodell, a man who proudly publicized the fact that he had never joined the Bar Association, who spoke disparagingly of lawyers and who suggested that the legal system be effectively abolished, even his subtitle for the *Life* article—"New York's Unlawyerlike Liberal Lawyer"—reveals that to an important degree, Rodell admired Ernst. To be "unlawyerlike" and liberal, in Rodell's eyes, was a plus.

Politically, however, Rodell was to the left of Ernst. When the two men met for dinner, they inevitably argued over politics. As a staunch liberal who doubted the policies of the Roosevelt administration, Rodell inevitably clashed with the comparatively politically moderate Ernst. "I was certainly intrigued by you," Ernst wrote Rodell the next day. "Even though you and I disagree with FDR on many issues, I cannot understand why you should be trying to embarrass him when you can do so much worse and see no hope of doing better." Rodell, in turn, responded that his problem with Roosevelt was that "the progressive cause is harmed even more by weak men of good will than by out and out bastards. You can fight the latter so much more easily and,

I believe, effectively."[17] It is not clear whether Rodell meant that Roosevelt was a weak man or a bastard. Either way, he was insulting Ernst's hero and, perhaps inadvertently, Ernst himself.

In a postscript to his letter, Ernst offered Rodell some free legal advice: "I should think that your friend, who is troubled with excessive alimony, is not without some relief. . . . If I can see the agreement and decree, I might have a bright idea as to procedure."[18] The "friend" he had offered to help, Ernst later complained bitterly, was Rodell himself. Rodell had divorced his first wife, Geraldine Watt, several years earlier.[19] After the issue was published, Ernst wrote *Life*'s counsel and made a point of mentioning Rodell's supposed request for help. "Incidentally, you will be interested to know that while Rodell had his knife out for me, and told me as much, he asked me to help him professionally in his own personal matrimonial matters," Ernst wrote. "At the time I was bewildered and do not know whether this was a frame-up or a bribe. I did, however, do some work in the matter because I thought he was needlessly bedeviled by life and that he could be helped, and I wrote him a line to that effect."[20]

If Ernst had hoped that a generous offer of legal advice for Rodell's personal problems might lead to a favorable portrait in *Life*, he was sorely disappointed. Rodell hailed Ernst's successes and included the obligatory greatest hits list: Ernst's defense of *Ulysses*, his work on civil rights, his association with celebrities and politicians, and so forth. But Rodell's portrait was no hagiography, and in fact some of Rodell's comments were a direct attack on Ernst's masculinity. In citing Ernst's intellectual influences, Rodell likened Ernst's adoration for Supreme Court Justice Louis Brandeis to "that of a small boy for his favorite baseball hero."[21] And though Rodell admired the work Ernst had done in civil liberties, he slighted Ernst's relationship with Roosevelt. Ernst was now visiting the White House monthly, he wrote, and pointed out that Ernst had not written a book since 1940 and had not argued a "headlined" civil liberties case in quite some time—presumably because he was focusing more energy on Roosevelt. Worst of all was Rodell's remark that Ernst was "a court jester—and today one of the President's favorites."[22] In this depiction, then, Ernst's successes were devalued by his boyish, immature behavior.

Despite such disparaging remarks, from a historical perspective—especially in light of Rodell's cutting remarks about lawyers in *Woe Unto You, Lawyer!*—the *Life* article as a whole reads as a fair and ultimately favorable portrait of Ernst. Rodell's conclusion was certainly positive. "His many diverse achievements," wrote Rodell, "add up to a substantial contribution to the public good. These, plus his generosity with his talents (many of his crusading cases are handled without a fee), should give him a solid inner satisfaction."[23] One legal historian actually cited the *Life* article as evidence that Rodell, despite his disdain of lawyers, occasionally did write positive essays about them.[24] Contemporaries generally viewed the coverage in a favorable light as well. In fact, in the week following publication, Ernst received numerous letters of congratulations on the article. Harold Young, the assistant to Vice President Henry Wallace, even joked that Ernst himself had ghostwritten the *Life* article: "You will be interested in knowing that I read the article in LIFE MAGAZINE written by Morris L. Ernst, about Morris L. Ernst, boosting Morris L. Ernst, and coyly admitting that Morris L. Ernst is a great citizen, a great sailor, a great farmer, a great lawyer, a great wit, and a very modest man."[25]

Young's intimation that Ernst had orchestrated the *Life* portrait is understandable. Ernst had, after all, enjoyed a long and fruitful relationship with the press. His clients and friends—which, in Ernst's case, were very frequently interchangeable categories—included opinion-makers like Broun and Winchell and critics such as Lippmann; the journalists Dorothy Thompson, Drew Pearson, and William L. Shirer; *New Yorker* writer E. B. White; the publisher of the *New York Times*, Arthur Hays Sulzberger; and *New York Herald Tribune* publisher Helen Reid. In addition, Ernst himself had written or dictated numerous articles to newspapers and magazines, even assuming a pseudonym, "Malachi Forsyte," for the *New York Post* in the 1930s, then bragging about his stunt in his books and to friends like Frankfurter.[26] Given his close ties to the press, the generally favorable coverage he had enjoyed for years in magazines such as *Scribner's*, and the positive reviews of his many books, Ernst may have indeed hoped for a hagiography—especially given the fact that he had won *Life* publicity and credibility in the 1938 "Birth of a Baby" case.

Though most of the letters Ernst received in response to the *Life* article were extremely positive, Ernst was so hurt and angry by the piece that he wrote a letter of complaint to *Life*'s publisher and addressed his former client as "Mr. Larsen—(formally known to me as Roy)."[27] According to Ernst, there were a "frightening number" of factual errors in the "anti-Roosevelt" piece.[28] For instance, contrary to Rodell's assertions, Ernst complained, "I have never had a pair of trunks that were other than one single color."[29] And despite Rodell's claim that Ernst's wife was often ill on his sailing trips, Ernst wrote that Maggie was seasick only once in her life.[30] Even Ernst recognized that he was pulling at straws, concluding his letter by saying, "Isn't it funny how the little things in life prick?"[31]

But Ernst found nothing funny about the article; in fact, he was so upset that two months later, he told *Life*'s counsel that the article was libelous and, in an eerie foreshadowing of the McCarthy era, claimed that *Life's* "dirty work" demonstrated that the company was infested with communists. "Is Life Magazine so innocent as to really play ball with the commies, or is it true, as

I am generally informed, that the Communists have planted in strategic positions in Life various minor employees to do some dirty work?"[32] In another letter, Ernst gossiped about Rodell's ethnicity. In doing so, Ernst suggested that one reason Rodell wrote a negative article was that he was a self-hating Jew. "I tried my best to prevent Life from writing this piece," Ernst wrote. "I knew that they had assigned a man who was a bitter anti-Roosevelt and who had changed his name because he was ashamed of being a Jew. But these are the things that one only whispers about."[33]

Two points in particular seemed to "prick" Ernst especially hard. First, Ernst was unhappy with Rodell's description of Ernst's father. As Ernst saw it, Rodell had claimed that Ernst's father had been wealthy and that Ernst had worked for him. To Ernst's thinking, Rodell was implying that Ernst was born with a silver spoon in his mouth. Ernst wrote that he had never had any business with his father or grandfather, and that his father had not been rich. "My father lost every nickel he ever had," he wrote. "I wish your statement were the truth."[34] In reality, Rodell wrote that Carl Ernst arrived in Uniontown, Alabama, "with a mattress, a spoon and an address tag around his neck," thus suggesting that the family was not born into money.[35] But Rodell's other suggestion—that Carl Ernst's family had enjoyed some financial success—was partially true. Whatever losses Carl Ernst himself suffered in his business dealings, the family had enough money to send Morris Ernst to private school, to summer camp in New Hampshire, and to Williams College; meanwhile Carl could afford to send his wife, Sarah, to the best health resorts in Europe.[36] By contemporary standards, the family *was* wealthy for some portion of Ernst's childhood. Though the Ernst family fortunes changed, forcing Morris Ernst to work full-time while taking night classes to get his law degree, Rodell was ultimately correct. Ernst, however, read malice in Rodell's comments. Such an image, Ernst perhaps believed, would undermine Ernst's credibility as a self-made man.

Second, Rodell claimed that Ernst's "mild and middle-age tendency" was to goose women. One male friend of Ernst's immediately telegrammed Ernst to facetiously protest this "libelous" denigration of Ernst's manliness. Ernst's "bottom-pinching," his friend insisted, was anything but mild:

> YOUR BOTTOM-PINCHING WAS DESCRIBED AS A "MILD AND MIDDLE-AGED TENDENCY." THAT'S A LIBELOUS ASPERSION ON YOUR BOTTOM-PINCHING . . . I'LL BE GLAD TO MOBILIZE THE PLAINTIFF'S WITNESSES, AND MARCH THEM INTO COURT IN COLUMNS, EIGHT ABREAST, TO OFFER THEIR EXPERIENCE AND LACERATED PERSONS AS EVIDENCE THAT HIS BOTTOM-PINCHING IS ABOUT AS "MILD AND MIDDLE-AGED" AS FERDINAND THE BULL WAS AFTER HE WAS BEE-STUNG.[37]

Whether or not his friend ever witnessed the aforementioned bottom-pinching, he clearly believed Ernst was capable of it. Ernst himself provided an intriguing and curious refutation to Larsen: "I have never pinched a bottom in my life. My sphere of influence, if any, is just the reverse."[38] By "reverse," Ernst might have meant that his "sphere of influence" was women's brains, breasts, or even their genitals.[39] Regardless of whether Ernst actually goosed women, that image of him had the potential of undermining his credibility as a modern, progressive man. But as evident from correspondence with Walter Winchell, together with a friend's poetic account of how Ernst "stopped to ogle" his associate, Harriet Pilpel, as well as Rodell's article, the above telegram, and the recollections of Ernst's former associate, Arthur Joel Katz, all suggest that Ernst was, indeed, a womanizer.[40] Ernst himself contributed to this growing reputation with joking insinuations in his private writings. "I wonder if your wife will remember me," Ernst wrote Felix Frankfurter. "I made some very lovely gentle passes at her one evening at Cambridge. She probably did not suspect anything."[41] In 1939, Ernst wrote and edited *The Nantucket Sun,* a homemade Ernst family newsletter. In the *Sun*'s jokey advertisements, Ernst portrayed himself as a flirt and a philanderer:

> ADVT-PERSONAL. MORRIS DARLING—Of course I want you to teach me how to float. Look for me at 9 p.m. – Geraldine
>
> ADVT-PERSONAL. GERALDINE-You had better mind your own damned business. –Maggie Samuels
>
> ADVT-PERSONAL. GERALDINE-Advise postponing engagement. You see how it is!-Morris[42]

But of course these were jokes, and Rodell's descriptions of Ernst's behavior were not meant in jest. Larsen, who found Rodell's article "delightful," responded to Ernst's protestations by pointing out that Ernst's inner circle had provided Rodell with the very details that Ernst found offensive: "you would be surprised to find how many of these 'inaccuracies' came from people very close to you as their best and friendly understanding of the various matters concerned," Larsen wrote. Then Larsen suggested that Ernst was a bit paranoid, since Larsen personally found nothing wrong with the article: "Maybe I just don't do enough reading between the lines."[43]

One person who had read between the lines was the famous novelist Edna Ferber, one of Ernst's closest friends. In her autobiography, Ferber had spoken glowingly of her friend, whom she often addressed as "Morrie," and she later wrote a blurb to an Ernst memoir that described him as "a gay and cerebral man." In a letter to another friend that she also sent to Ernst, she labeled the *Life* piece "a shocking thing, deliberate, destructive, vicious." Like Ernst, Ferber envisioned the article as "a knife into Roosevelt," but she dedicated most of the letter to praising her friend. "Morris Ernst is a really good man who has lived with integrity, courage, and industry; who has unselfishly fought for the rights of his fellow men; whose compassion is limitless, whose sense of justice is profound." Her one concession: Ernst "has some rather boyish traits," though those behaviors, she explained, "serve to make him more human."[44]

Those boyish traits—a certain glee for publicity, an excitement about meeting new people, a profound interest in everything from woodcarving to wildlife—hint at Ernst's slow, forced departure from power and celebrity. His boyishness, which many had found endearing, could also make Ernst an object of ridicule. The image Rodell painted of Ernst as a little boy apparently stuck. In 1952, after meeting with Ernst, FBI agent L. B. Nichols included details of the meeting that could only serve to disparage Ernst. "Ernst had just had a visit with the President who gave him one of the new plastic Rite Point lighters which had the President's picture in the fuel tank," Nichols wrote. "He was like a little boy."[45] Even in 1962, when Ernst was in his seventies, one friend described Ernst as a "perennially young angry man."[46] It is telling that Ernst himself joked that he hadn't fully developed, and as evidence cited his personal and professional loyalties, saying in 1975, "I'm a case of arrested development—the same law firm, the same city, the same wife—who could say I was daring?"[47]

It is ironic that during that last year of his life, Ernst may have unwittingly put his finger on the cause of his loss of influence and recognition. Before World War II, Ernst *was* daring: he had defended very controversial free speech cases relating to sexuality, and he had done so in innovative ways. After the war, however, Ernst tried to kindle relationships with an FBI director and, later, a Caribbean dictator. His joke on himself here—that for a twentieth-century man, a long-term dedication to one's wife and career is boring—may suggest that Ernst knew on some level that his "arrested development," or his inability to change with the times, ultimately cut him out of the recognition he sought. And, as a final irony, though by every account, Morris and Margaret Ernst clearly loved one another, and though their marriage lasted until Margaret's death, he would in fact have amorous relationships with other women—and, according to family lore, so would she.[48]

Beyond his anti-communist stance, which went above and beyond the usual liberal support for democracy and into fanboy territory, Ernst's interactions with women increasingly seemed to come into conflict with the pro-feminist (or, at least, pro-woman) image he had projected to the general public. In 1938, his friend, the scenic designer Lee Simonson, was moved to commemorate Ernst's attentions to the women in Ernst's office:

> When Morris got through giving Hague hell
>
> He stopped to ogle Harriet Pilpel
>
> And Harriet, giving him the glad eye,
>
> (You guessed it) said, "Boy, you're a swell guy."[49]

Hiring and mentoring Harriet Pilpel, who became an outstanding attorney in her own right, was proof that Ernst put his money where his mouth was, as he had persuaded his partners to hire her by promising that he'd personally pay out her salary if she didn't earn her own way. Pilpel herself recalled that when Ernst had brought her into the firm in 1936, she had asked for $30 per week, because that was the same amount the men in her class were making. Ernst's response, according to Pilpel: "If the men are getting it, then you should get it too, absolutely."[50] But Simonson's poem, together with Winchell's letter, presents an image of Ernst that he never publicly challenged: despite all of his work to further women's causes, and his public stances on allowing women to serve as jurors and lawyers, he was a womanizer and a documented rump pincher.

Ernst's behavior, however, took a back seat to his incredible stretch of important achievements in the 1930s and 1940s. In addition to his landmark victory in the *Ulysses* case, Ernst could boast triumphs not just in the *Birth of a Baby* trial, but in freeing Marie Stopes' *Contraception* (1930) and *Married Love* (1932); and defending several other authors. In the late 1930s, he burnished his progressive bona fides by representing the labor union in its fight against Jersey City Mayor Frank Hague, who had denied the CIO the right to publicly assemble. Between 1930 and 1949, he wrote or co-wrote a dozen books, on subjects as wide ranging as libel and slander; the monopolization of the media; how oversized businesses and governments may threaten democracy; and sexuality. At the same time, he published two books which largely told the story of his life, both personal and professional, and reflected his myriad interests, both legal and non-legal: *The Best Is Yet* (1945) and *So Far, So Good (*1948). These somewhat stream-of-consciousness memoirs told of his life and family, and his many interests: woodworking, sailing, bowling, with plenty of famous politicians and celebrities sprinkled through.

He published numerous articles, too, in large-circulation magazines, like *The New Yorker, Harper's,* and *Variety,* but also in law journals and newspapers. Ernst had so many stories to tell (and opinions to debate), and he was in great demand as a speaker, both on the radio and at women's clubs and colleges.

The general public, it seemed, couldn't get enough of Ernst, and those who wrote about him increasingly referred to him as "famous." His close relationship to reporters helped, too. As just one example, Walter Winchell, the powerful columnist and commentator and gossipmonger devoted both column space and airtime to promoting Ernst. That relationship was clearly symbiotic. In 1938, Winchell, who both Ernst's client and his friend, wrote a "Dear Morris" letter to claim that the selfsame letter "mentions that I am supposed to get an item from you more than once a year. You give me an item, that I can use, once a year and I'll introduce you to some very pretty white girls."[51] This tit-for-tat relationship continued into at least the 1950s. In 1945, Ernst sent Winchell a telegram thanking him for promoting his memoirs . . . and asking him to do so again: "Your boost on the radio of THE BEST IS YET emptied the bookstores of all the books. At long last there are some books in the bookstores. If you feel free to give it another push I would be truly grateful."[52] In an undated letter, Winchell responded: "I will plug the book, of course. I'm glad its a hit [*sic*]. I wish you would keep me in mind more with stuff. I hope you are convinced that I kept you in mind but big! W.W."[53] In these years, Ernst was already getting known for name-dropping—part of his exhibitionist strategy. It is easy to imagine that, in fact, Ernst was providing Winchell with information (or "items"), the reporting of which benefited both men, as it delighted Ernst to get his name in the newspaper. This habit of gossiping—or informing—would continue into the Cold War, when Ernst acted as an informant to J. Edgar Hoover's FBI. In fact, the three men were often spotted together at the Stork Club's "Cub Room," at Winchell's table.[54]

After the death of Franklin D. Roosevelt, whom Ernst occasionally advised and frequently promoted as an intimate friend, Ernst looked to Hoover as another powerful insider. The closer Ernst tried to get to the FBI, the less in step he was with the general public's interest in civil liberties. Whereas his earlier work highlighted his dedication to progressive social issues and his willingness to challenge the establishment, he now allocated more and more effort to defending the existing power structure. Though Ernst exchanged some 300 letters with Hoover, the FBI director mistrusted him, and the FBI agents who served as Ernst's contacts came to belittle Ernst and mocked his lack of maturity. Ernst's insatiable thirst for access and influence ultimately rendered him impotent.

## SISSY COMMUNISTS, "PENIS ENVY," AND BLIND ADVOCACY FOR THE FBI

Ernst faced a conundrum that many liberals faced during the early Cold War era: he was decidedly anti-communist, but were he to criticize American institutions, he risked being labeled *as* a communist. Those concerns were justified. Ernst had, in fact, been accused of being a communist in the 1930s, and the political identity of American Jews came under particular scrutiny during the first decade of the Cold War. By 1950, the American Jewish community had adopted what Edward Shapiro calls a "siege mentality" and sought out signs of a coming pogrom.[55] In response to both social and institutional anti-Semitism, Jews learned to view their Cold War world with extreme vigilance. Although public surveys had suggested that anti-Semitism in postwar America was on the wane, Jews were unable to relax their guard. Jews only had to think back to the anti-Semitic diatribes of radio demagogue Father Charles E. Coughlin in the 1930s, to the rise of Nazism in Germany, and to the tragic stories of concentration camp victims. Lest they forget, Jewish leaders reminded American Jews repeatedly about the hostility of non-Jews and the past evidence of anti-Semitism, even warning that the apparent decline of anti-Semitism in the late 1940s was a camouflage for anti-Semites searching for new ways to spread their hate.[56] Many Jewish Americans felt that they were being suspiciously eyed by anti-Semites concealing themselves as anti-communists.[57] In recalling the era, Arnold Forster, who was then the general counsel to the Anti-Defamation League, said that "Jews . . . were automatically suspect," and recalled that "the general mood was that the people felt if you scratch a Jew, you can find a Communist."[58] During the early Cold War, anti-Semites exploited this perception in order to slur prominent Jews. In 1950, for instance, hate groups attempted to prevent the appointment of Anna Rosenberg as assistant secretary of defense by suggesting that she had links to communist organizations. Eventually, the U.S. Congress approved Rosenberg, but only after the American Jewish Committee and the Anti-Defamation League exposed her accusers' anti-Semitic background.[59]

This had a more generally political aspect as well. In light of changing post–World War II attitudes toward gender and masculinity, this reinterpretation of Ernst's boyishness is understandable. Prior to the Cold War, Ernst's enthusiasm for new ideas and his excitement about publicity must have seemed refreshing. After World War II, however, an intense culture of conformity, which emerged from anxieties about military and psychological threats from communism, rendered this performance dated.[60] The threat of communism "put a new premium on hard masculine toughness and rendered anything less than that soft, timid, feminine, and as such a real or potential threat to the security of the nation."[61] Though there were many creative and iconoclastic figures who emerged out of the early Cold War and gained followings—the writers of the so-called Beat Generation come immediately to mind—the culture of consensus may have made outspokenness such as Ernst's seem oddly childish, rather than boldly youthful.

While World War II raged on, however, Ernst's brand of wit and enthusiasm was certainly being welcomed in the popular restaurants and nightclubs, in the media, and even in the White House, where an idea man like him was recognized for his efforts. Franklin D. Roosevelt, whom Ernst had first counseled when Roosevelt was governor of New York, encouraged Ernst's advice and his visits to the White House during his presidency, and Ernst capitalized on his relationship with FDR. In his autobiographies, Ernst wrote affectionately about his experiences with the president. Ernst frequently offered FDR what Ernst called "tidbits," which were ideas, both brilliant and silly, for improving America, and the president encouraged Ernst to keep the tidbits coming. "I love the 'tidbits,'" Roosevelt wrote Ernst in April 1943; "be sure to keep them up."[62] Sometimes Ernst's tidbits directly influenced Roosevelt's policies. For instance, in one such memo, Ernst persuaded Roosevelt that postal rates unfairly discriminated against literature. According to Ernst, to make his case, he sent two separate packages of equal weight to the White House: one contained a two-pound Bible, and the other contained two pounds of the raciest pornography he could get his hands on.[63] Was it fair, Ernst asked, that the Bible cost more to send?[64] There is no further record of the whereabouts of either package. The story Ernst told differed somewhat from the version described by Rodell in *Life* (Rodell reported that the second package contained three sex booklets) but whatever the contents, Roosevelt changed the postal rates, and Ernst told the story to further expand his reputation as an intimate of the president.[65]

While Samuel Walker rightly points out that Ernst "exaggerated" his influence on Roosevelt, historian Richard W. Steele notes that Ernst did, in fact, serve as an important conduit of information between the president and the New York mainstream politicians and journalists:

> Ernst was well connected in New York and Washington society, and was a mine of gossip, rumour [*sic*], and stories of the sort Roosevelt prized. Much of this he collected at his justly famous parties. . . . Ernst visited the White House frequently during the war, supplementing these visits with occasional written tips on impending political problems. No tidbit, no matter how bizarre, went without a personal response and follow-up by the President.[66]

Ernst rewarded Roosevelt's encouragement with blind loyalty. Ernst argued in favor of Roosevelt's policies at his dinner parties, at clubs, and on the radio. As the general co-counsel for the ACLU, Ernst was part of a coalition that supported Roosevelt's Japanese internment policy.[67] And, with Roosevelt's support, Ernst drew up a proposal to change Internal Revenue Service regulations so that anti-Roosevelt factions and communists would be forced to reveal the names of all directors and members. While Ernst's recommendations were never implemented, his dedication to the president, his talent for brainstorming, and his gung-ho boyishness ultimately fit the character of an administration tackling war and economic depression.[68]

With the death of Roosevelt, Ernst focused on ingratiating himself with other power brokers. Ernst attempted to act as an advisor to the new president, Harry S. Truman. His main contribution to the Truman administration related to civil rights, a subject dear to Ernst's heart. In 1931, Ernst had worked with James Weldon Johnson, author of *Autobiography of an Ex-Colored Man*, Lewis Gannett of the *Herald Tribune* and others on a civil rights program.[69] His progressive credentials and past legal work on civil rights landed Ernst a position on a blue-ribbon committee in Truman's White House in 1947.[70] Though he would continue to write to the White House over the course of the next decades, however, he never again had the proximity to the Oval Office that he had enjoyed and publicized during World War II.[71]

But in J. Edgar Hoover, Ernst found a new, powerful Washington relationship he could promote. Under Roosevelt, Ernst had first worked with Hoover on what Richard W. Steele describes as "countersubversive activities of an undisclosed nature."[72] The relationship between Hoover and Ernst was clearly desirable to both; from 1939 to 1964, the two men exchanged over 300 letters.[73] Harrison Salisbury, who reported on these letters in 1984, wrote that the basic feature of the exchange between Ernst and Hoover over the course of three decades is "the secret, unauthorized sharing of letters from third parties."[74] After the war, Ernst wooed Hoover with flattery and information. Calling himself "Hoover's personal attorney"—which, as Walker points out, was another exaggeration—Ernst became perhaps Hoover's greatest public cheerleader. As Salisbury documented in a famous 1984 article for *The Nation*, the relationship between Ernst and Hoover was, to an extent, symbiotic. Ernst used his position as general co-counsel of the ACLU to glean information about clients, which he then passed onto the FBI. In addition, he wrote several articles and co-wrote a book which lauded the FBI generally and its director specifically. "On balance," wrote Salisbury, "it seems clear that Ernst's greatest value to the Bureau was as a publicist, a kind of Good Housekeeping seal of approval."[75]

The greatest value of this relationship to Ernst was that it enabled him to flaunt his proximity to power. But in the process, Ernst disregarded the very elements of his exhibitionist strategy which had brought him fame and recognition in the first place. As an FBI booster, Ernst could no longer persuasively depict himself as a modern man who was in step with the general public's interest in civil liberties. His suggestions, years before, that the legal profession was a "racket" and that he was on the side of the common man would no longer ring true once he became the FBI's biggest cheerleader. Whereas before he highlighted his eagerness to challenge power, his dedication to progressive social issues, and his sexual expertise, he ceased defending the kinds of cases that amplified these features to the public. Furthermore, to an important extent, Ernst had abandoned the integrity behind his actions. As much as he might have dropped names before the war, his exhibitionism had usually been entwined with the purity of his causes. After the 1940s, he neglected this feature of the script. "He protected the FBI whenever possible," writes Roger K. Newman, "and he alerted the FBI to antibureau sentiments among ACLU members and to their plans to condemn it. While he may not have given specific names, he did pass confidential ACLU material to the FBI."[76] Newman's findings suggest that Ernst's integrity was second to his dedication to Hoover and anti-communism. "His relationship with Hoover compromised his law practice," Newman argues, since Ernst "would not sue Red Channels magazine for possibly libelous comments it made about one of his clients, journalist William L. Shirer."[77] Ernst, as Curt Gentry described it, brought a pro-FBI atmosphere to the ACLU, having "effectively neutralized criticism of the FBI" within their organization.[78]

Ernst, it should be reiterated, had consistently opposed communism, and he had associated it with weakness and femininity long before the Cold War made liberal anti-communism *de rigueur*. In the 1920s and 1930s, Ernst had worked with communists and even invited them to his home for dinner parties, and his association with communists imbued him with a sense of manly superiority. Throughout his life, he loved to recall how his "good friend," the author and socialist H. G. Wells, asked to meet a real, live American Communist. Ernst obliged by introducing Wells to American Communist Party leader Earl Browder at a dinner party. The next morning, Ernst gleefully reported, Ernst asked his son Roger what he thought of Earl Browder. "He's a sissy!" exclaimed Roger.[79] This oft-told tale reveals much about Ernst. Though he promoted progressive views about women in his roles as author, speaker, and lawyer, and though he personally benefited from the more flexible image of masculinity he presented in the courtroom and in many of his writings, his prejudice against communists displaced that modern attitude toward gender identity. It is even more telling that he crafted these prejudices into a pseudo-psychological explanation for communist behavior. He surmised, in 1948, "that the factor of impotence is higher among American communists than among the general population. The women, suffering from penis envy, want to be men, and the men want to be bossed around by someone who can relieve them of the necessity and pain of making decisions. They need a Papa—omnipotent and always at hand."[80]

These assumptions later had real consequences, and may have even contributed, albeit indirectly, to the 1953 execution of Julius and Ethel Rosenberg. In 1952, after the Rosenbergs had been convicted of giving atomic secrets to the Soviet Union, Eleanor Roosevelt suggested that family members consult with Ernst who was, she said, a great civil rights attorney.[81] Drawing on FBI reports, Ronald Radosh and Joyce Milton wrote that Ernst was delighted about the opportunity to defend the Rosenbergs—to help out the FBI. Radosh and Milton cite an FBI report of Ernst's comments on this exciting prospect: "this would be a terrific story," Ernst is reported to have declared, "and probably would be most helpful to the Bureau." During his sole meeting with the family, Ernst urged Julius Rosenberg's brother and sister to get Julius and Ethel to confess, and then lectured the family on the perils of communism. According to one FBI agent's account, Ernst later psychoanalyzed the Rosenbergs: "Julius is the slave and his wife, Ethel, the master." Though Ernst had no training in psychoanalysis, Rodell reported in 1944 that "one of Ernst's favorite hobbies is amateur psychoanalysis which he practices on friends and chance acquaintances."[82] In Ernst's evaluation, communists like Julius Rosenberg were usually wimpy and easily controlled. Ernst was apparently very convincing. Though Ernst had never actually met Julius or Ethel, Radosh and Milton believe that the FBI may have used his amateur, long-distance psychoanalysis of the Rosenbergs as justification for Ethel's execution.[83] Whatever fluidity Ernst had formally attributed to masculinity in the past, when it came to communists, Ernst clearly believed that gender stereotypes were fixed.

Ernst's hard stance distanced some liberals, and certainly made some friends anxious. To some extent, Hoover found Ernst useful in same way as Roosevelt had—as a promoter—but unlike Roosevelt, Hoover kept Ernst at arm's length. The driving part of Ernst's script—the exhibitionist in him—ultimately undermined his credibility. In Gentry's analysis, Hoover and Nichols were well aware of Ernst's need for celebrity and proximity to power. So they allowed him to suggest himself to be a kind of fixer behind the scenes and exploited Ernst's "very human weaknesses" for their own ends.[84] "Because of [Ernst]," Gentry explains, "for nearly twenty-five years the one organization in the American Left which had the resources, prestige, and independence to investigate and expose the many illegal acts committed by the FBI . . . chose not criticism or even silent acquiescence but blind advocacy."[85] Meanwhile, Ernst boasted about his relationship with Hoover, and while such exaggerations were endearing in the past, when it came to Hoover, these claims were not well taken. Hoover trusted neither Ernst nor the ACLU.[86] The more Ernst emphasized his influence on Hoover, the more Hoover kept Ernst out of the loop. By the mid-1950s, when Ernst actively helped whitewash murder accusations against the dictator Rafael Trujillo, Hoover was, for all practical purposes, done with him.[87] When the FBI cut off ties in 1964, Gentry writes, Ernst was "shattered."[88] And yet, Ernst would continue exaggerating his own influence. As late as 1971, Ernst assured a lawyer that he could get some information on a government mob informant, but that information, of course, never materialized.[89] On some level, this was magical thinking, and an odd perversion of Ernst's perception of himself as a "glandular optimist." Five decades earlier, when friends and clients approached Ernst with problems, he'd churn out scores of ideas and seemingly will them into solutions. This was part of his exhibitionism, a kind of "fake-it-'til-you-make-it" strategy. But as those friends and clients distanced themselves from Ernst's embrace of anti-democratic authority, the effectiveness of that exhibitionist strategy, along with his access to powerful colleagues who could help put such ideas into practice, steadily dissolved.

## NOTES

1. Morris L. Ernst, *A Love Affair With the Law: A Legal Sampler* (New York: The Macmillan Company, 1968), 149. See also "AP v Guild," *Time,* December 16, 1935.

2. See, for example, Russell B. Porter, "Hague Interview on Radicals Brings Contempt Charge," *New York Times* (June 18, 1938): 1.

3. Mayor Hague used a city ordinance to prohibit the CIO from holding meetings in Jersey City. Ernst and the ACLU ask the court for an injunction, which was granted. The case went to the U.S. Supreme Court, which upheld the injunction, ruled that Hague had violated the CIO's right to free speech, and established parks and streets as public forums protected under the First Amendment. Hague later became Ernst's client; as Rodell writes, "Ernst, after trouncing Hague in the Supreme Court, turned right around and accepted the mayor's shrewd invitation to help draft a restrictive yet constitutional soap-box-orator ordinance for Jersey City." See Rodell, "Morris Ernst," 97. For more on *Hague v. CIO.*, see McAlister Coleman, "Hague's Army Falls Back," *The Nation* (1938-11–26), vol. 147, issue 22, 557; and *Samuel Walker, In Defense of American Liberties: A History of the ACLU* (New York: Oxford University Press, 1990), 110–111.

4. Robert S. Allen and Drew Pearson, "The Washington Merry-Go-Around," *Capital Times* (Madison, Wisconsin), June 26, 1938, 4.

5. Anonymous, *The Smiling Corpse. Wherein G.K. Chesterton, S.S. Van Dine, Sax Rohmer and Dashiell Hammett Are Surprised to Find Themselves at a Murder* (New York: Farrar & Rinehart, 1935).

6. Dewitt Stetten, Jr., *How My Light Is Spent: The Memoirs of DeWitt Stetten, Jr.*, Office of NIH History, 1983, x-2. history.nih.gov/articles/DeWittStettenMemoirs.pdf. NIH.

7. H. W. Ross to Morris Ernst. The letter is undated, but the article is from February 1934. At the request of Fiorello LaGuardia, the Mayor of New York, Ernst had mediated an end to the city's tax strike. Box 127, MLE.

8. Morris Ernst to Roy Larsen, Jan 20, 1944, Box 128, MLE.

9. Roy Larsen to Morris Ernst, January 27, 1944, Box 128, MLE.

10. Fred Rodell to Morris Ernst, June 21, 1944, Box 128, MLE.

11. Michael H. Hoffheimer, "Rodell, Fred (1907–1980), legal educator and journalist," *American National Biography*, February 1, 2000, https://doi.org/10.1093/anb/9780198606697.article.1101128. Though some writers have spelled his birth name "Rodelheim," the *New York Times* obituary of Rodell's father and the Haverford collection of Rodell's papers spell it "Roedelheim." We know from the Haverford collection that Rodell still identified himself as "Roedelheim" as an undergraduate. Interestingly, some writers have claimed that Rodell's parents changed their family name when he was a child. Had it in fact been imposed on Rodell, rather than made by his own free will, the change in his name would have of course undermined Ernst's claim that Rodell was "ashamed" of his Jewishness. See G. Beth Packert, "The Relentless Realist: Fred Rodell's Life and Writings," *University of Illinois Law Review* (1984): 824n7; and Neil Duxbury, "In the Twilight of Legal Realism: Fred Rodell and the Limits of Legal Critique," *Oxford Journal of Legal Studies 11*, no. 3 (1991).

12. Ibid.

13. Ibid. Ernst had advised many governors and mayors, including Franklin D. Roosevelt, Herbert Lehman, and Fiorello LaGuardia of New York and Governor George Earle of Pennsylvania.

14. Marisa Anne Pagnattaro, "Carving a Literary Exception: The Obscenity Standard and Ulysses," *Twentieth-Century Literature* 47, no. 2 (Summer 2001), 227–278.

15. "Jurisprudence," *West's Encyclopedia of American Law*, second ed., edited by Shirelle Phelps and Jeffrey Lehman, 73–78. Vol. 6, Detroit, MI: Gale, 2005, *Gale eBooks*, https://link.gale.com/apps/doc/CX3437702502/GVRL?u=29002&sid=bookmark-GVRL&xid=3fc8f383.

16. Fred Rodell, *Woe Unto You, Lawyers!* (New York: Reynal & Hitchcock, 1939), 15, 239, 249.

17. Fred Rodell to Ernst, January 26, 1944, Box 128, MLE.

18. Morris Ernst to Fred Rodell, January 25, 1944, Box 128, MLE.

19. Hoffheimer, "Rodell, Fred."

20. Morris Ernst to Bruce Bromley, Esq., March 11, 1944, Box 128, MLE.

21. Rodell, "Morris Ernst," 102.

22. Ibid.

23. Ibid., 107.

24. Packert, "Relentless Realist," 836n138.

25. Harold Young to Morris Ernst, February 26, 1944, Box 128, MLE.

26. Morris Ernst to Felix Frankfurter, March 30, 1934, Box 127, MLE. One possible meaning of the pseudonym: "I'm Lacking Foresight."

27. Morris L. Ernst to Roy Larsen, February 18, 1944, Box 128, MLE.

28. Ibid.

29. Ibid.

30. Ibid.

31. Ibid.

32. Ernst to Bromley, March 11, 1944.

33. Morris Ernst to Harry Lissauer, March 1, 1944, Box 128, MLE. Lissauer was connected to the jewelry industry, and it is likely that the two men met back when Ernst was representing jewelers in the early 1920s.

34. Ernst to Larsen, February 18, 1944.

35. Rodell, "Morris Ernst," 100.

36. "Mrs. Carl Ernst Dead," *New York Times*, February 15, 1908, 14.

37. Ralph Hayes, Telegram to Morris Ernst, January 28, 1944, Box 128, MLE. Hayes' identity is not certain, though he may have been the secretary to Newton Baker, who was Secretary of War, in 1916. The book Hayes refers to is the classic children's story, *Ferdinand the Bull*, in which a mild-manner bull who enjoys sniffing flowers suddenly explodes into savage bucking after accidentally sitting on a bee.

38. Ernst to Larsen; Ibid.

39. One might be reminded, regrettably, of the 2005 recorded comments of future U.S. president Donald J. Trump: "And when you're a star they let you do it. You can do anything. Grab them by the pussy." Cited in Alex Shephard, "Donald Trump's way of hitting on women is to 'grab them by the p**sy,'" *New Republic,* October 7, 2016, https://newrepublic.com/article/137579/donald-trumps-way-hitting-women-grab-psy.

40. Arthur Joel Katz, email message to the author, July 20, 2005.

41. Morris Ernst to Felix Frankfurter, March 5, 1934, Box 127, MLE.

42. *The Nantucket Sun* (homemade newsletter), July 22, 1939, Box 171, MLE. "Maggie Samuels" was Margaret Ernst's maiden name.

43. Roy Larsen to Morris Ernst, February 29, 1944, Box 128, MLE.

44. Edna Ferber to Morris Ernst, March 6, 1944, Box 128, MLE.

45. Memorandum from L. B. Nichols to Clyde Tolson, January 23, 1952, Morris Ernst files, FBI. Tolson was the Associate Director of the FBI.

46. Richard Starnes. "The Very Earnest Ernst." *New York World-Telegram*, December 6, 1962, Box 564, MLE. Originally cited in John Paul Balz, "Fuel for the Fire: Law and Capitalism in the Birth Control Movements," Master's Thesis, The University of Texas at Austin, 2004, n13.

47. Stephen Hochberg, "Dedication to Morris Leopold Ernst," *New York Law Forum,* XX, no. 3 (Winter 1975).

48. According to one Ernst relative, family lore has it that Ernst's wife, Margaret, may have had an intimate relationship with Eleanor Roosevelt. Anonymous, personal interview by author, June 11, 2006.

49. Lee Simonson to Morris Ernst, June 16, 1938, Box 157, MLE. Simonson was an influential set designer and artist. See "Lee Simonson, Set Designer, 78; Theater Guild Co-Founder Dies," *New York Times*, January 24, 1967: 28. See n50 for more on Pilpel.

50. "General Counsel Harriet Pilpel," American Civil Liberties Union, no. 333, 1980, 4. Archives of Sexuality and Gender, link.gale.com/apps/doc/CWPMJR701377084/DSLAB?u=29002&sid=DSLAB&xid=f41e3134.

51. Walter Winchell to Morris Ernst, April 13, 1938, Box 123, MLE. For more on the powerful and influential Winchell, see Neal Gabler, *Winchell: Gossip, Power and the Culture of Celebrity* (New York: Knopf, 1994).

52. Morris Ernst to Walter Winchell, July 10, 1945, MLE, Box 477.

53. Walter Winchell to Morris Ernst, undated, MLE, Box 477. This letter was found together with the July 10, 1945 telegram from Ernst to Winchell.

54. Gentry, 233.

55. Edward S. Shapiro, *A Time for Healing: American Jewry since World War II*, The Jewish People in America series, Vol. V. (Baltimore: Johns Hopkins University Press, 1992), 29.

56. Ibid., 30–31. Shapiro cites Isaiah M. Minkoff, then the executive director of the National Community Relations Advisory Board, who in 1947 stated that anti-Semites were "involved in their own postwar reconversion, seeking for and experimenting with new avenues of attack, exploring the possibilities of exploiting new issues."

57. Certain anti-communists actually *were* anti-Semites (Congressman John E. Rankin, Sen. Jack B. Tenney, Sen. Patrick McCarran). Still, numerous anti-communists were not anti-Semitic, and numerous Jewish Americans (Leslie Fiedler, Irving Kristol, the staff at *Commentary*) were themselves outspoken anti-communists. For Jews and anti-Semites, see Howard M. Sachar, *A History of the Jews in America* (New York: Alfred A. Knopf, 1992); for communists and anti-communists, see Richard Pells, *The Liberal Mind in a Conservative Age: American Intellectuals in the 1940s and 1950s* (Middletown: Wesleyan University Press, 1989).

58. Cited in Shapiro, 35.

59. Sachar, *A History of the Jews in America,* 638–639.

60. For a good overview of Cold War culture, see Stephen J. Whitfield, *The Culture of the Cold War* (Baltimore: Johns Hopkins, 1992).

61. K. A. Cuordileone, *Manhood and American Political Culture in the Cold War* (Taylor & Francis Group, 2005), ProQuest Ebook Central, http://ebookcentral.proquest.com/lib/yale-ebooks/detail.action?docID=1075256.

62. Franklin D. Roosevelt to Morris L. Ernst, October 7, 1943, President Secretary's File, Box 132, Morris Ernst Folder, FDR. For more on these "tidbits," and their role in Ernst's interaction with FDR regarding the Holocaust, see Laurel Leff, "News of the Holocaust: Why FDR Didn't Tell and the Press Didn't Ask," *Hakirah: A Journal of Jewish and Ethnic Studies* (Vol. 2 2006): 31–61.

63. Ernst, *Love Affair With the Law*, 109.

64. Ibid.

65. Ibid.; Rodell, "Morris Ernst," 105.

66. Richard W. Steele, "The Pulse of the People: Franklin D. Roosevelt and the Gauging of American Public Opinion," *Journal of Contemporary History, 9*, no. 4 (1974): 201.

67. Walker, *In Defense of American Liberties*, 139.

68. Richard W. Steele, "Franklin D. Roosevelt and His Foreign Policy Critics," *Political Science Quarterly,* 94, no. 1 (1979): 24.

69. Walker, *In Defense of American Liberties*, 88–90.

70. Samuel Walker. "Ernst, Morris Leopold (1888–1976), attorney," *American National Biography*. Feb. 1, 2000, https://doi.org/10.1093/anb/9780198606697.article.1100982.

71. Ibid.

72. Steele, "Franklin D. Roosevelt," 24. Harrison E. Salisbury cites a June 1, 1940, letter from Ernst to FDR that documents Ernst's "countersubversion" work with Hoover. Salisbury suggests that this work grew out of an Ernst scheme to use the Internal Revenue Service to force disclosure of the members of subversive groups. FDR apparently like the idea, but the plan stalled in the Treasury Department. Harrison E. Salisbury, "The Strange Correspondence of Morris Ernst and John Edgar Hoover, 1939–1964," *The Nation,* December 1, 1984.

73. Salisbury, "The Strange Correspondence of Morris Ernst and John Edgar Hoover."

74. Ibid.

75. Ibid.

76. Roger K. Newman, "Morris Leopold Ernst," *Dictionary of American Biography*, New York: Charles Scribner's Sons, 1995, Gale in Context: U.S. History, https://link.gale.com/apps/doc/BT2310013962/UHIC?u=29002&sid=bookmark-UHIC&xid=29bdbed3.

77. Ibid.

78. Curt Gentry, *J. Edgar Hoover* (New York: W.W. Norton, 1991), 234.

79. Ernst, *Love Affair With the Law*, 147. The "good friend" comment comes from Hochberg, "Dedication to Morris Leopold Ernst."

80. Morris L. Ernst, *So Far So Good* (New York: Harper & Brothers, 1948), 63.

81. Cited in Salisbury, para. 74.

82. Rodell, "Morris Ernst," 106.

83. Cited in Alan M. Dershowitz, Review of *The Rosenberg File: A Search for the Truth*, by Ronald Radosh and Joyce Milton; *New York Times*, August 14, 1983. Dershowitz, pointing out that Radosh and Milton's charge is extremely grave, wonders aloud whether Ernst's actions might have actually been a strategy to help the Rosenbergs: "Ernst, who died in 1976, cannot respond to these serious charges of perfidy, the legal analogue of espionage and treason. It is, of course, possible that the F.B.I. memorandums do not accurately reflect his motivations or his precise words; possibly he was using unorthodox measures in a desperate effort to save the Rosenbergs' lives. Perhaps some rebuttal or explanation will be forthcoming from his legion of friends and admirers. If not, this revelation will require some reassessment of Ernst's important place in the history of American civil liberties." Though Ernst was frequently "unorthodox," it seems unlikely that he would attempt such a stunt with Hoover's FBI. In addition, Ernst's comment that his defense of the Rosenbergs "would make a terrific story," unfortunately, rings very true with Ernst's exhibitionism.

84. Gentry, 235.

85. Ibid., 236.

86. Ibid.

87. Handwritten comment by J. Edgar Hoover, Memorandum to Clyde Tolson from L. B. Nichols, July 11, 1957, FBI.

88. Gentry, 237.

89. Daniel Rezneck, telephone interview by the author, May 16, 2006. Along with Sam Dash (who would later prosecute the Watergate hearings), Rezneck was defending Carmine DeSapio, the former boss of the Tammany Hall political machine, against bribery and conspiracy charges. Rezneck and Dash hoped to damage the credibility of the government's witness. Ernst told Rezneck he could get FBI information that would expose the government's witness. Instead, he sent Rezneck a signed copy of his latest book. DeSapio was convicted and served two years in jail.

# Conclusion

## THE LEGAL EXHIBITIONIST

Morris Ernst was the consummate name-dropper and publicity hound, the confidant of movie stars and mayors, the brilliant Jewish man from the South who connected with the masses. Ernst's exhibitionist strategy served him extremely well for three decades, enabling him to present himself as a truly modern man. He gained fame and fortune and, perhaps most importantly, respect and recognition by turning his boyhood insecurities on their head and by presenting himself as a man of the people. He also played with the truth and exaggerated his influence, a trait that friends like Henry Wallace considered playful, even attractive, during the decades of his greatest fame. Until the end of the war, Ernst's outstanding work in civil liberties and free speech cases, his genius for using the media to promote himself and his causes, his uncanny ability to master a myriad of legal topics, his nonstop production of articles and books, and his daily contact with the country's cultural and political movers and shakers seemed to merit Morris Ernst the right to any exaggerations, name-dropping, and exhibitionism.

After World War II, perhaps due to his boyish enthusiasm or boredom, Ernst looked beyond his past sources of success for stimulation. With the publication of Kinsey's bestselling studies of the sexual life of the American man and woman, Ernst's own expertise of sexuality became common knowledge, even passé. He increasingly focused his talents and energy on battling communism. Unlike sex education, birth control, lesbianism, or pregnancy, anti-communism did not provide Ernst with the kind of theater he had mastered in the courtroom or the kind of influence he had enjoyed in the media. Though Ernst's friends and associates had tolerated Ernst's habit of inflating his influence during the 1930s and 1940s, and though Ernst aggressively flattered J. Edgar Hoover, the FBI director came to view Ernst as an irritant. In the late

1950s, perhaps in part to impress Hoover, Ernst accepted an enormous salary to produce a report defending Rafael Trujillo, the dictator of the Dominican Republic, after one of Trujillo's political enemies was disappeared in New York City. That report was largely seen as a whitewash, and Ernst was subsequently viewed as naïve at best and opportunistic at worst. Ernst's credibility, already shaken among some progressives by his unyielding anti-communist rhetoric and his avowed close relationship with Hoover, was so damaged that even Hoover wanted nothing more to do with him.

## "CHARACTER ASSASSINATION FOR A FEE"

Fred Rodell was the first to highlight the less attractive side to Ernst's personality for the public. Rodell had publicly identified Ernst's sense of inferiority and insecurity as early as 1944 in his *Life* profile of Ernst. "His most obvious surface characteristic," Rodell wrote, "is the constant mouthing of well-known names, the anxiety lest his listener not know in what select circles he moves. Here is clearly indicated some innate sense of insecurity, some feeling of inferiority turned inside out for self-protection."[1] Perhaps that take down of Ernst was a license for some of Ernst's colleagues to begin distancing themselves from him. More likely, as with President Roosevelt and Vice President Wallace, Rodell's comments simply confirmed what friends and associates already knew but found charming at the time. Yet the success stories Ernst told were mainly confined to the first three decades of his law career. Several of his many books and articles from the 1930s through the 1960s contain very similar anecdotes and war stories. Rodell, again, was the first to identify this trait publicly. In Rodell's harsh, yet accurate, review of *The Best is Yet,* Ernst's bestselling 1945 memoir, Rodell labels Ernst's stories "about his clever clashes with stupid censors" as "twice-told tales."[2] Rodell suggested that Ernst's exhibitionism, which Rodell reframed as Ernst's "less than modesty," was less than endearing. Citing Ernst's tendency to drop names, Rodell wrote that "[s]imilar instances of self-advertisement crowd Mr. Ernst's book." "[W]hen opened at random," Rodell criticized, the book "will reveal ten or fifteen 'I's' on almost every page."[3] Though the review is full of barbs, the most devastating attack on Ernst's credibility indirectly relates to Ernst's attempts to appeal to a general audience:

> [Ernst] makes the rather startling statement that the legal game is "truly non-competitive." His correlative claim that the law is utterly free of "the curse of advertising" may perhaps amuse certain bar members who have long unkindly commented that Mr. Ernst's own often unpaid but always highly publicized

> forays in the field of civil liberties have never perceptibly decreased his more lucrative practise [*sic*] nor kept his name unknown to potential clients.[4]

So long as Ernst associated with popular and controversial causes, such as civil liberties and censorship cases, he retained his appeal with the public, and his motives were overlooked. But in the above critique, Rodell indicates that Ernst was wrong about the very nature of the law, was disingenuous about his use of publicity, and had "long" been criticized by other lawyers. Put in other terms, by 1945, Ernst's use of exhibitionism was already being devalued by his colleagues. Though Ernst's talent and intellect were never in question, and though his work in free speech cases would always merit him respect, this strategy, and his very credibility, came under question as he increasingly associated himself with Hoover and anti-communism.

During the 1950s, Ernst also sought excitement and recognition in his personal life. Ernst was engaged in extramarital relationships, including one with the prominent psychoanalyst, Marie Jahoda.[5] The duration and extent of such affairs are unclear, but according to one of Ernst's relatives, Morris and Margaret had an "open marriage," an arrangement with which, apparently, Morris was much more enthusiastic than Maggie.[6] "Margaret had an affair, and Morris had multiple affairs. The Nantucket house was used for that."[7] In his books, Ernst had used Kinsey's research to push the idea that married men frequently had intercourse outside of marriage. Ernst wrote, for instance, that Kinsey had demonstrated that "30 to 45 per cent of married men have had extramarital relationships, and this percentage is in no way related to the number of broken marriages."[8] In other words, Ernst applied his wit, charisma, and expansive knowledge of sexuality to both personal and professional endeavors. Despite any such extramarital affairs, however, the couple was always a team, and Ernst was discreet about his other relationships. "Attractive to women (and attracted to them) he was, nevertheless, a family man," Salisbury wrote of Ernst.[9] Mary Batten, who lived down the hall from the Ernsts at 2 Fifth Avenue in New York, saw no evidence of any difficulty in their relationship. "It seemed to me that they had a really good working marriage," she wrote. "They complemented each other beautifully. Morris greatly respected her and told me how much she had influenced his interest in etymology. I got the impression that he loved her dearly."[10]

In January 1956, the couple appeared together on the nationally broadcast *Person to Person* television show. Edward R. Murrow, Morris Ernst's friend and client, interviewed him and Maggie Ernst for what would be Ernst's last wink of positive celebrity.[11] Murrow called Ernst one of America's "best known lawyers," and gave him a platform to promote Ernst's latest book, *Utopia 1976*, in which Ernst predicted what life would be like in 20 years. The 11-minute, commercial-free segment was pure fluff, and Murrow had

**Figure 8.1. In his beloved Nantucket. Photo by Arthur Griffin; date unknown.**

only praise for his lawyer. Murrow, whom both Morris and Maggie called "Ed," seemed unphased by some odd responses from Morris Ernst, perhaps because the segment was clearly scripted. For instance, when Murrow asked how he liked living in Washington Square, Ernst replied, "I think life is only good when you live less than 6 stories above the ground, because if you live above 6 stories, you haven't got your roots in our great country."[12] When

Murrow asked him, with a chuckle: "What are your credentials for peering into the future, you glandular optimist?" Ernst responded, "Well, I reread all of the utopians, and I got very irritated at the people who look with despair at our great republic. And I've had a love affair with this republic for over a half a century. And so I wanted to predict for my grandchildren at least what this country will be like."[13] Ernst's predictions of what life in the U.S. in 1976 were truly fantastical—all diseases would be cured ("there will only be one disease left: old age"); airlines would no longer use more gasoline ("either atomic energy or solar energy, or maybe ionic batteries"); certain utilities would be close to free ("energy for the home will come in so cheap that it won't pay to put a meter in for light and heat.") Notably, Ernst mentioned nothing about communism or the FBI. Prompted by Murrow, Ernst mentioned that he had correspondence from several presidents, including one framed letter from Roosevelt, that Ernst showed to the camera. When Murrow asked what he was focusing on now, Ernst replied that he wanted to defend "talent"—meaning artists and baseball players—against unfair taxation.[14]

Three months later, on March 12, 1956, Jesús de Galíndez, a Basque exile and intellectual, disappeared from the streets of New York after teaching a night class at Columbia University. Galíndez was set to publish a book that accused the leader of the Dominican Republic, General Rafael Trujillo, of horrific crimes, including at least 140 political assassinations, since taking power in 1930.[15] *Life* magazine, suggesting that he had been kidnapped, tracked Galíndez to the Dominican Republic, where it was thought that he had been murdered by Trujillo.[16] The prevailing theory: Galíndez was accosted at the entrance of a subway station; drugged, bandaged, and dragged into an ambulance; and then taken to a plane awaiting in Long Island and flown first to Florida, and then to the Dominican Republic, where he was assassinated. *Life* claimed that the Dominican Republic's counsel general in New York had enticed Gerald Murphy, a 23-year-old American pilot from Oregon "with bad eyesight" to fly someone Murphy thought was "a wealthy invalid" (i.e., Galíndez) to the Dominican Republic.[17] According to *Life*, after delivering Galíndez to the Dominican authorities, Murphy decided to stay in the Dominican Republic, where he secured a job with the Dominican Republic's national airline. Supposedly Murphy purchased a convertible and talked about his flight from Florida to the Dominican Republic. In December 1957, one day after Murphy had posted a newspaper advertisement to sell his "household goods," his abandoned car was found.[18] A Dominican pilot was charged with Murphy's murder, and was later found hanged in his jail cell, along with a suicide note. The State Department, Murphy's family, various Congressmen, and anti-Trujillo activists demanded an explanation from the Dominican government.[19] Trujillo's government hired the New York City publicist Sidney Baron to handle the negative backlash.[20] Baron, in turn, sought out Ernst to lead an investigation into Galíndez's disappearance.

Ernst agreed to a fact-finding mission to report on the disappearance. The *Village Voice* stated that the assignment of Ernst to the case was "unprecedented in the history of an independent country,"[21] and posited that the Dominican Republic's motive in restoring its reputation was financial: "It is reported the Dominican government took the surprising step of asking Mr. Ernst to investigate in an attempt to clear up a situation which had become disastrous financially to the island republic. As an aftermath of the Galíndez case becoming headline news early last year, there was a steady decline in revenues from American tourists who crossed the Caribbean island off their travel itineraries."[22] The newspaper continued, "Mr. Ernst is said to have exacted a promise of full cooperation from the Dominican government," but that "it is expected that he will face a very difficult task." Ernst's trump card? His proximity to power: "Mr. Ernst has the advantage, however, of close personal ties with FBI director J. Edgar Hoover. The government of the little republic is not cooperating with investigations now being carried on by the Departments of Justice and State, and the New York City Police Department."[23] The use of the passive voice and the reference to J. Edgar Hoover suggests that either Ernst himself or a loyal associate fed the details of the case to the newspaper's reporter. Perhaps Ernst had hoped his involvement would impress Hoover. But Hoover himself had washed his hands of Ernst. The FBI director never completely trusted Ernst, and by this point pegged Ernst as an opportunist. A few days before Sidney S. Baron and Co. publicly announced that it had hired Ernst to review allegations against the Dominican Government, Hoover wrote, in an internal report, "Ernst is always maneuvering—in his own interest."[24]

Ten months after Ernst took on the investigation, Baron published Ernst's report. Unsurprisingly, Ernst's main conclusions were, first, that none of the evidence supported any accusation connecting the Dominican Republic or any of its officials with the disappearance of Galíndez; and second, that "We find not a scintilla of evidence connecting Galíndez with Murphy's plane, N68100, on any flight of the plane."[25] The media widely panned this report. *Newsday* was typical. On the one hand, the newspaper recognized Ernst's qualities: the "dedicated liberal Morris Ernst," *Newsday* stated, was "a man of the utmost probity." But the report was a mistake: "We could wish that a lawyer who has in the past fought so vigilantly against censorship, for freedom of speech and every other cause held dear by liberals, had rejected this opportunity to investigate Trujillo's behavior." But *Newsday* concluded by voicing regret that this "fine liberal permitted himself to be mixed up with this particular odoriferous dictator."[26] Similarly, Robert G. Spivack of the *Daily Defender* praised the past achievements of Ernst before lamenting his work on behalf of Trujillo. "I have known Morris Ernst for a great many years," Spivack began. "He is an able attorney. He is an able debater. He has a good mind. . . . He has fought some good fights over the years; he has helped to keep the American Civil Liberties Union going during some of its shakier moments." But, Spivack continued, while Ernst argues that a client's crimes shouldn't "rub off" on that client's attorney, "[t]here is, of course, no law which says a lawyer must accept a client; nor that he must accept a fee for his services."[27] *Life*, which 14 years earlier had published a largely positive profile of Ernst, titled its story on the report, "Costly Whitewash of Black Charges," and described the report this way: "it turned out to be an obvious attempt to get Trujillo off the hook."[28] The *New York Times* went even further, stating that Ernst's report "took the published accusations against the Dominicans, threw confusion and doubt upon them, and strove mightily to depict the Dominican dictator as unjustly accused by enemies."[29] The common thread in the press coverage: that Ernst was brilliant; that he accepted an enormous amount of money for his work; and that his report was nothing more than a whitewash. As Ernst's report was panned, his credibility was torpedoed along with it. *Newsweek* made that fact the thesis of its article on the case: after stating that Morris Ernst "was the liberals' liberal," and listing off some of his many contributions to progressive causes, the magazine delivered the boom: "Last week, however, there wasn't an old-time liberal in the U.S. with a good word for Morris Ernst." It cited an unnamed "distinguished champion of civil rights" as calling Ernst "a publicity hound," and included dismissive comments about Ernst's report from Sidney Hook, Norman Thomas, and "the militarily liberal" *New York Post.*[30]

In July 1958, soon after the release of the report, one congressman gave an hour-long speech on the floor of the House of Representatives to vigorously attack both the report and Ernst's tactics in drafting it. Representative Charles O. Porter of Oregon took Ernst titled his speech, "THE ERNST REPORT: CHARACTER ASSASSINATION FOR A FEE," and dissected Ernst's findings, both on Galíndez and on Murphy, whom Porter called "Gerry" and "my constituent." While Porter dismissed the "bought and paid for lawyers' brief," he focused most of his wrath at Ernst's "brilliant and trained mind"; even as Ernst attacked the character of the victims in the case, Ernst was "careful to avoid grounds for libel suits, a specialty of his." Ernst's "weapons of attack," Porter said, were "innuendo, implication, inference." Porter read aloud the following passage from Ernst's report as an example: "We know that free-lance pilots live lives of terrific temptation. It is profitable to smuggle nylon, drugs, guns, immigrants and people who want to enter or leave our shores illegally. We are inclined to believe that the Border Patrol of the United States Government must have a substantial dossier on Murphy."[31] Homing in on the phrase *we are inclined to believe*, Porter pointed out that "Ernst does not say, 'We know.' A check with the border patrol, as I made, would have relieved Ernst of any speculation in the matter. The border patrol does not have any dossier on Gerry. Moreover, to the knowledge of the Department of Justice, Gerry had never engaged in any such activities."[32] Porter later cited an even more damning passage from Ernst's report:

> With a catch in his voice and a tear in his eye, [Ernst] states: "We have understanding and deep sympathy for Mrs. Murphy, the mother of Gerald. In fact, we understand her grief. And since this evidence (regarding the alleged de la Maza suicide note's reference to homosexuality) bears no relation to the Galíndez affair, we see no point or duty which impels us to spread on the record documentation which would have little value other than to satisfy the purveyors of scandal. Furthermore, much of our information came to us under the cloak of privileged communication, without which a lawyer could not wisely counsel any client."[33]

One can almost feel Porter's outrage. "How touching," Porter said. "Ernst's sensitivity for Mrs. Murphy's feelings. [*sic*] Yet in the same breath, he hints that his information, if he were callous enough to reveal his facts, is salacious and most damaging to Gerry. And how despicably clever. Ernst skirts a libelous statement by protesting that his tender feelings prevent him from going on record."[34] At this point in his life and career, Ernst still had fans, many of whom considered him to be a progressive man of integrity. Some, after hearing Porter's hour-long speech—or after reading the six-page excerpt Porter published in the *New Leader*, or the letters he wrote to newspapers—would likely have been disappointed, at a minimum, by Ernst's McCarthyist slurs.

Porter emphasized how much money went into the report, stating that the Dominican Republic had, over the course of six months, paid Sidney Baron, Inc. $262,854 "to organize the whitewash job."[35] That Ernst was paid handsomely for his work on Trujillo's behalf was uncontested.[36] Different sources put the payment, including expenses, starting at $90,000. The government's own report in June 1960 put his two-year earnings from the Dominican Republic as a "foreign agent" at $201,793.[37] Moreover, Ernst's motivation for agreeing to defend Trujillo could not have been financial. By 1957, the year that Ernst agreed to defend Trujillo, Ernst was an extremely wealthy man. Almost twenty years earlier, in 1938, Marquis James noted that Ernst was already earning at least $40,000 annually.[38] With his added lifelong *Ulysses* royalties, his salary from Greenbaum, Wolff, & Ernst, as well as the additional profits from speeches and from the numerous books and articles he had written (not to mention Margaret Ernst's income as a teacher and author), Ernst was able to construct a compound on Nantucket, where he spent nearly every summer of his professional life. He owned three houses by 1938, and when his three children grew up, he built one house for each of them in Nantucket.

Ernst's real motive in accepting Trujillo's offer was an itch for excitement and publicity. "Ernst certainly knew that Trujillo would not put up the money if he expected an unfavorable verdict," wrote Salisbury. "Ernst also knew that his critics—and he had plenty by this time—would gather like crows in a barnyard and peck at every grain of evidence, looking for bias or special favors. It was the hottest potato he had ever been offered, and that made it irresistible." Trujillo, of course, had not been formally accused of a crime. There was no court case and Trujillo was not on trial; Ernst's work amounted to a fact-finding mission, and Trujillo happily fed Ernst the information he wanted to publicize. "The whole episode dismayed many of Ernst's friends and allies," writes Roger K. Newman.[39] During Porter's scathing takedown of Ernst, as he cited one passage of Ernst's report, Porter made a curious observation: that Ernst's description of Galíndez actually applied to Ernst himself. Porter then again read directly from Ernst's report: "It must be remembered that there attaches to all men, and especially to men in public prominence, the possibility that beneath the facade which they show to the world there lurks a secret and very private self which seeks strange bedfellows. • • • For now, it suffices to say that the part of his life which he kept hidden may well have been the most important part."[40] Porter's conclusion, accurately and devastatingly revealed the consequences of Ernst's work. "Morris Ernst," Porter proclaimed, "great defender of civil liberties, is now character assassin for a fee from Trujillo. The characters of the intended victims of his venal and unworthy report emerge, when the facts are known, unscathed, and triumphant. The character of one unintended victim, however, is smashed perhaps beyond repair. This victim's name? Morris Ernst."[41]

## MORRIS ERNST AND THE MODERN CELEBRITY LAWYER SOUNDBITE

Decades after his streak of successes, many of Ernst's famous friends had died, or had shied away from Ernst's ever-more rabid pro-FBI and anti-communist stance, or had simply been replaced on the gossip circuit. In 1962, Paul Boyer arranged a 30-minute interview with Ernst. Boyer noted that Ernst could be simultaneously confident and insecure:

> [Ernst] was very brash and assertive, with a rather brusque and impatient manner, absolutely sure of himself, as I suppose one would expect of a famous trial lawyer and litigator. On the wall behind him were photographs—possibly autographed—of Louis D. Brandeis and (as I recall) Franklin D. Roosevelt. For what

> it's worth, I got the impression of a somewhat insecure person who compensated by being very aggressive and rather condescending, and by stressing his connections to influential and powerful people.[42]

Boyer attributes his negative impression of Ernst in part to the fact that, at the time of the interview, Boyer was a young dissertation student and that, "from (Ernst's) perspective, although I had made an appointment, I was no doubt just an annoyance in the midst of a busy day."[43] If Boyer is correct about Ernst's motives for name-dropping and posting those autographed photograph, then Ernst's "annoyance" and underlying lack of confidence might also be attributed to the fact that the young Boyer had questioned the aging attorney about events that had taken place over three decades earlier. If Ernst drew confidence from his fame and his connections with the powerful and famous, those connections had largely dried up by 1964; the photographs Boyer mentions were several decades old. Ernst's exhibitionism, which had helped him to reach the bestseller lists, pay frequent visits to the White House, argue before the Supreme Court, and earn a spotlight in the pages of *Life* magazine, now seemed dated and out of place.

By the 1960s, Ernst's days of legal relevance were long past. As David Garrow writes in his history of *Roe v. Wade*, "[a]fter more than thirty years on the front lines, Morris Ernst would spend his remaining years talking mostly to himself."[44] When Margaret died in 1964, Ernst was shattered. His handwritten, unpublished diary of the time is crushingly sad, a side of Ernst that the self-proclaimed "glandular optimist" had never displayed in his public writings.[45] Three years after her death, he remained depressed and desperate over his loss. It is touching and pathetic that during this unrelenting period of grief and pain, Ernst decided to go on the Merv Griffin show to promote his latest book, *The Teacher*. "Last night, for no reason I can fathom, I went to appear on T.V.—the Merv Griffin Show. Was I vain, wanting excitement?"[46] To the end, Ernst yearned for the attention and recognition, and when suffering the most, he instinctively sought the balm of celebrity. Though he received kudos from friends and admirers, he watched his own performance on Merv Griffin's show and, in a surprising moment of self-reflection, questioned his own motives. "I should not have observed myself on the TV show," he wrote, "for what is more depressing than looking at oneself when all alone. No Maggie to kid me, correct me—to share. And still, I'm so vain and curious that I just had to observe me on a show. Childish??"[47] The public appearances continued, however, and Ernst remained wed to the image of the everyday man. During a 1966 WNYC radio show titled, "Bringing City Hall Closer to People and Problems," Ernst—the same man that the mayor of New York had asked to resolve the 1937 taxi strike—claimed, """I don't know anything about transportation or anything big in New York . . . I think I'm like most citizens." Then, calling New York City "hopeless," he proposed bringing multiple city halls to the city: "The only way to save taxes and get better service is by breaking up New York as London broke up."[48] Though Ernst suggested during the radio appearance, that his main strength was asking questions, and hoped for a New York City that was "less glib," his WYNC performance was not unlike his memoirs, where he jumped from topic to topic:

> I think we ought to get together in each neighborhood . . . in our neighborhood we have thirty schools, private and public, they're responsible for the upbringing of the youth of our neighborhood; we can get those principals to meet. Just to have them meet is a great advance. Then they can start thinking of what do you do about children? For example, I'm [now] in favor of child labor, having fought it all my life, because when we automated the homes, we threw our kids of twelve to sixteen out of work and they're bums, hanging around street corners. When you're bored, you're next door to juvenile delinquency and violence. Well now, these school principals can get together, and they can start working out, "what do you do with twelve to sixteens?" In the countryside, they can paint a fence, they can shoot a rabbit.[49]

Ernst here moves from the topic at hand (namely, a proposal for neighborhood city halls) to the recommendation that school principals should gather to solve the problems of juvenile delinquency. He then suggests, based on no cited evidence, that automation has left children bereft of responsibility and is therefore responsible for juvenile crime and violence. He's certain enough of his stance that he is willing to stand in favor of child labor, even though he'd fought against it for decades. Ernst is unwittingly on display *himself* as glib, and while the full radio program is 24 minutes long, his performance is the precursor to the twenty-first century soundbite, anticipating the behavior of today's pundits and talking heads, who voice offhand ideas, with little forethought. This offhand commentary is the diametric opposite to the careful, well-researched legal presentations he made prior to the 1950s.

In the 1960s and 1970s, Ernst may have seemed publicly enthusiastic and engaged, whether on the page and in his television and radio appearances. In fact, he never recovered from the death of his wife. Ernst's family attempted to set him up on dates, but he refused the possibility of romance after losing his wife. "For some reason, since Maggie's death I can't feel close to anyone—no matter how much I try," he wrote in 1967. "My real problem is I care about few things or people and then only a tiny bit. Is it possible that caring is a habit and I have lost it with Maggie's death?"[50] Batten wrote that "he was like a ship without a rudder when she died. He would tell me that he just didn't know what to do without Margaret. . . . Margaret was like an anchor for him. Without her he was drifting."[51] In 1968, Ernst added a short, handwritten entry to a diary of events Margaret had kept for several years that serves as a poignant illustration of his misery: "1968 April 2 – 3:22 p.m. "AWFUL!! Old Man Finished No No No No."[52] Ernst, whom Rodell once said was rarely in the absence of company, was lonely.[53] He may have lived his last years, as Garrow writes, simply talking to himself, and the only true bright spots in his final, unpublished diaries, are his entries about Stephanie, his granddaughter by his daughter Joan. Morris Ernst died on May 21, 1976.

**Figure 8.2. Morris Ernst, in his later years. Photo by Blackstone Studios; date unknown.**

Though there was no official finding that the 87-year-old Ernst was a suicide, his son Roger suspected that Morris Ernst saved up heart medication until he had enough to kill himself.[54] "My feeling was that he grieved himself to death," wrote Batten.[55] Perhaps, in part, it was the return to the solitude of his youth, and the need to be recognized, that finally led to Ernst's death.

For better or for worse, Morris Ernst paved the way for the emergence of the modern celebrity lawyer. He opined on the cases he handled, of course, as well as the laws and politics surrounding those cases. But he also became a regular commentator, in the press, through his books, on the radio, and later on television on a myriad of other subjects that interested him, where his authority came not from years of study or experience before the court, but from his celebrity. John Balz, who studied Ernst's career (and who, as the son of the storied *Washington Post* reporter Dan Balz, knows a thing or two about the media), proclaimed in 2004 that "[i]f Ernst were alive today, I do not doubt we would see him regularly on a Larry King Live roundtable."[56] Ernst yearned for recognition and respect, and to get close enough to power that he could capitalize on those relationships to boost his own currency. More often than not, up through World War II, that self-promotion benefited his clients and friends: it is evident that he was generous and enormously supportive of friends and clients alike, especially because the two categories frequently blended in the environment of Ernst's charisma, energy, and optimism. But after World War II, Ernst's strategy of exhibitionism wore thin, particularly as his attentions wandered away from the progressive, common man themes, like birth control, sex education, and censorship. Suddenly, it seemed, the man who called himself a "glandular optimist" was acting in ways that appeared cynical: throwing his credibility first behind J. Edgar Hoover and then a Dominican tyrant; offering to represent Julius and Ethel Rosenberg so that he could get a "terrific story" and possibly help out the FBI; informing, possibly, on his ACLU colleagues.

In his essay on celebrity lawyers and the cult of personality, law professor Richard K. Sherman laments the transformation, from Tocqueville's ideal of lawyers as "an essential bulwark against the tyranny of the majority," to today's perception of lawyers as "luminaries in the culture of celebrity." "The lawyer as celebrity," Sherman writes, "has become a willing participant in the mutually assured seduction that goes on between TV journalists and producers and the lawyer pundits, anchors, and screen personalities who help make entertainment king. . . . As perceived by the American public, law today is becoming entertainment, and entertainment law."[57] Ernst himself helped engender this idea. Two quotations, both cited in earlier chapters, speak to this strategy. In 1928, Ernst and his co-author wrote: "Jury antagonism is easily aroused by boredom, and the first duty of the defense is entertainment."[58] The context of this statement was the prosecution's decision, in some censorship cases, to read the book aloud, which could potentially annoy the jury; trials were usually boring affairs anyway, and Ernst saw that by entertaining the jury, he might be able to get them on his side. And in 1945, as he reflected back on obscenity cases, he declared: "We had fun educating juries and judges."[59] While the key action here is *educating*, Ernst proved to be a witty defense attorney, and his energy and excitement before the court was indubitably entertaining.

But perhaps even more importantly, Ernst helped create the opportunity, and even the expectation, for celebrity lawyers to address just about any topic under the sun. Whether he was arguing about bigotry, proposing pie-in-the-sky predictions of the future on television with Edward R. Murrow, or writing about sailing, or carpentry, or the migration of birds, or the rise of the human race in his memoirs, Ernst presented himself, in this role of celebrity, as an authority on most anything, and he was accepted as such. It is interesting to see how that exhibitionist streak in Ernst compares with Jeffrey Toobin's description of the consummate celebrity lawyer, Alan Dershowitz, in Toobin's *The Run of His Life:* The People v. OJ Simpson:

> Whenever any legal or criminal proceeding makes news, talk-show bookers instantly summon the Harvard Law School professor for analysis, and Dershowitz gladly delivers the goods in well-rounded sound bites. Alan Dershowitz has an enviable life—a prestigious professorship, lucrative deals for books and speeches, a full plate of wealthy clients eager to pay him for legal work—and yet he seemingly will appear on any program and talk about anything. His lust for publicity has a manic quality, as if the bookish yeshiva boy from Brooklyn still cannot believe that others care what he thinks. So when the calls came from the media in the immediate aftermath of the murders in Brentwood, Dershowitz was, as usual, available.[60]

The similarities, if we accept Toobin's description at face value, are intriguing: like Dershowitz, Ernst was a somewhat bookish Jewish American; like Dershowitz, Ernst had no financial need for the extracurricular forays onto radio and television; and like Dershowitz, Ernst's lust for publicity *was* manic. Ernst helped cement the expectation that lawyers could be a ready news-making source, and that the bigger the celebrity, the more entertaining the resulting publication or broadcast would be.

For decades, Ernst's name and influence were largely forgotten. It remains unclear whether Dershowitz's defense of Donald Trump during the 2020 presidential impeachment will damage Dershowitz's reputation in the same way that Ernst's 1958 defense of Raphael Trujillo damaged his. And yet over this last year, three authors have brought out books about Ernst's life and legacy. Ernst is again relevant, both for his work to advance women's causes, and for his regrettable exaggerations. In the television and internet age, with ample opportunity for nonstop instant commentary, Ernst's stories, proposals, and exaggerations would prove compelling. Furthermore, in the current political and cultural environment of conservative assaults on civil liberties, Ernst's experiences would be eerily relevant. After all, he was, in historian Samuel Walker's words, "the greatest civil libertarian of the first-half of the twentieth century"—a "pioneer," as Harriet Pilpel remarked, in the legal defense of issues relating to reproductive rights. Ernst freed *Ulysses,* which the prolific and acclaimed novelist Michael Chabon considers his favorite novel. Ernst argued in favor of *The Well of Loneliness,* a novel that is still taught in university classrooms and still considered by some to be the "lesbian Bible" of literature. He challenged restrictions on sexual education and contraception. And he popularized law for the masses, even arguing that it was the duty of the general public to challenge lawyers, since the main function of lawyers, in his view, was to slow down society. Many of the debates he entered into are very much alive today.[61]

Morris Ernst ought to be remembered as more than just the lawyer who freed *Ulysses*. At a tribute to Morris Ernst, held in December 1976, Ernst's longtime associate, law partner at the firm and friend, cited an unnamed columnist's declaration that "even Shea Stadium would not hold the people who were forever in debt to Morris."[62] And it is true that he made a difference in the lives of so many: women who could not afford birth control; married couples seeking accurate sex education; parents who sought to educate their children about sex but found no literature that provided those tools; LGBT Americans seeking any representation—any positive representation—in books; and countless others, who were assisted by the legal and personal work Ernst did. Though Ernst undermined his own credibility and his hard-won integrity when he abandoned the core features of his exhibitionist strategy, scholars, historians, and civil libertarians who analyze current challenges to civil liberties should consider the applicability of his work on women's issues and his take on gender and identity, which was progressive in his own time. By joining publicity with a passion for civil liberties and a clear emphasis on the ideal of the common man, Ernst won numerous freedoms in the 1920s and 1930s, and his winning strategy deserves to be reexamined today.

## NOTES

1. Fred Rodell, "Morris Ernst," *Life*, Feb 21, 1944, 106.
2. Fred Rodell, *Harvard Law Review* 58, no. 7 (1945): 1102–105, doi:10.2307/1335690.
3. Ibid.

4. Ibid.

5. One of Ernst's junior associates, Arthur Joel Katz, recalled an overnight sailing trip with Ernst, Jahoda, and Katz's girlfriend in the early 1950s. According to Katz, Jahoda and Ernst shared a berth. Arthur Joel Katz, email message to the author, July 20, 2005.

6. Anonymous, personal interview by author, June 11. 2006.

7. Ibid.

8. Morris L. Ernst, *So Far So Good*, (New York: Harper and Brothers, 1948), 81.

9. Harrison E. Salisbury, "The Strange Correspondence of Morris Ernst and John Edgar Hoover, 1939–1964," *The Nation*, December 1, 1984, v. 239, para. 16.

10. Mary Batten, email message to the author, August 20, 2006.

11. As with most of his clients, Murrow had become a friend; two years earlier, according to Margaret Ernst's unpublished diary, the two men had traveled to Germany together. Unpublished diary of Margaret Ernst, February 1954, SB.

12. *Person to Person*, January 6, 1956, CBS, hosted by Edward R. Murrow, with Morris L. Ernst and Margaret S. Ernst.

13. Ibid.

14. Ibid.

15. Milton Bracker, "Trujillo's Rule Denounced In Missing Scholar's Book: Galíndez Says Dominican Republic is Operated as Feudal Tyranny," *New York Times,* May 29, 1956, 1, ProQuest Historical Newspapers.

16. "The Story of a Dark International Conspiracy," *Life*, Feb 25, 1957, 25.

17. Ibid., 29.

18. "Costly Whitewash of Black Charges," *Life*, June 9, 1958, 105.

19. "The Story of a Dark International Conspiracy," *Life*, 30.

20. Jonathan Marshall, "The Dictator and The Mafia: How Rafael Trujillo Partnered With US Criminals to Extend His Power," *Journal of Global South Studies*, March 22, 2018, Vol. 35, no 1, 56(31). Marshall, citing Stuart McKeever's book *Galíndez*, adds that Baron was hired "on the advice of mob lawyer Francis Rosenbaum." See n44.

21. "Noted Village Lawyer Takes on Top Mystery," *Village Voice*, July 24, 1957, Vol. II, No. 39, 1.

22. Ibid.

23. Ibid.

24. Handwritten comment by J. Edgar Hoover, Memorandum to Clyde Tolson from L. B. Nichols, July 11, 1957, FBI.

25. Representative Charles Porter, speaking on "THE ERNST REPORT: CHARACTER ASSASSINATION FOR A FEE," on July 1, 1958, 85th Cong., 2nd sess., *Congressional Record* 104, pt. 10:12861.

26. "Scotch Verdict," *Newsday*, June 3, 1958, 31.

27. Robert G. Spivack, "Watch on the POTOMAC," *Daily Defender*, June 10, 1958, A4.

28. "Costly Whitewash of Black Charges," *Life*, June 9, 1958, 10.

29. "Galíndez, Murphy, Ernst," *New York Times*, June 24, 1958, 30.

30. *Newsweek*; New York Vol. 51, Iss. 27, (Jul 7, 1958): 26–27. Sidney Hook, who taught at New York University, was an influential political philosopher who had

supported the communist candidate William Z. Foster for president in the early 1930s but later became a leading anti-communist. Norman Thomas, who had considered Ernst a friend, had helped found the National Civil Liberties Union (which later was reorganized to become the ACLU) and a frequent presidential candidate for the American Socialist Party.

31. "Report and Opinion in the Matter of Galíndez" (New York: Sidney S. Baron & Company, 1958), 39.

32. Porter, "THE ERNST REPORT," 12861

33. "Report and Opinion," 51.

34. Porter, "THE ERNST REPORT," 12861

35. Porter, "THE ERNST REPORT," 12860. According to inflationtool.com, this would be equivalent to about $2,411,163.26 in 2021.

36. Ernst reportedly received $70,000 for his work and another $101,000 for expenses. Salisbury, para. 105.

37. U.S. Department of Justice, Report of the Attorney General to the Congress of the United States on the Administration of The Foreign Agents Registration Act of 1938, As Amended, for the Period January 1, 1955 to December 31, 1959 (June 1960), Appendix IV, 343, https://www.justice.gov/nsd-fara/page/file/991956/download. This report cites the $90,000 payment reported in many newspaper accounts, paid to Ernst in 1957, but also includes a second payment of $ 111,793 in 1958. This amount is listed apart from the $562,855.39 paid to Sidney S. Baron & Company during those same years.

38. Marquis James, "Morris L. Ernst," *Scribner's*, July 1938, 7–11, 57–58.

39. Newman, "Morris Leopold Ernst."

40. "Report and Opinion," 60.

41. Porter, "THE ERNST REPORT," 12865.

42. Paul S. Boyer, email message to the author, July 5, 2005.

43. Ibid.

44. Garrow, *Liberty and Sexuality, 159.*

45. Ernst, *So Far So Good, 8.*

46. Typescript of unpublished diary, 58, n.d., Box 774, MLE.

47. Ibid.

48. Morris Ernst, "Bringing City Hall Closer to People and Problems," WNYC radio, May 18, 1966, https://www.wnyc.org/story/bringing-city-hall-closer-to-people-and-problems/.

49. Ibid.

50. Typescript of unpublished diary, 56, 41, n.d., Box 774, MLE.

51. Mary Batten, email message to the author, August 20, 2006.

52. Unpublished diary of Margaret Ernst, SB.

53. Rodell, "Morris Ernst," 106.

54. Roger Ernst, telephone interview by author, July 24, 2005.

55. Mary Batten, email message to the author, August 20, 2006.

56. John Balz, "Legally Yours: The 'Unlawyerlike' Lawyer Morris Ernst Goes Public with Birth Control," 4, Remarks Prepared for the American Society of Legal History Conference, October 28–30, 2004. See also John Paul Balz, "Fuel for the

Fire: Law and Capitalism in the Birth Control Movements," Master's Thesis, The University of Texas at Austin, 2004.

57. Richard K. Sherwin, "Celebrity Lawyers and the Cult of Personality," *New York Law School Law Review,* v. 46, issue 3, (2002–2003), 517–519.

58. Morris L. Ernst and William Seagle, *To the Pure . . . A Study of Obscenity and the Censor* (New York, Viking Press, 1928), 6.

59. Ernst, "The Best is Yet," 114.

60. Jeffrey Toobin, *The Run of His Life:* The People v. O.J. Simpson (New York: Random House, 1996), 129.

61. See, for instance, Reid J. Epstein, "Abortion Arrives at the Center of the American Political Maelstrom," *New York Times*, Sept 2, 2021; Emma Schartz, "The Birds, Bees And Everything between: Nebraska Goes to War over Sex Education," *The Reader,* September 1, 2021; Ian Millhiser, "Justice Thomas launches an utterly bizarre attack on birth control," *ThinkProgress,* May 28, 2019; Jamie L. Manson, "The Catholic Church's Reproductive Fight Is About Controlling Women's Freedom," *New York Times*, May 27, 2021; Suzanne Nossel, "Thirteen Ways of Looking at Censorship," *New York Times Sunday Book Review,* July 16, 2021; Caleb Daniel, "Library removes LGBTQ books from kids' section," *Ruston Daily Leader* (Louisiana), December 4, 2020.

62. Transcript of "Tribute to Morris L. Ernst, 12/15/76," SB.

# Key to Archives Cited

| | |
|---|---|
| FBI | Federal Bureau of Investigation, Washington, DC |
| FDR | Franklin D. Roosevelt Library, Hyde Park, NY |
| NIH | Office of NIH History, National Institutes of Health, Washington, DC |
| MLE | Morris Leopold Ernst Papers, MS-1331, Harry Ransom Center, University of Texas at Austin, Austin, TX |
| SB | Stephanie G. Begen Collection, Rocky Hill, CT |

# Selected Bibliography


Adams, Rachel and David Savran, eds. *The Masculinity Studies Reader*. Malden: Blackwell Publishers, Inc., 2002.

Anonymous. *The Smiling Corpse: Wherein G.K. Chesterton, S.S. Van Dine, Sax Rohmer and Dashiell Hammett Are Surprised to Find Themselves at a Murder*. New York: Farrar and Rinehart Incorporated, 1935.

Auerbach, Jerald S. "From Rags to Robes: The Legal Profession, Social Mobility and the American Jewish Experience." *American Jewish Historical Quarterly* 66, no. 2 (1976).

———. *Unequal Justice: Lawyers and Social Change in Modern America*. Cary, NC: Oxford University Press, 1977.

Bacon, Peggy. *Off With Their Heads!* New York: Robert M. McBride and Company, 1934.

Baker, Michael. *Our Three Selves: The Life of Radclyffe Hall*. New York: Morrow, 1985.

Barbas, Samantha. *The Rise and Fall of Morris Ernst, Free Speech Renegade*. Chicago: University of Chicago Press, 2021.

Bauer, Heike. "Richard von Krafft-Ebing's *Psychopathia Sexualis* as Sexual Sourcebook for Radclyffe Hall's *The Well of Loneliness*." *Critical Survey* 15, no. 3 (2003).

Bederman, Gail. *Manliness and Civilization: A Cultural History of Gender and Race in the United States, 1880–1917*. Chicago: The University of Chicago Press, 1995.

Behling, Laura L. *The Masculine Woman in America, 1890–1935*. Urbana: University of Illinois Press, 2001.

Beisel, Nicola. *Imperiled Innocents: Anthony Comstock and Family Reproduction in Victorian America*. Princeton: Princeton University Press, 1997.

Boyer, Paul. *Purity in Print: Book Censorship in America From the Gilded Age to the Computer Age,* Second ed. Madison: The University of Wisconsin Press, 2002.

Brandt, Allan M. *No Magic Bullet: A Social History of Venereal Disease in the United States Since 1880*. New York: Oxford University Press, 1987.

Breger, Claudia. "Feminine Masculinities: Scientific and Literary Representations of 'Female Inversion' at the Turn of the Twentieth Century." *Journal of the History of Sexuality* 14, no. 1–2 (2005): 76(31).

Brod, Harry. "The Case for Men's Studies." In *The Making of Masculinities: The New Men's Studies*. Edited by Harry Brod. Boston: Allen and Unwin, 1987.

———. "To Be a Man, or Not to Be a Man—That Is the Feminist Question." In *Men Doing Feminism*. Edited by Tom Digby. New York: Routledge, 1998; 197–212.

Butler, Judith. *Gender Trouble: Feminism and the Subversion of Identity*. New York: Routledge, 1990.

———. *Undoing Gender*. New York: Routledge, 2004.

Capshew, James H., Matthew H. Adamson, Patricia A. Buchanan, Narisara Murray, and Naoko Wake. "Kinsey's Biographers: A Historiographical Reconnaissance." *Journal of the History of Sexuality,* July 2003 v12 i3 p465(22).

Cerf, Bennett. *At Random: The Reminiscences of Bennett Cerf.* New York: Random House, 1977.

Chabon, Michael. "*United States v. One Book Called 'Ulysses'* (1933)." In *Fight of the Century: Writers Reflect on 100 Years of Landmark ACLU Cases.* Edited by Michael Chabon and Ayelet Waldman. New York: Avid Reader Press, 2020.

Chauncey, George. *Gay New York: Gender, Urban Culture, and the Making of the Gay Male World 1890–1940*. New York: BasicBooks, 1994.

Chauncey, George, Jr. "From Sexual Inversion to Homosexuality: Medicine and the Changing Conceptualization of Female Deviance." In *History of Women in the United States, v.10: Sexuality and Sexual Behavior*. Edited by Nancy F. Cott. New Providence: K.G. Saur, 1993.

Chen, Constance M. *"The Sex Side of Life": Mary Ware Dennett's Pioneering Battle for Birth Control and Sex Education*. New York: The New Press, 1996.

Cott, Nancy F. *The Bonds of Womanhood: "Woman's Sphere" in New England, 1780–1835*. New Haven: Yale University Press, 1977.

———. *The Grounding of Modern Feminism*. New Haven: Yale University Press, 1987.

Crowley, Vicki. "Within the New Moment—An Interview with Judith Halberstam," *Discourse* Vol. 25, no. 4 (2004).

Cuordileone, K. A. *Manhood and American Political Culture in the Cold War*. Taylor and Francis Group, 2005. ProQuest Ebook Central. http://ebookcentral.proquest.com/lib/yale-ebooks/detail.action?docID=1075256.

de Grazia, Edward. *Girls Lean Back Everywhere: The Law of Obscenity and the Assault on Genius*. New York: Vintage Books, 1993.

D'Emilio, John, and Estelle B. Freedman. *Intimate Matters: A History of Sexuality in America*. New York: Harper and Row, 1988.

Doan, Laura. "'The Outcast of One Age Is the Hero of Another': Radclyffe Hall, Edward Carpenter and the Intermediate Sex." In *Palatable Poison: Critical Perspectives on The Well of Loneliness*. Edited by Laura Doan and Jay Prosser. 162–178. New York: Columbia University Press, 2001.

———. "Passing Fashions: Reading Female Masculinities in the 1920s." *Feminist Studies* 24, no. 3 (1998): 663(3).

———. "Sappho's Apotheosis? Radclyffe Hall's Queer Kinship With the Watchdogs of the Lord." *Sexuality & Culture* 8, no. 2 (Spring 2004): 80–106.

Dorr, Lisa Lindquist. "Arm in Arm: Gender, Eugenics, and Virginia's Racial Integrity Acts of the 1920s." *Journal of Women's History* 11, no. 1 (1999): 143.

Dubbert, Joe L. "Progressivism and the Masculinity Crisis." In *The American Man*. Edited by Elizabeth H. Pleck and Joseph H. Pleck. Englewood Cliffs: Prentice-Hall, Inc., 1980.

Duxbury, Neil. "In the Twilight of Legal Realism: Fred Rodell and the Limits of Legal Critique." *Oxford Journal of Legal Studies* 11, no. 3 (1991): 354–395.

Ernst, Morris L. *The Best is Yet . . .* New York: Harper and Brothers, 1945.

———. Foreword to *Ulysses,* by James Joyce. New York: Vintage Press, 1961.

———. "The Kinsey Report and the Law." *The Scientific Monthly* Vol. 70, No. 5 (May 1950): 279–282. JSTOR.

———. *A Love Affair With the Law: A Legal Sampler*. New York: The Macmillan Company, 1968.

———. "Recollections on the 'Ulysses' Trial and Censorship." *James Joyce Quarterly*, Fall 1965, Vol. 3, No. 1, 6, https://www.jstor.org/stable/25486535.

———. *So Far So Good*. New York: Harper and Brothers, 1948.

———. *Touch Wood: A Year's Diary*. New York: Atheneum, 1960.

———. *Untitled: The Diary of My 72nd Year*. New York: Robert B. Luce, Inc., 1962.

Ernst, Morris L., ed. *The Teacher*. New York: Prentice Hall, 1967.

Ernst, Morris L., and Alexander Lindey. *The Censor Marches On: Recent Milestones in the Administration of the Obscenity Law in the United States*. New York: Doubleday, Doran and Company, Inc., 1940.

Ernst, Morris L., and Pare Lorentz. *Censored: The Private Life of the Movie*. New York: Jonathan Cape and Harrison Smith, 1930.

Ernst, Morris L., and David Loth. *American Sexual Behavior and the Kinsey Report*. New York: The Greystone Press, 1948.

Ernst, Morris L., and Alan U. Schwartz. *Censorship: The Search for the Obscene*. New York: The Macmillan Company, 1964.

———. *Lawyers and What They Do*. New York: Franklin Watts, Inc., 1964.

Ernst, Morris L. and William Seagle. *To the Pure: A Study of Obscenity and the Censor*. New York: The Viking Press, 1928.

Fairchild, Amy L., James Colgrove, and Ronald Bayer. "The Myth of Exceptionalism: the History of Venereal Disease Reporting in the Twentieth Century (Emerging Issues in Population Health: National and Global Perspectives)." *Journal of Law, Medicine & Ethics* 31, no. 4 (Winter 2003): 624(15).

Faludi, Susan. *Stiffed: The Betrayal of the American Man*. New York: William Morrow and Company, Inc., 1999.

Fogarty, Robert S., and H. Roger Grant. "Free Love in Ohio: Jacob Beilhart and the Spirit Fruit Colony." *Ohio History: The Scholarly Journal of the Ohio Historical Society,* Volume 89, 206–221.

Freedman, Estelle B. "'Uncontrolled Desires': The Response to the Sexual Psychopath, 1920–1960." In *Passion and Power: Sexuality in History*. Edited by Kathy Peiss and Christina Simmons. Philadelphia: Temple University Press, 1989.

Friedman, Andrea. *Prurient Interests: Gender, Democracy, and Obscenity in New York City, 1909–1945*. New York: Columbia University Press, 2000.

Garrow, David J. *Liberty and Sexuality: The Right to Privacy and the Making of Roe v. Wade*. New York: Macmillan Publishing Company, 1994.

Gary, Brett. *Dirty works: Obscenity on Trial in America's First Sexual Revolution.* Stanford: Stanford University Press, 2021.

Gentry, Curt *J. Edgar Hoover.* New York: W.W. Norton, 1991.

Gillers, Stephen. "A Tendency to Deprave and Corrupt: The Transformation of American Obscenity Law from Hicklin to Ulysses II." *Washington University Law Review* 85, no. 2 (2007): 215–296

Gillespie, Michael Patrick. "'Prying into the Family Life of a Great Man': A Survey of the Joyce/Léon Papers at the National Library of Ireland." *James Joyce Quarterly*, Vol. 30, No. 2 (Winter, 1993), 277–294. https://www.jstor.org/stable/25485376.

Halberstam, Judith. "An Introduction to Female Masculinity: Masculinity without Men." In *The Masculinity Studies Reader.* Edited by Rachel Adams and David Savran. 355–374. Malden: Blackwell Publishers Inc, 2002.

———. "'A Writer of Misfits': 'John' Radclyffe Hall and the Discourse of Inversion." In *Palatable Poison: Critical Perspectives on The Well of Loneliness.* Edited by Laura Doan and Jay Prosser. 145–161. New York: Columbia University Press, 2001.

Hall, Kermit L. *The Magic Mirror: Law in American History*. New York: Oxford University Press, 1989.

Haltunen, Karen. *Confidence Men and Painted Women: A Study of Middle-Class Culture in America 1830–1870*. New Haven: Yale University Press, 1982.

Hantover, Jeffrey P. "The Boy Scouts and the Validation of Masculinity." In *The American Man*. Edited by Elizabeth H. Pleck and Joseph H. Pleck. 285–301. New York: Prentice-Hall, Inc., 1978.

Hardiman, Adrian. "The Trial of Ulysses, 1933." *Dublin University Law Journal* 33 (2011): 50.

Hassett, Joseph M. *The Ulysses Trials: Beauty and Truth Meet the Law*. Dublin: The Lilliput Press, 2016.

Hochberg, Stephen. "Dedication to Morris Leopold Ernst." *New York Law Forum* XX, no. 3 (Winter 1975): 447–451.

Hoffheimer, Michael H. "Rodell, Fred (1907–1980), Legal Educator and Journalist." *American National Biography*. February 1, 2000. https://doi.org/10.1093/anb/9780198606697.article.1101128.

Hoffman, Warren. "The Rise (and Fall) of David Levinsky: Performing Jewish American Heterosexuality." *Modern Fiction Studies*, Volume 51 number 2, Summer 2005.

hooks, bell. *Feminist Theory: From Margin to Center*. Second ed. Cambridge: South End Press, 2000.

Houston, Ruth. "A Dream Come True: Papa Tuthill and Memphis Music," Unpublished fellowship thesis, Rhodes College, 2005. https://dlynx.rhodes.edu/jspui/bitstream/10267/23927/1/2005-Ruth_Houston-A_Dream_Come_True-Sharp.pdf.

Jones, James H. *Alfred C. Kinsey: A Public/Private Life.* New York: W.W. Norton & Company, 1997.

Kalman, Laura. *Abe Fortas: A Biography*. New Haven: Yale University Press, 1990.

Kasson, John F. *Houdini, Tarzan, and the Perfect Man: The White Male Body and the Challenge of Modernity in America*. New York: Hill and Wang, 2001.

Keire, Mara L. "The Vice Trust: A Reinterpretation of The White Slavery Scare in The United States, 1907–1917." *Journal of Social History* 35.1: Fall 2001.

Kimmel, Michael S. "The Contemporary 'Crisis' of Masculinity in Historical Perspective." In *The Making of Masculinities: The New Men's Studies*. Edited by Harry Brod. 121–153. Boston: Allen & Unwin, 1987.

———. "Masculinity as Homophobia: Fear, Shame, and Silence in the Construction of Gender Identity." In *The Masculinities Reader*. Edited by Stephen M. Whitehead and Frank J. Barrett. Malden: Polity Press/Blackwell Publishers, 2001.

———. *Manhood in America: A Cultural History*. New York: The Free Press, 1996.

Knauer, Nancy J. "Homosexuality as Contagion: From the *Well of Loneliness* to the Boy Scouts." *Hofstra Law Review* 29, no. 2 (2000).

LaMay, Craig L. "America's Censor: Anthony Comstock and Free Speech." *Communications and the Law* 19, no. 3 (September 1997): 1–59.

Leff, Laurel. "News of the Holocaust: Why FDR Didn't Tell and the Press Didn't Ask." *Hakirah: A Journal of Jewish and Ethnic Studies* 2 (2006): 31–61.

Link, Arthur S. and Richard L. McCormick. *Progressivism*. Arlington Heights, IL: Harlan Davidson, 1983.

Marchand, Roland. *Advertising the American Dream: Making Way for Modernity, 1920–1940*. Berkeley: University of California Press, 1986.

Marshall, Jonathan. *Journal of Global South Studies*. "The Dictator and The Mafia: How Rafael Trujillo Partnered With US Criminals to Extend His Power." March 22, 2018, Vol. 35, no 1, 56(31).

McGovern, James R. "The American Woman's Pre-World War I Freedom in Manners and Morals." In *History of Women in the United States, v.10: Sexuality and Sexual Behavior*. Edited by Nancy F. Cott. New Providence: K.G. Saur, 1993.

Moore, Jacqueline. "'Them's Fighting Words': Violence, Masculinity, and the Texas Cowboy in the Late Nineteenth Century." *The Journal of the Gilded Age and Progressive Era* 13(01). doi:doi:10.1017/S1537781413000479.

Moran, Jeffrey P. "'Modernism Gone Mad': Sex Education Comes to Chicago, 1913." *Journal of American History* 83 (1996): 481–513.

———. *Teaching Sex: The Shaping of Adolescence in the 20th Century*. Cambridge: Harvard University Press, 2000.

Morrow, Prince A. *Social Diseases and Marriage: Social Prophylaxis*. Philadelphia: Lea Brothers and Co., 1904.

Moscato, Michael and Leslie LeBlanc, eds. *The United States of America v. One Book Entitled Ulysses By James Joyce: Documents and Commentary—a 50-Year Retrospective.* Frederick, MD: University Publications of America, Inc., 1984.

Newman, Roger K. "Morris Leopold Ernst." In *Dictionary of American Biography.* New York: Charles Scribner's Sons, 1995; Reproduced in *Gale in Context: U.S. History*, https://link.gale.com/apps/doc/BT2310013962/UHIC?u=29002&sid=bookmark-UHIC&xid=.

Norwood, Stephen H. "'American Jewish Muscle': Forging a New Masculinity in the Streets and in the Ring, 1890–1940." *Modern Judaism* 29, Number 2, May 2009.

Nye, Robert A. "Locating Masculinity: Some Recent Work on Men." *Signs* 3 (Spring 2005): 1937(26).

O'Shea, Michael J. Review of *"Ulysses" as a Comic Novel,* by Zack Bowen. *James Joyce Quarterly*, Vol. 29, No. 2 (Winter, 1992): 421–424. https://www.jstor.org/stable/25485275.

Packert, G. Beth. "The Relentless Realist: Fred Rodell's Life and Writings." *University of Illinois Law Review* (1984): 823–856.

Pagnattaro, Marisa Anne. "Carving a Literary Exception: The Obscenity Standard and *Ulysses*." *Twentieth-Century Literature* 47, no. 2 (Summer 2001): 216–240.

Peiss, Kathy. "'Charity Girls' and City Pleasures: Historical Notes on Working-Class Sexuality, 1880–1920." In *Passion and Power: Sexuality in History*. Edited by Kathy Peiss and Christina Simmons. 57–69. Philadelphia: Temple University Press, 1989.

Pleck, Joseph H. "American Fathering in Historical Perspective." In *Changing Men: New Directions in Research on Men and Masculinity*. Edited by Michael S. Kimmel. 83–97. Newbury Park: Sage Publications, Inc., 1987.

Polenberg, Richard. *Fighting Faiths: The Abrams Case, the Supreme Court and Free Speech*. Ithaca: Cornell University Press, 1999.

Rodell, Fred. "Morris Ernst: New York's Unlawyerlike Liberal Lawyer Is the Censor's Enemy, the President's Friend." *Life*, February 21, 1944, 96–107.

———. *Woe Unto You, Lawyers!* New York: Reynal & Hitchcock, 1939.

Rotundo, E. Anthony. *American Manhood: Transformations in Masculinity from the Revolution to the Modern Era*. New York: BasicBooks, 1993.

———. "Patriarchs and Participants: A Historical Perspective on Fatherhood in the United States." In *Beyond Patriarchy: Essays By Men on Pleasure, Power, and Change*. Edited by Michael Kaufman. 64–80. New York: Oxford University Press, 1987.

Salisbury, Harrison E. "The Strange Correspondence of Morris Ernst and John Edgar Hoover, 1939–1964." *The Nation,* December 1, 1984: 575(15).

Schwartzburg, Molly. "The Writer and His Lawyer: James Joyce, Morris Ernst, and *Ulysses.*" In *Other People's Books: Association Copies and the Stories They Tell.* Edited by Susan F. Rossen. 175–179. Chicago: Caxton Club, 2011.

Schwarz, Judith. *The Radical Feminists of Heterodoxy.* Lebanon, NH: New Victoria Publishers, Summer 1986.

Shapiro, Edward S. *A Time for Healing: American Jewry Since World War II*. Edited by Henry L. Feingold. 5 vols. Vol. V, *The Jewish People in America*. Baltimore: The Johns Hopkins University Press, 1992.

Sherwin, Richard K. "Celebrity Lawyers and the Cult of Personality." *New York Law School Law Review,* v. 46, issue 3, (2002–2003).

Silverman, Joel. "*Krieger v. Mittelman*: A Matter of Perceptions." *Judaism: A Journal of Jewish Life & Thought* 55, no. 217/218 (2006): 40–54.

Smith-Rosenberg, Caroll. "The Female World of Love and Ritual: Relations between Women in Nineteenth-Century America." In *History of Women in the United*

*States, v.10: Sexuality and Sexual Behavior*. Edited by Nancy F. Cott. 55–83. New Providence: K.G. Saur, 1993.

Souhami, Diana. *The Trials of Radclyffe Hall*. London: Weidenfeld & Nicolson, 1998.

Spoo, Robert. "Judging Woolsey Judging Obscenity: Elitism, Aestheticism, and the Reasonable Libido in the 'Ulysses' Customs Case." *James Joyce Quarterly*, Summer 2013, Vol. 50, No. 4.

Stansell, Christine. *American Moderns: Bohemian New York and the Creation of a New Century*. New York: Owl Books, 2001.

Steele, Richard W. "Franklin D. Roosevelt and His Foreign Policy Critics." *Political Science Quarterly* 94, no. 1 (1979): 15–32.

———. "The Pulse of the People: Franklin D. Roosevelt and the Gauging of American Public Opinion." *Journal of Contemporary History* 9, no. 4 (1974): 195–216.

Stetten, Dewitt, Jr. *How My Light Is Spent: The Memoirs of DeWitt Stetten, Jr.* Office of NIH History, 1983. https://history.nih.gov/download/attachments/1016824/DeWittStettenMemoirs.pdf?version=1&modificationDate=1550592737757&api=v2.

Taylor, Leslie A. "'I Made Up My Mind to Get It': The American Trial of The Well of Loneliness, New York City, 1928–1929." *Journal of the History of Sexuality* 10, no. 2 (April 2001).

Tone, Andrea. "Contraceptive Consumers: Gender and the Political Economy of Birth Control in the 1930s." *Journal of Social History* 29, no. 3: 485(22).

Toobin, Jeffrey. *The Run of His Life: The People v. O.J. Simpson.* New York: Random House, 1996.

Traister, Bryce. "American Viagra: The Rise of American Masculinity Studies." *American Quarterly* 52, no. 2 (2000): 274–304.

Vanderham, Paul. *James Joyce and Censorship: The Trials of Ulysses.* London: Macmillan Press Ltd., 1998.

Walker, Samuel. *In Defense of American Liberties: A History of the ACLU*. New York: Oxford University Press, 1990.

———. "Ernst, Morris Leopold (1888–1976), Attorney." *American National Biography*. Feb. 1, 2000. https://doi.org/10.1093/anb/9780198606697.article.1100982.

Weinrib, Laura. "From Left to Rights: Civil Liberties Lawyering between the World Wars." *University of Chicago Public Law & Legal Theory Working Paper* No. 571, 2016.

———. "The Sex Side of Civil Liberties: *United States v. Dennett* and the Changing Face of Free Speech." *University of Chicago Public Law & Legal Theory Working Paper* No. 385, 2012.

White, Kevin. *The First Sexual Revolution: The Emergence of Male Heterosexuality in Modern America.* New York: New York University Press, 1993.

# Index

# About the Author

**Joel Silverman** earned his PhD in American studies at the University of Texas at Austin and has published articles in *Masculinities* and *Judaism*. He is Director of Academic and Educational Affairs for Yale College, and lives in New Haven, Connecticut.

www.ingramcontent.com/pod-product-compliance
Lightning Source LLC
LaVergne TN
LVHW011814200926
848484LV00005B/1185
* 9 7 8 1 6 8 3 9 3 3 3 5 9 *